Theologizing in
BLACK

Theologizing in
BLACK

On Africana Theological
Ethics and Anthropology

Celucien L. Joseph

PICKWICK *Publications* · Eugene, Oregon

THEOLOGIZING IN BLACK
On Africana Theological Ethics and Anthropology

Pickwick Publications
An Imprint of Wipf and Stock Publishers
199 W. 8th Ave., Suite 3
Eugene, OR 97401

www.wipfandstock.com

PAPERBACK ISBN: 978-1-5326-9995-5
HARDCOVER ISBN: 978-1-5326-9996-2
EBOOK ISBN: 978-1-5326-9997-9

Cataloguing-in-Publication data:

Names: Joseph, Celucien L., author.
Title: Theologizing in black : on Africana theological ethics and anthropology / Celucien L. Joseph.
Description: Eugene, OR : Pickwick Publications, 2020 | Includes bibliographical references and index.
Identifiers: ISBN 978-1-5326-9995-5 (paperback) | ISBN 978-1-5326-9996-2 (hardcover) | ISBN 978-1-5326-9997-9 (ebook)
Subjects: LCSH: Ethics—Africa. | Christian ethics. | Christian ethics—Africa. | African American—Religion. | Religious thought—Africa. | Philosophy, African.
Classification: BR1360 .J66 2020 (print) | BR1360 .J66 (ebook)

Manufactured in the U.S.A.   APRIL 13, 2020

In memory of my wonderful and godly mother Hélène Joseph (January 3, 1947—May 31, 2019). You went home too soon to be with Jesus, your Lord and Savior.

May we love like you; may we show compassion and empathy toward people like you; may we show hospitality and care to the poor and strangers like you; may we be virtuous, faithful, and reconcilable like you; and may we walk in godliness and the fear of the Lord and be peacemaker like you.

We love you, manmi cherie.

Contents

Preface

THIS PRESENT TEXT, *THEOLOGIZING in Black: On Africana Theological Ethics and Anthropology*, attempts to articulate five broad objectives. First, it is about how African theologians in continental Africa and Black theologians in the African diaspora (i.e., the United States and the Caribbean) think theologically about the relationship between the African people and their descendants in the Diaspora with God and the social order which they inhabit, as well as their connection with the white world. Second, the book undertakes a comparative approach to religion and theology to examine both the religious experience and the theological experience of the African people and their descendants. The Black experience in religion is critical as it has paved the way for thinking theologically or *theologizing in black*. The idea here is that religious thinking leads to theological musing, and the two are inseparable, but not the same phenomenon.

While scholars of religion have distinctively identified the elementary forms of religion, theologians have idiosyncratically theorized theological categories and markers which place God as the starting point for theological conversation and contemplation. In other words, in the traditional theological discourse of Christian orthodoxy, God is the originator of theological imagination and thinking since he deliberately took the initiative to disclose his God-self to human beings he created, and this same God willingly informed both man and woman about his character and his attributes, and his moral demands revealed in his law. In brief, God's self-revelatory expression as divine gift is the starting point of all theological order and creativity without undermining the importance of the human experience in relation to God. Therefore, human beings must respond promptly to their Creator-God in view of what God has graciously made them to them. It is within this theological angle that both Barth and Tillich could interpret the Christ event in the history of salvation as "The universal basis for all divine-human interaction. Not that all religions are mediated through Christianity, but that Christianity is the most accessible instantiation of the divine self-manifestation that, when properly understood, can guide our understanding of divine self-revelation in all traditions."[1]

While some Liberation and Constructive theologians have argued that the human experience in history and culture is the opening for all theological conversations, they also recognize that this intellectual orientation is predicated upon the divine revelation to human beings throughout human history. As James Cone reminds us, it is God who communicates to Black people and the poor that they are special and beautiful and have dignity and worth. Hence lies the third objective of this book. Latin American theologian Ruben Rosario Rodriguez candidly observes that "Revelation is a divine possibility; the closet corresponding human reality is to *bear witness* to divine revelation, since even the sacred Scriptures themselves are properly categorized as bearing witness to revelation."[2]

Fourth, the book chronicles how Black theologians and thinkers discuss the issue of theological anthropology and ethics as they relate to the Black experience in continental Africa and the African Diaspora. Africana theological ethics and anthropology is a lament and protest theological discourse that reflects critically on the history of suffering and dehumanization of the African people and their descendants in the African Diaspora. This politico-theological narrative contemplates on the practice of racial segregation in public spaces and Christian meetings (Mays), Caribbean slavery and American imperialism (Price-Mars, Hamid, Aristide, Erskine), American slavery and lynching (Cone), the colonial legacy and European hegemony in continental Africa (Mbiti, Idowu, Megasa), and each of these transforming-life events shaped Black intellectual discourse and theological musings.

It is good to note here in African traditional religion, African theological ethics and anthropology was not a late development in the sense that it was a reaction to Western theology that excludes the Africans and people of African descent from God's global family. In fact, the African people have articulated their concept of personhood and humanhood

---

1. Rodriguez, *Dogmatics After Babel*, 48.
2. Ibid., 49.

in relation to their understanding of God and their religious ethical system, and their rapport with their ancestors and the community which they belong. Perhaps, we should call this ancient tradition the "African theological ethics and anthropology proper" because it is not derivative of Western theological ethical tradition nor is it a counter response to Western philosophical and theological anthropology. Hence lies the fifth objective of this book.

Theologizing in Black also examines the legacy of colonial Christianity and imperial Christianity, which have introduced agonizing pain and horror in the African and diasporic experience. The historic misuse of Christianity by slave masters, colonialists, and agents of American and European imperialism has contributed to the underdevelopment of Africa and the economic regress of black-populated countries like Haiti and Jamaica or in the zones of the darker nations where Christianity was also misappropriated an ambivalent vehicle of colonization, neo-colonization, and imperialism. Similarly, in the American context, white theologians, anti-black racists, and Christians who championed racial segregation in public spaces and ecclesiastical meetings have deployed the Christian faith as a resource to dehumanize black people and withhold from them the benefits and promises of American democracy. Consequently, one can infer that the witness of Christianity in the public sphere in the American society has been the antithesis of the liberative message and teachings of Jesus Christ. Racialized or colonial Christianity has brought a great dishonor to the message of the Gospel and is indeed the opposition to the biblical doctrine of the fatherhood of God and the brotherhood of man.

My fascination with Black theological tradition began in a Biblical Hermeneutics class with the prominent New Testament scholar Dr. Robert Stein at The Southern Baptist Theological Seminary (SBTS). While I learned helpful and insightful principles to assist me in interpreting the Bible theologically and exegetically, "the Black voice" in this White European Hermeneutical and Theological tradition was absent in the course. Similarly, in an introductory course on Systematic Theology (Part I) with the well-respected public theologian and President of SBTS R. Albert Mohler, again "the Black voice" was also missing in the white European Theological tradition. I decided to search elsewhere, to drink from other cisterns, the non-white male European sources, and I discovered on my own both Liberation Theology and Black Liberation Theology. Hence, I could assert that the preliminary foundations for this book occurred in this very specific seminary setting and as a response to satisfy my own intellectual hunger and thirst and to hear from the voices from the margins and correspondingly, from those who live underside of modernity.

Nonetheless, it was not until I became a doctoral student at the University of Texas at Dallas, and particularly in the process of choosing a topic for dissertation, that I was drawn to the Africana intellectual tradition and decided to write my long dissertation on a complex topic that intersects two major intellectual currents: the Black Atlantic intellectual tradition and the African (Anglophone and Francophone) intellectual tradition, within the academic disciplines of (Black) literature and (Black) intellectual history. Eventually, my first published article in 2011 laid the foundation for all the subsequent research and writing projects I will be undertaking in Africana Studies—with a special interest in Black theology and Black religion.

I am thankful to all my friends who have provided constructive feedback and shaped my theological ideas and intellectual trajectories in writing this book. I am grateful to my amazing and supportive spouse Katia and our wonderful four children: Terrence, Josh, Emily, and Abigal, who are and have been a source of inspiration, empowerment, and joy to me. I love you eternally and beyond the printed words in this book. However, I dedicate this book to this wonderful and godly woman Hélène Joseph (January 3, 1947—May 31, 2019)—my unforgettable mother—who recently left this world for a better and more promising world, where Jesus her Redeemer lives and the place in which she will experience the greatest and eternal joy and the greatest and eternal delight in the abundant and satisfying presence of God, her Savior and King.

Joseph decided to write this essay in order to bring black voices back into the narrative of Christian history - it was used to back the horrifying treatment of africans and left them with pain and the remnents of religion to work with.

Introduction

Bearing Witness: On Black Theological Musings and Liberative Theological Contemplation

THEOLOGIZING IN BLACK IS a rigorous comparative study of black theological musings and liberative theological contemplation engaging the theological ethics and anthropology of both continental African theologians (Tanzania, Kenya, Democratic Republic of the Congo) and Black theologians in the African Diaspora (Haiti, Trinidad, Jamaica, Antigua and Barbuda, the United States). Using the pluralist approach to religion promoted by the philosopher of religion John Hick, the book is also an attempt to bridge an important gap in the comparative study of religion, Africana Studies, and (Black) Liberation theology, both in Africa and its Diaspora. Few current studies have attempted to undertake this intellectual challenge of comparative study of both continental and diasporic Black theologians and thinkers and their thought on Africana theological anthropology and ethics. Contemporary scholarship in African American Studies and Black Diaspora Studies either focus on Black theological ethics in the United States or Black theological anthropology in Western Africa. It is very rare in Black Studies to find theological studies that transcend geographical boundary, national theological thinking, and the American-centric theological narrative.

Theological works produced in the United States emphasize the American-based theological enterprise, whether they are written by Black theologians, Asian theologians, White theologians, what have you?

Another important issue in contemporary theological studies in the United States is the language barrier which prevents American theologians to engage theological writings in other languages than English. The problem is prevalent in Black theological writing and education. A complementary problem is the seemingly American theological hegemony as well as theological arrogance in American theological landscape; many American theologians and biblical scholars, whether Black, White, Hispanic, or Asian do not explicitly engage other theologians writing from another side of the world—especially those from the developing nations. Unfortunately, these American thinkers do not even cite non-American theological thinkers who are writing in the same English language. Race-based theological writing has also influenced this lack of intellectual engagement and interaction among theologians and biblical scholars of the same theological discipline or cognate areas. For example, rarely do white theologians engage or cite black or brown biblical scholars and theologians in their theological writings.

This phenomenon of theological distance is creating further division in intercontinental, cross-cultural, and interracial theological discourse or conversations. This book offers another route by providing an alternative way to do theological engagement and theological confrontation, in a creative and relational way. Toward this goal, it will require that we practice an interdisciplinary methodological approach to study our subject matter.

The Nature of Religion and the Comparative Method

Caribbean Liberation theologian Idris Hamid in his seminal essay on the logic of Caribbean theology and to connect it to the development of the Caribbean people notes that everything in life is theological and that theology pervades every area of human existence. He writes, "Life's meaning, destiny, and relationships, are all governed or informed by our theologies. Furthermore, man's perpetual yearning and search after the meaning and truth lead him to examine his faith continually, to interpret it anew for life, and to 'search the scriptures' to test the validity and authenticity of it all."[1] In his important book, *Dogmatics After Babel*, Rodriguez argues with intellectual rigor and clarity that "The discipline of systematic (or constructive) theology needs to adapt to the increasing

---

1. Hamid, "Theology and Caribbean Development," 121.

diversity within Christian religious thought while simultaneously contending with the realities of religious pluralism in global context and the prevailing secularism with the academy."[2] In his tour-de-force *Ainsi Parla L'Oncle,* published in 1928, Jean Price-Mars of Haiti identifies the basic elements of all religion: the reverence for the Sacred or God, priesthood, dance, sacrifice, trance, a system of ethics, and faithful adherents, which he insists form "the most preserving parts of religious rites and that we experience them, either joined together or separately, in the most exalted religions."[3] Price-Mars concurs that these elementary forms of the religious life result in cases of mysticism, such as in the case of spirit possession; what remains a high possibility is that the religious phenomenon is transfigured universally.[4] This book considers various theological voices and religious perspectives in the Africana intellectual communities to sing a song of Black freedom and a polyphonic hymn that sustains black dignity, agency, and worth.

Philosopher of religion John Hick advances the idea that we live in a religious universe. Religion is a human phenomenon; however, the concept of religion as interpreted in modern scholarship is an academic invention. Some thinkers have argued that there was never a time in human history in which people have not been religious or committed to a religious faith. Even those who are deemed irreligious or anti-religious have somewhat had a religious encounter or possibly once committed to a religious tradition. This same Hick explains the ambivalence of religion and irreligion in this language:

> It is also true that we have to speak today of post-Buddhists, post-Muslims, post-Christians . . . However the post-religious are still deeply influenced by their religio-cultural past and it remains true that much of the life of humanity flows through the channels of thought and imagination formed by the ancient traditions that we know, in rough order of antiquity, as Hinduism, Judaism, Buddhism, Taoism, Confucianism, Christianity and Islam.[5]

Nonetheless, the religious experience is as complex and ambivalent as the human experience in the modern world. Hick identifies two major

2. Rodriguez, *Dogmatics After Babel,* 65.

3. Price-Mars, *So Spoke the Uncle,* 125.

4. Ibid., 107.

5. Hick, *An Interpretation of Religion,* 2.

responses to the religious life explaining the human experience in the cosmos: religious and naturalistic definitions.

> According to the form, religion (or a particular religious tradition) centres upon an awareness of and response to a reality that transcends ourselves and our world, whether the "direction" of transcendence be beyond or within or both. Such definitions presuppose the reality of the intentional object of religious thought and experience; and they are broader or narrower according as this object is characteristic upon generally, for example as a cosmic power, or more specifically, for example as a personal God. Naturalistic definitions on the other hand describe religion as a purely human activity or state of mind. Such definitions have been phenomenological, psychological and sociological.[6]

Generally, religion is good for society and human interactions. Various religious traditions could help enhance the human condition in the modern world. Because religion interweaves with human culture and worldview, learning about various religious traditions could assist us in gaining better understanding and insights about the people who embody cultural practices and traditions that are different from ours. Charles Kimball's engaging remark in the opening paragraph of his excellent text on the complexity and neutrality of religion is noteworthy:

> Religion is arguably the most powerful and pervasive force on earth. Throughout history religious ideas and commitments have inspired individuals and communities of faith to transcend narrow self-interest in pursuit of higher values and truths. The record of history shows that noble acts of love, self-sacrifice, and service to others are frequently rooted in deeply held religious worldviews. At the same time, history clearly shows that religion has often been linked directly to the worst examples of human behavior. It is somewhat trite, but nevertheless sadly true, to say that more wars have been waged, more people killed, and these days more evil perpetrated in the name of religion than by other institutional force in human history.[7]

In other words, religion may influence human actions, social interactions, and human behavior. Geoffrey Parrinder observes that "the intellectual and emotional sides of religion affect behavior. Religion has

---

6. Ibid., 3.

7. Kimball, *When Religion Becomes Evil*, 1.

always been linked with morality, though moral systems differ greatly from place to place. Whether morals can exist without religion or some supernatural belief has been debated, but at least all religions have important moral commandments."[8] Within this backdrop, we suggest that the religions of the world should be studied comparatively and contrastively, as this method could assist in identifying shared ideas and common ethical values, and points of difference or disaccord between them. In addition, the religions of the world that articulate different conceptions of God in their own terms help us to connect with God, the Divine, and in the words of John Hick, "the Real." Not only have these religions embody "different forms of life in response to the Real,"[9] they also express different responses to God and showcase different revelations and manifestations of God. From a pluralistic approach to religious traditions, Hick defines the Real as "ineffable" and that which is "having a nature that is beyond the scope of our networks of human concepts." David Tracy could assert that "Any act of interpretation involves at least three realities: some phenomenon to be interpreted, someone interpreting that phenomenon, and some interaction between these first two realities."[10]

Thus, the Real in itself cannot properly be said to be personal or impersonal, purposive or non-purposed, good or evil, substance or process, even one or many."[11] Contrary to Hick's claim, in the theology of the Abrahamic religions (Judaism, Christianity, and Islam), God is a personal Being who has revealed himself to humanity in a personal way, and his creation is geared toward the designated telos, according to his plan, will, and purpose. In their doctrine of God, most Jews, Christians, and Muslims believe that God is actively involved in the world and his ultimate goal is the cosmic redemption of all people and all created things, both seen and unseen, visible and invisible. While he employs the subject pronoun "it" as a reference to the "Real," which most adherents to the Abrahamic religions would reject, Hick, however, maintains the idea that "The Real is the source and ground of everything, and which is such that in so far as the religious traditions are in soteriological alignment

8. Parrinder, *World Religions*, 10.

9. Hick, *An Interpretation of Religion*, 27.

10. Tracy, *Plurality and Ambiguity*, 10.

11. Hick, *An Interpretation of Religion*, 27.

with it they are contexts of salvation/liberation."[12] The Real, for Hick, is a mystery because

> We cannot describe it as it is, but only as it is thought and ex-perienced in human terms—in traditional scholastic language, not *quoad se* but always *quoad nos* . . . The difference between there being and there not being an ultimate Reality, which is variously conceived and experienced through the "lenses" of the different religions is thus the difference between a religious and a naturalistic interpretation of religion.[13]

Like John Hick, Jean Price-Mars believes in the plurality of divine revelations, the idea that God's self-disclosure is clearly known in vari-ous practicing religious traditions in the world. As a religious pluralist, he sustains that the revelation of God is not exclusive to any particular religious tradition or any peculiar people; rather, it is hypothesized that God has intentionally made himself known inclusively to all religions and to all people regardless of culture, ethnicity, race, language, and geo-graphical location. In the same line of thought, Price-Mars postulates the notion that God's revelation was not monolithic, homogeneous, and ex-clusive; through divine revelation, God interrupted the human narrative and global history through different means and in different ways. This claim does not mean God's revelation is communicated solely through the religious traditions of the world. The revelation of God is also outside the realm of religion. For example, some scholars of religion have identi-fied some religions without revelation, and that there are religions that do not affirm theism. The transcendent and immanent God who defines reality is not bound by human convention, invention, or tradition.

The revelation of God had imposed "a religious content" to the universe and human existence. Consequently, Hick could theorize this phenomenon in this paragraph:

> When we look back into the past we find that religion has been a virtually universal dimension of human life—so much so that man has been defined as the religious animal. For he has displayed an innate tendency to experience his environment as being religiously as well as naturally significant, and to feel required to live in it as such . . . In the life of primitive man this religious tendency is expressed in a belief in sacred objects,

12. Ibid.

13. Ibid., 28.

endowed with mana, and in a multitude of nature and ancestral spirits needing to be carefully propitiated. The divine was here crudely apprehended as a plurality of quasi-animal forces which could to some extent be controlled by ritualistic and magical procedures.[14]

While it is possible to periodize the history of most functioning religions in the world today, it is, however, problematic to pinpoint with accuracy the exact time of the very first divine revelation. (However, some people have argued that Kemet predates this idea in terms of writing as well as religious, ethical, and moral texts.) Because religion always links to civilization and culture, we are able to approximate the beginning of religion and religions through the study of human civilizations. Most religious scholars have concluded that "The development of religion and religious begins to emerge into the light of recorded history as the third millennium B.C. moves towards the period around 2000 B.C."[15] According to Hick, historically, we can trace the very religious phenomenon and activities to "the Mesopotamia in the Near East and the Indus valley of northern India."[16] From an evolutionary theory perspective, the elements of religion or religious ideas began from the lowest-form of religious concepts to the highest religious ideas ever conceived by individuals.

The Golden Age of religious actions and innovation began around 800 B.C, in which different cultures and peoples transformatively experienced the various modes of divine revelation through the interruption of the mediatory Spirit of God, and as God attempted to impart his life in the soul of humanity.[17] Hick provides an informative analysis of what he has phrased "the golden age of religious creativity":

> This consisted in a remarkable series of revelatory experiences occurring during the next five hundred or so years in different parts of the world, experiences which deepened and purified men's conceptions of the ultimate, and which religious faith can only attribute to the pressure of the divine Spirit upon the human spirit.[18]

14. Hick, *God and the Universe of Faiths*, 133–34.

15. Ibid., 134.

16. Ibid.

17. Ibid., 135.

18. Ibid.

Hick goes on to list the different stages of this religious creativity of God's self-disclosure to his creation—from Judaism to Islam—and human response to God:

> First came the early Jewish prophets, Amos, Hosea and first Isaiah, declaring that they had heard the Word of the Lord . . . Then in Persia the great prophet Zoroaster appeared; China produced Lao-tzu and then Confucius; in India the Upanishads were written, and Gotama the Buddha lived, and Mahavira, the founder of the Jain religion and, probably about the end of this period, the writing of the Bhagavad Gita; and Greece produced Pythagoras and then, ending this golden age . . . Then after the gap of some three hundred years came Jesus of Nazareth and the emergence of Christianity; and after another gap the prophet Mohammed and the rise of Islam.[19]

The first revelation of God, according to Hick's (Eurocentric) analysis, came in the form of divine speech, which he appropriately named "The Word of God." He contends that the Bible is an aspect of God's self-disclosure; in the same line of thought, the final revelation of God ended with the Quran directed to Prophet Mohammed. Hick infers in all of these religious traditions we can witness "moments of divine revelation" in which God communicated his will to humanity not in a single mighty act; his revelations were multiple, progressive, partial, and at different times and places in human history.[20] Hick's interpretation of divine revelation follows the context and chronology of the Abrahamic religious traditions (Judaism, Christianity, and Islam).

Price-Mars associates the various forms of religious with divine revelation (s). For him, religious mysticism has its roots in God's natural revelation to people. For example, in *Ainsi parla l'Oncle* and other religious writings, Price-Mars studies comparatively the phenomena of Vodou mysticism on a par with Christian mysticism and Islamic mysticism of the Sufi sect. He also offers a comparative analysis of the music and dance of Vodou to the sacred music and dance in Judaism and those of Islam. The religious sacrifice in Dahomean-Vodou is compared to the rite performed in Asia, and the Assyria-Chaldean religious traditions. About the nature of sacrifice in Vodou, he concurs that there are some possible connections or filiation which lead us to believe in almost identical phenomena in a number of ceremonies of worship of different religions in

19. Ibid., 135–36.
20. Ibid., 136.

Israelite and Greco-Roman antiquity; that does not mean, however, that each community of faith does not exploit its own inclinations.[21]

It is a speculation, he sustains, to suggest that in the beginning of the religious life, a revelation was made to all peoples which had now been lost in the obscurity of time; consequently, we can "establish that the human specificity of mystical sentiment and its inevitable consequence, the sacrifice, and that the sacrifice matter itself, in the form of the victim, has scarcely changed from people to people, from religion to religion . . . with innumerable variants in Greco-Roman paganism, in Egypt, Persia, China, Japan, India, Africa."[22]

There is not one revelation, but revelations throughout human history. There is not one single center of divine revelation, but centers of divine revelation; there is not one location of divine revelation, but locations of God's revelation; there is not one recipient of God's revelation, but recipients of God's revelation; there is not one human-mediator or agent of divine revelation, but human-mediators or agents of divine revelation.

> If there was to be a revelation of the divine reality to mankind it had to be a pluriform revelation, a series of revealing experiences occurring independently within the different streams of human history . . . None of these expansions from different centres of revelation has of course been simple and uncontested, and a number of alternatives which proved less durable have perished or been absorbed in the process.[23]

The revelation of God to different geographical spheres and human agents has generated different religious responses and interpretations to what was revealed, leading to paradoxically complementary and competing religious traditions. God is the One who has revealed. Consequently, we can conclude that revelation is plural, varied, diverse, trans-ethnic, trans-cultural, trans-racial, trans-national, and global. We can then speak of a "global God-Revealer" who is not limited by space and time. This cosmic Deity is the God of all people and all culture; he is very much concerned about the welfare of everyone. We should be careful not to speak of a "polytheistic God," but of "one God" whose self-disclosure has generated different and multiple concepts of God.

21. Price-Mars, *So Spoke the Uncle*, 146.
22. Ibid., 146–47.
23. Hick, *God and the Universe of Faiths*, 137.

This detailed analysis above is an attempt to establish the intellectual context or a roadmap to better grasp Price-Mars's interpretation of the workings and nature of religion, and his appreciation of African traditional religion and contribution to Africana theological studies; this interpretive grid is also significant to make sense of Price-Mars' underlying thesis that God has revealed himself in the historical past to African people through their religious experience. For Price-Mars, African traditional religion must be investigated comparatively with other religions in the world. Each religion in its way distinctly adds meaning or significance to human reality and our experience in the world. According to Price-Mars, the shared vision of various religious traditions is that "The religious sentiment of the popular masses derives from the same psychological substratum which forged the faith of the humble and ignorant in every country in the world."[24] He goes on to articulate the universal religious language in this manner:

> Everywhere man similarly employs the same behavior to attract supernatural grace for himself and that by hardly changing the quality of his offering he obeys the same psychological injunction of employing everywhere the sacrificial matter most to his liking in order to seal his pact with the divinity, except to insert in each ritual gift the mystical qualities which heighten their value in the eyes of the gods.[25]

We already identified above the religious markers Price-Mars has recognized. For example, about the general nature of the ritual of religious sacrifice, he writes informatively that "The idea of oblation, of mystical communion, of reverential homage, of participation of the faithful in the life of the god or intercommunication between the profane and the sacred worlds. Each of these aforesaid considerations envisage an aspect of the rite, and together they bring about a sacrifice so rich in content that it expresses the general sense and the perfect symbol of the ceremony."[26] In the African religious context, the sacrifice bears various objectives:

> It is fulfilled in acts of thanksgiving to the gods for their attention, their benevolence toward the sacrifice, individual or group. It is an act of expiation to appease the wrath of the divinity irritated by some voluntary or unconscious offense the effects of

24. Price-Mars, *So Spoke the Uncle*, 107.
25. Ibid., 147.
26. Ibid., 136.

which had been translated into calamities of all sorts: maladies, sorrows, unsuccessful enterprises, and so forth.[27]

Next, we consider the phenomenon of the religious trance, and its "religious purpose" in fostering spiritual awakening. Fundamentally, the trance or crisis of possession is the highest and ultimate religious experience in which the individual is empowered by the Divine, or as it is said in Vodou, the *sevite* (adherent or "worshipper") is mounted by a lwa (spirit)—that is the possession of the divine spirit. Price-Mars describes the mystical possession in the supporting details below:

> Through these different words we are identifying a universal phenomenon in the diversity of religious and one in which the individual, under the influence of ill-determined causes, is plunged into a crisis sometimes manifested by confused movements of clonic agitation [spasmodic convulsion], accompanied by cries or a flood of unintelligible words. Other times, the individual is the object of sudden transformation: his body trembles, his face changes for the worse, his eyes protrude, and his foaming lips utter hoarse, inarticulate sounds, or even predictions and prophecies . . . The realization of crisis operates only on the level of the subconscious, therefore beyond any participation of the will of the believer. Here also such a course of action is only possible in a mentality where psychological hypotension plays the principal role . . . It is in fact eh phenomenon of glossolalia [gift of tongue]. It is common to all religions, at least in their beginnings, and is perpetuated in the mystical theology of the cults. And it is because the voodooistic "servants" are mystics that we find again in them the self-same phenomenon just as it is revealed elsewhere.[28]

Price-Mars interprets the religious trance or spirit possession as a "manifestation of divine beatitude." In this manner of revelation, the Divine invades the human being, both bodily and spiritually. Next, he establishes the connection of the spectacle of spirit possession in African traditional religion such as in the Afro-Haitian Vodou to spirit possession in Christianity. He pronounces: "Does not obeying the laws of the Church, humbling oneself before the *Mysteres* of Religion, performing one's devotion to the angels and saints of Paradise, form part of the

27. Ibid.

28. Ibid., 116, 121–25.

teaching of the Church?"[29] What remains a fundamental religious fact for Price-Mars is that Black people are equal partners in God's kingdom, and that God has not hidden himself from them. To a certain degree, Price-Mars would appeal to the idea of "spiritual equality" to dispel the narrative of white superiority and the myth of racial hierarchy. Moreover, he provides the supplementary details to enrich our understanding of religion:

> Superior religions, even the most advanced, have all been marked in their origins by this elementary process of posses- sion by the divine, by these accounts of strangely close relations between the god and his worshippers, and although they glory now in having attained a high state of spirituality they will retain these encumbrances which from time to time cause them to ret- rogress toward old forms of cultic worship.[30]

Like the contemporary thinkers of his era, Price-Mars was heavily influenced by the Darwinian evolutionary theory, which would shape his understanding of religion and the different stages of the religious life. Throughout human history, Price-Mars explains that people have deliberately modified their religious practices, rituals, moral codes, and dogmas to enhance the human experience in religion, and accommodate the changes and uncertainties of life. For example, Price-Mars had sub- scribed to the theory of the so-called "superior religions" and "lesser reli- gions" because of the belief that some religions have evolved from a lesser ethical system to a higher ethical system, which contributes to spiritual growth and human flourishing. In the same line of thought, Price-Mars has embraced the scholarly consensus that there exists both "revelatory religions" and "non-revelatory religions."

As will be observed in our analysis in subsequent paragraphs in this essay, Price-Mars would contend that African traditional religion is equally valid to any of the world's religions. It is good to note here that in the first half of the twentieth-century, it was uncommon for scholars of religion to make an apologetic defense for the legitimacy of African religion. A final component he identifies in African traditional religion, Judaism, and Christianity is the performative aspect of religion through ritual of dance. Sacred music and dance are linked to the various mani- festations of the religious sentiment.

29. Ibid., 116.
30. Ibid., 128–29.

Need be reminded that in Greco-Roman antiquity, that the dance very often had a sacred character? Did not the Nabis, the Nazirs of Israel, resort to music to provoke possession of the Spirit so that the Eternal God could speak through their line? Since the Hebrew used the world "chag" to express both festival and dance, does not the Bible teach us that David danced and leaped before the ark of the Eternal God, at Obed-Edom and that the ceremony was consummated with a burnt offering and sacrifices of riches.[31]

Despite the common religious practices and rituals African traditional religion shares with other religions, previous studies on African traditional religion, produced by Western thinkers and writers, have denigrated the religious experience of African people, and considered their experience in religion as non-religious and rubbish. A central objective of this book is to bridge this intellectual gap. The book is also an attempt to bring in candid conversation the discipline of Black religion and Black theology, as this is an important void that must be filled in contemporary Africana Studies and Black Diasporic Studies. A promising intellectual exploration that could assist us in achieving this objective is to deploy various methodological models such as the comparative study of religion, which we already alluded above, postcolonial strategies, and decolonial approaches.

The Significance of Postcolonial and Decolonial Methodologies

Fernando Segovia argues that all reconstructions of history are dependent upon reading strategies and theoretical models, suggesting that all such strategies and models and the resultant recreations and reconstructions as construct on the part of real readers.[32] Hence, hermeneutical interpretation demands reconstruction and recreation of the text and the historical past. The "postcolonial optic" paradigm, as Segovia framed it, "concerns a view of real or flesh-and-blood readers as variously positioned and engaged within their respective social locations, with a further

---

31. Ibid., 115.

32. Segovia, *Decolonizing Biblical Studies*, 119.

view of all such contextualizations and perspectives as constructs on the pare of real readers as well."[33]

Furthermore, Segovia outlines four ideas embedded in the postcolonial optic:

> First, "The task of interpretation is viewed in terms of the application of different reading strategies and theoretical models— whether produced or borrowed—by different real readers in different ways, at different times, and with different results (different readings and interpretations) in the light of their different and highly complex situations and perspectives. Second, a critical analysis of real readers and their readings (their representations of themselves as well as their representations of the ancient texts and the ancient world) becomes as important and necessary as a critical analysis of the ancient texts themselves (the remains of the ancient world). Third, all recreations of meaning and all reconstructions of history are in the end regarded as representations of the past—re-creations and reconstructions—on the part of readers who are themselves situated and interested to the core. Finally, given the paradigm's overriding focus on contextualization and perspective, social location and agenda, and thus on the political character of all compositions and texts, all readings and interpretations, all readers and interpreters, its mode of discourse may be described as profoundly ideological."[34]

The postcolonial optic forces the writer, reader and the text itself to engage critically in the process of "emancipation" and "decolonization," considering the social structures that jettison cultures and dehumanize people. By *postcolonial*, we mean

> ideological reflection on the discourse and practice of imperialism and colonialism from the vantage point of a situation where imperialism and colonialism have come—by and large, though by no means altogether so—to a formal end, but remains very much at work, in practice, as neoimperialism and neocolonialism. Thus, the postcolonial optic is a field of vision forged in the wake of imperialism and colonialism but still very much conscious of their continuing, even if transformed, power.[35]

---

33. Ibid.
34. Ibid, 119–20.
35. Ibid., 126.

Sugirtharajah remarks that "Colonialism is not simply a system of economic and military control, but a systematic cultural penetration and domination. Most damaging is not the historical, political, and economic domination, but the psychological, intellectual, and cultural colonization."[36] V. Y. Mudimble complements that colonialism or colonization means to "organize and transform non-European areas into fundamentally European constructs . . . [it also promotes] the domination of space, the reformation of natives' minds, and the integration of local economic histories into Western perspective."[37]

In addition, we must remember, however, the *postcolonial subjects* are "people whose perceptions of each other and of economic, political, and cultural relationships cannot be separated from the global impact and constructions of Western/Modern imperialism, which still remain potent in forms of neocolonialism, military arrogance, and globalization." [38]

The postcolonial model is useful as it welcomes direct and indirect engagement and dialogue with Caribbean theology, political theology, constructive theology, Christian ethics, and cultural studies, as they pertain to the theological worldview and ethical demands of these four Caribbean thinkers. The promise of the postcolonial method and decolonial paradigm is that they "counteract the oppressive dualisms and hierarchies of imperialism."[39] In other words, the decolonizing method seeks to cultivate new spaces of liberation and new zone of agency. The underlying idea of the postcolonial optic is the engagement of the human condition that has been affected by violence and human-orchestrated oppression and dehumanization. Hence, both liberation theology and postcolonial theology as models and theoretical tools of analysis will be implemented strategically in order to be able to restore the *imago dei*, foster emancipative future possibilities, and orchestrate post-western futures in the Caribbean Region. The ultimate goal is to fashion a new revolutionary humanism, to paraphrase Frantz Fanon, and correspondingly, to create a decolonized condition so the human person in the Caribbean, Africa, and the greater Black Diaspora can flourish and live in complete shalom.

36. Sugirtharajah, *Asian Biblical Hermeneutics*, 126.
37. Mudimbe, *The Invention of Africa*, 1–4.
38. Dube, *Postcolonial Feminist Interpretation*, 16.
39. Ibid., 105.

In bringing liberation theology, political theology, postcoloniality, and decolonization in close conversation, this article emphasizes human hope and eschatological wholeness in the present order as the ultimate objective of an ethics of liberation and cosmopolitan communism in Africa, the Caribbean, and the Black Diaspora. We contend that it is a false dream to conceive hope as simply an historical change in the pattern of life; rather, we promote a revolutionary hope and comprehensive liberation that will inevitably lead to "a radical renewal of the present system with a view to an historical liberation movement as a true sign of eschatological advance."[40]

The Case for Black Africana Liberation Theology

Black liberation theology is a subset of Africana Liberation Theology. Like Africana liberation Theology, Black liberation theology is a critique of western global dominance and the hegemony of Eurocentric theological discourse. While Black liberation emerged out of the Black experience in the United States, Africana liberation theology is primarily concerned with both the experience of the people of Africa and their descendants in the African diaspora. One can infer that Black Africana liberation theology has a pan-Africanist leaning. Liberation theology is anticolonial, anti-imperial, and anti-oppression. As Christopher Rowland reminds us, "The key thing is that one first of all does liberation theology rather than learns about it. Or, to put it another way, one can only learn about it by embarking on it."[41] In other words, black liberation theology is emancipative praxis, and argues that liberation of the poor and the oppressed is the heart of Christian theology and the message of Jesus. It is a relational form of theological discourse on the thought of and about God and God's relationship with the social order and the poor. A constructive theology of liberation calls for democratic intervention, "provides a basis for the radical democratic social transformation of contemporary society . . . and is also rooted in the social and political realities of poor and marginalized people."[42]

Constructive liberation theology insists on the principles of justice, truth, peace, and the participation of the most disheartened in the

---

40. Dussell, *Beyond Philosophy*, 33.

41. Rowland, *The Cambridge Companion to Liberation Theology*, 322.

42. Rabaka, *Against Epistemic Apartheid*, 249.

political order. Constructive liberation theology contends that the commitment to the liberation of the poor is not an "option," and the ultimate objective of a theology of liberation is the social salvation of the poor.[43] As Gustavo Gutierrez argues, liberation theology considers the conditions of oppression and the marginalization of the disheartened. Liberation theology as personal and collective transformation allows us to "live with profound inner freedom in the face of every kind of servitude . . . "[44] and liberation from sin attacks which attacks the deepest of all servitude. Suffice to say, liberation theology denounces all kinds of human oppression, marginalization, and discrimination, and stresses human dignity, "the option for the poor," and argues that the will of the (poor) as the expression of the will of God. Therefore, God of liberation is the God of the oppressed. It is within this context that James Cone, in the context of the Black experience in the United States, could assert that the God of the oppressed is a Black God because he sympathizes with the pain and suffering of Black people through the American history.[45]

For Cone, "the affirmation of the black Christ [God] can be understood when the significance of Jesus' past Jewishness is related dialectically to the significance of his present blackness."[46] As it is followed, "The Jewishness of Jesus located him in the context of the Exodus, thereby connecting his appearance in Palestine with God's liberation of the oppressed Israelites from Egypt."[47] In the same vein, the blackness of God situated him in the historical trajectory of the Black experience, both in continental Africa, and the African Diaspora, wherein God's acting and liberating presence provided hope for the future world of the enslaved. An understanding of God's identity with the suffering poor, the marginalized, and the economically-disadvantaged groups, as well as those who fight on behalf of the emancipation of humanity in this world is a central theme in Africana theological ethics and anthropology. Therefore, the blackness of God, accordingly, is not a mere statement about skin color, but rather, the transcendent assertion that God has not left the oppressed alone in their struggle.

---

43. Dupuy, *Haiti in the New World Order*, 83–84.

44. Ellis and Maduro, *Expanding the View*, 12–25.

45. Joseph, "Freedom from Below," 29.

46. Cone, *God of the Oppressed*, 122.

47. Ibid.

Reflecting about Africana theological ethics and anthropology bring to the complex issue of black theodicy. As will be observed in the subsequent chapters on Cone, Cone attempts to solve the theodicy crisis in Black theology through his Black Christology and the theology of atonement. He also justifies it within the doctrine of God and that because God is righteous and holy, he will render justice to the poor and the oppressed. For example, he declares, "If God is going to be true to himself, his righteousness must be directed to the helpless and the poor, whose who can expect no security from this world."[48] God will unquestionably vindicate the poor. As Cone also observes, "In the ongoing struggle for meaning in the midst of suffering, there is not intellectual or theoretical answer that will ease the pain of evil and injustice. We solve the mystery of evil's existence by fighting it. And faith is real only to the degree it endows us with the courage to fight."[49] God establishes the right by punishing the wicked and setting free their victims from oppression.

In Africana Critical Liberation Theology, God's righteousness is identical with the punishment of the oppressors and the colonizers, and divine deliverance is synonymous with the emancipation of the oppressed and the colonized from the bondage of slavery and imperial colonialism. Cone and other Caribbean theologians in conversation in this book articulate that the theme of divine justice is intimately connected to the notion of future hope. The God who establishes the right and eradicates the wrong is the sole basis for the hope that the suffering and dehumanization of victims will be eliminated.[50] Africana Theologians and thinkers maintain that the affirmation of God's liberating presence in the lives of the poor and the enslaved Africans in their fight for freedom and a dignified life might redirect our theological thinking of a radical understanding of God's righteousness and faithfulness. As Blount reiterates:

> This people who believed in a liberating God hacked out a liberating space for themselves in the strangling midst of a lethal human jungle. In the protective shelter of this worship and praying space they came to believe—despite what their owners and white theologians, legislators, and scientists maintained—that they were God's children and that God demanded their freedom . . . The result, from sundown to sunup *and* sunup to sum down,

48. Cone, *Black Theology and Black Power*, 45.
49. Cone, "God and the Black Suffering," 701–12.
50. Ibid., 703.

was the genesis of a culture of resistance shored up by a completely reconfigured understanding of ethics.[51]

God's righteousness vindication is reserved only for those who come empty-handed, without any economic, political, or social power and status. This is also an important theme found in the work of theologian Benjamin E. Mays, a forerunner of Liberation Theology, and John S. Mbiti. Remarkably, black suffering and white violence are critical concerns in this book, and for the articulation of a theology of liberation that fosters optimism in the midst of human suffering and the struggle to live in a just world. Any constructive theology such as black liberation theology, political theology, or postcolonial theology, should engage in an anti-colonial/imperial politics as much as it engages an anti-white supremacist politics. Critical theory of liberation theology is a critique of all forms of (social) domination and (social) inequalities. This project as theological imagination, which is rooted in the sociopolitical and existential realties of the disheartened and marginalized people, should also provide a basis for effective activism and "the radical democratic socialist transformation of contemporary society" and the welfare of humanity."[52]

The Cry for Black Justice and Democracy

At the core of Africana Theological Ethics and Anthropology is the central question of black dignity, justice, and democracy. Africana people search for liberation because they have been subject to violence, oppression, racism, abuse, exploitation, based on their race, class, and sex. Hence, Africana theological ethics is a liberative ethics of (black) human rights that emerges out of the experience of the Africana people. Theologian J. Deotis Roberts advises that Black ethics should be cosmopolitan and humanistic as it addresses the contours of God's revelation and ethics.[53] Africana theological ethics considers the mass of Africana folk in their respective country and other marginalized people in the developing nations with whom they are connected by a common history of imperialism, racism, and poverty.[54]

51. Blount, *Then the Whisper Put on Flesh*, 38–39.
52. Rabaka, *Against Epistemic Apartheid*, 249.
53. Roberts, *Black Religion, Black Theology*, 54.
54. Ibid, 55.

One of our important interlocutors in this book is Benjamin E. Mays who wrote about these various issues named above. Mays was a fierce critic of American segregation and anti-black racism, as both practices challenged black humanity and justice, and deferred the human rights of black people. Racial segregation in public spaces, for example, challenges the very idea of American democratic values and principles, and American Christianity was complicit in this societal and racial arrangement. The underlying issue for Mays was the question of justice and its role in interracial relations. John Rawls describes the role of justice in social cooperation and writes:

> Although, a society is a cooperative venture for mutual advantage, it is typically marked by a conflict as well as by an identity of interests. There is an identity of interest since social cooperation makes possible a better life for all than any would have if each were to live solely by his own efforts. There is a conflict of interests since persons are not indifferent as how the greater benefits produced by their collaboration are distributed, for in order to pursue their ends they each prefer a larger to a lesser share. A set of principles is required for choosing among the various social arrangements which determine this division of advantages and for underwriting an agreement on the proper distributive shares. These principles are the principles of social justice: they provide a way of assigning rights and duties in the basic institutions of society and they define the appropriate distribution of the benefits and burdens of social cooperation.[55]

For Mays, since the issue of Black theological and ethics comprised of moral, ethical, religious, economic, and political matters, he argued that the people in the church needed to be "Christianized" and that the American government did not extend democracy to its black citizens. In order for black people to experience their full humanity, there must be a rearrangement in the civil and political societies that will prize justice and promote the welfare of Black people. He also insisted in the public role of American Christianity in actualizing democracy to all people, especially America's marginalized and minoritized populations.

Mays was very hopeful about the future of Black people and the destiny of American Christians in the United States. Africana theological anthropology is a discourse on black hope and human optimism comprising of various Africana communities and vulnerable people in the

55. Rawls, *A Theory of Justice*, 4.

world. It rejects nihilism and despair. Roberts's statement on the relationship between hope and eschatology is significant for our conversation on Africana theological anthropology and ethics.

> Hope requires a strong emphasis upon the future. Belief in progress, which has provided the presuppositions of science and technology in the West, is akin to the theological perspective on hope. Man has to believe that things can be otherwise if he is to involve himself in changing things, it is true of the scientist as it is for the politician. There is to be teleology in hope. we take the responsibility to map the future of hope.[56]

The welfare of Africana communities and the wellbeing of marginalized races and groups is the subject of inquiry and concern of this present book. In the spirit of Caribbean postcolonial theology, Cone's Black theology of liberation, Bujo and Magasa's Ubuntu philosophy, Hamid and Erskine's decolonial theology, and Mays and Aristide's call for black democracy and human rights, this present work cries for justice and dignity on the best interest of Africana communities and the marginalized in God's global village.

Africana Studies and Africana Liberation Theology

What Is Africana Studies?

The term "Africana" has been used by scholars and researchers as well as academic programs and departments to discuss interdisciplinary methodologies associated with the field of Africana Studies. The concept signals a comparative approach to the history, culture, and experience of the African people and their descendants in the African Diaspora. Theoretically and pedagogically, the emphasis is on global blackness and this comparative analysis comprises of engaging various diasporic perspectives in the black world, whether it is in the geographical setting of continental Africa or the political nation-states where diasporic Black people reside.[57] For example, the discipline of Africana Studies considers pertinent issues relating to continental Africa, the Black Diaspora in the Caribbean, Afro-Latin-America, the United States, and elsewhere in the world.[58]

56. Roberts, *A Black Political Theology*, 186.

57. "History of Africana Studies at Cornell," https://africana.cornell.edu/history.

58. Azevedo, *Africana Studies*.

At this junction in this analysis, I will provide various definitions and descriptions of Africana Studies, as reported in selected universities' Africana Studies Departments. I will limit my survey to six schools, chiefly the University of Massachusetts Boston, University of Pittsburg, Williams College, University of Notre Dame, Cornell University, and Brown University. According to the Department's website at University of Massachusetts Boston,

> The Africana Studies Department is a multidisciplinary and interdisciplinary field of inquiry which is focused upon the social and cultural histories, politics, literatures, economics, environment, and psychology of African Diasporas' people in the Americas, Africa, and the Caribbean. Its broad educational goal is to document and disseminate a specialized body of knowledge about the Pan-African experience with a special emphasis on human equality in American society.[59]

The Africana Studies at the University of Pittsburg provides a broad definition of the field as "the study of the history and culture of African peoples."[60] Its goal includes the critical examination of "the problems, and perspectives of Blacks in Africa and the African Diaspora, which the African Union defined as the "people [and communities] of African origin living outside the [African] continent, irrespective of their citizenship and nationality." Most Africana departments in the U.S. grew out of Black Studies departments. As a result, "Africana Studies" at Pitt centers on the three-tier thrust of our Africana department: 1. African, 2. African American, and 3. Caribbean social sciences and humanities."[61] The department makes a distinction between African Studies and Africana Studies. While African Studies focuses on the African experience in continental Africa, Africana Studies brings together "Africa and the African diaspora (which includes Afro-Latin American studies, African American studies, and Black studies) into a concept of an "African experience" or cultural ideology with an Afrocentric perspective."[62]

The Africana Studies at Williams College is described as "a thriving interdisciplinary academic concentration that critically and systematically

---

59. "Africana Studies Department at the University of Massachusetts Boston," https://www.umb.edu/academics/cla/africana.

60. African Studies and African Country Resources @ Pitt: African VS. Africana Studies," https://pitt.libguides.com/c.php?g=12378&p=65819.

61. Ibid.

62. Ibid.

examines the cultures, histories, and experiences of people of African descent globally, and that grounds students in their multiple ways of knowing."[63] In its cross-disciplinary philosophy, the program aims at the educational needs of its diverse student body by blending scholarship and service. The program recognizes" the importance of grounding intellectual engagement with activism and life experience, and we assist students in finding unique and compelling perspectives from which to pursue and to make their own contributions to the field of Africana Studies."[64] Similarly the Department of Africana Studies program at the University of Notre Dame studies "the African American experience, Africa, and the African Diaspora—the global dispersion of peoples of African descent."[65] It claims an interdisciplinary approach to coursework and research and broad vision includes the promotion of "a critical engagement with the whole of human culture."[66]

In its attempt to define Africana Studies in its broad dimension and cross-disciplinary focus, the Africana Studies program at Cornell University alludes to the valuable definition provided by Robert L. Harris:

> Africana studies is the multidisciplinary analysis of the lives and thought of people of African ancestry on the African continent and throughout the world. It embraces Africa, Afro-America and the Caribbean but does not confine itself to those three geographical areas. Africana studies examines people of African ancestry wherever they may be found — for example, in Central and South America, Asia and the Pacific Islands. Its primary means of organization are racial and cultural. Many of the themes of Africana studies are derived from the historical position of African peoples in relation to Western societies and in the dynamics of slavery, oppression, colonization, imperialism, emancipation, self-determination, liberation and socioeconomic and political development.[67]

63. "Africana Studies at Williams," https://africana-studies.williams.edu/.

64. Ibid.

65. "Why Africana Studies," Department of Africana Studies at the University of Notre Dame, https://africana.nd.edu/undergraduate-programs/why-africana-studies/.

66. Ibid.

67. "History of Africana Studies at Cornell," https://africana.cornell.edu/history; for further details, see Jacqueline Bobo, Cynthia Hudley, and Claudine Michel's anthology, *The Black Studies Reader*.

Finally, the Africana Studies at Brown University claims a multiple theoretical and methodological perspective to studying critically "the intersections of class, gender, nation, race, and sexuality as well as the histories, experiences, and ideas of the cultures of Africa and the African diaspora as well as other cultures from around the world."[68] Disciplines in the Humanities, the arts, and the Social Sciences such as philosophy, theology, religion, history, sociology, psychology, anthropology, ethics, mathematics, etc., are the objects of academic study in the field of Africana Studies.

Moreover, the interdisciplinary Africana scholar and thinker Reiland Rabaka, who has published a multiple volume work on Africana Critical Theory,[69] defines Africana Studies "as a transdisciplinary human science;"[70] elsewhere, he cogently supplies this helpful articulation to this field of study: "Africana studies is the body of knowledge based on critically and systematically studying a specific human group, continental and diaspora Africans, and their particular and peculiar life-worlds and life-struggles."[71] Rabaka construes the concept of human sciences as an inclusive and open intellectual trajectory that "includes non-traditional 'disciplines' or areas of human studies, such as, of course, Africana studies, gender studies, sexuality studies, and postcolonial studies."[72] Furthermore, he makes this helpful elaboration:

> At their heart, human sciences deeply endeavor to extend and expand human beings' knowledge and consciousness of their existence, their interrelationship with non-human species and systems, and their distinct ability to develop artifacts to immortalize human thought and culture. In other words, human sciences are areas of inquiry where human phenomena are systematically and critically studies, which also means that they are simultaneously historical and current, classical and

---

68. "Africana Studies at Brown University," https://www.brown.edu/academics/africana-studies/.

69. For example, Rabaka, *Du Bois's Dialectics*; *Africana Critical Theory*; *Against Epistemic Apartheid: W.E.B. Du Bois and the Disciplinary Decadence of Sociology*; *Forms of Fanonism: Frantz Fanon's Critical Theory and the Dialectics of Decolonization*; *Concepts of Cabralism: Amilcar Cabral and Africana Critical Theory*; *The Negritude Movement*.

70. Rabaka, *Forms of Fanonism*, xvi.

71. Rabaka, *Concepts of Cabralism*, 20.

72. Ibid., 17.

contemporary in their concerns and in the questions and an-
swers they raise and offer.[73]

Human sciences as a theatrical framework challenges "the rules
of epistemic apartheid of the European and European American ivory
towers of academia."[74] Thus, Rabaka could conceive Africana critical
theory as "a school of radical/revolutionary thought or a radical revolutionary thought-tradition primarily preoccupied with radical/revo-
lutionary praxis, which decidedly goes above and beyond the influence
of a single intellectual-activist ancestor."[75] Africana Critical Theory not
only engages in an intellectual battle with the anti-blackness narrative
advanced by White American and European thinkers, it also seeks to
dismantle acts of white violence, fear, and terrorism launched toward
black and brown people.

Africana Critical Theory, both as a field and theory of knowledge,
critically assesses the interconnections and inextricability of colonialism
and capitalism, and incorporates the dialectical deconstruction and reconstruction, as well as radical politics and critical social theory toward
the emancipation of the African people, their descendants in the Diaspora, and the total freedom of the wretched of the earth.[76]

Finally, Rabaka establishes the important rapport between Africana
Studies and Africana Critical Theory by asserting that "Africana studies provides Africana critical theory with its philosophical foundation
(s) and primary point (s) of departure, as it, Africana studies, decidedly
moves beyond single-subject, one-dimensional, monodisciplinary approaches to, quite frequently, multidimensional and multifactorial Africana phenomena."[77] Africana philosopher Lewis R. Gordon also links
Africana philosophical tradition with the wider discipline of Africana
Studies. For example, he defines African thought as

> an area of thought that focuses on theoretical questions raised
> by struggles over ideas in African cultures and their hybrid and
> creolized forms in Europe, North America, Central and South
> America, and the Caribbean. Africana thought also refers to the
> set of questions raised by the historical project of conquest and

73. Ibid.

74. Rabaka, *Forms of Fanonism*, 35.

75. Ibid., xi.

76. Ibid., 35.

77. Rabaka, *Concepts of Cabralism*, 20.

colonization that has emerged since 1492 and the subsequent struggle for emancipation that continue to this day.[78]

Based on Gordon's pan-Africanist leaning, Africana philosophy engages the multiple terrain and zones of struggle of Africana communities. In particular, existential philosophy in Africana intellectual tradition gives careful attention to "the problems of anguish and despair, freedom, dread, degradation, responsibility, embodied agency, sociality, and liberation" facing the Africana populations globally."[79] He posits that the racial impact on the Africana people is twofold: "On the one hand, it is the question of exclusion in the face of an ethos of assimilation. On the other hand, there is the complex conformation with the fact of such exclusion in a world that portends commitment to rational resolutions of evil."[80] Not only problems of existence address the complexity and meaning of Africana anthropology and ethics; they also affect the black human condition and challenge us to look for an answer in the fields of moral theology and ethical philosophy.

In his important work, *A Pan-African Theology*, Josiah Young defines Pan-African theology as a theological tradition that "seeks to valorize what blacks have in common: African descent, cultural modalities, and especially the poor, radical similarity in socioeconomic suffering."[81] This book departs from Young's thesis; I do not believe that the Africana communities everywhere share a monolithic history nor do I hold that they are a homogeneous group. Young, however, focuses "on the transatlantic dimension of blacks in Africa and the United States,"[82] while neglecting the black experience in the Caribbean and Latin-America, a crucial matter I analyze in Chapter five in the book. Like Young, I try to make transcontextual dialogue through critical interaction with black theological ideas and texts and other forms of black literary expressions. Young defines transcontextuality as a perspective that "focuses on diverse situations and seeks to transform them in a praxis that does not annul the distinctiveness of those situations. Pan-African theology seeks

---

78. Gordon, *Existentia Africana*, 1.

79. Ibid., 7.

80. Ibid., 8.

81. Young, *A Pan-African Theology*, 10–11.

82. Ibid., 11.

to join distinct options for the poor in order to see, through them, the benefits of black solidarity."[83]

Our emphasis in this book on Africana theological ethics and anthropology is a long intellectual journey whose request is to find "the moral understanding, i.e., a reflection over action that gives an answer to the question of "why" this particular norm is valid."[84] This quest for justification takes into consideration the four constitutive spheres of Africana experience: God, community, ancestor, and person. The question of "why" may relate, for example, to the problems of slavery and colonial legacy in Africana history and communal experience, economic injustice, miscarriage of justice in the legal field, mass incarceration of black males in the United States, Police brutality, anti-black racism in the world, and acts of terror and violence toward the global Africana communities, the poor, and the wretched of the earth. This book seeks to find an answer to these existential problems by suggesting an alternative way to life and human relationships toward an ethics of human understanding, interconnectedness, reconciliation, and interracial unity. To achieve these goals in Africana critical theology, we must first decolonize God and deconstruct the theological practices that are anti-black and detrimental to the wellbeing of Africana communities. This decolonization process might involve a series of mental and intellectual steps as well as existential practices:

> First, it must explore and expose the extent to which God has been mis-represented or "colonized." Secondly, it must to discover him anew and proclaim faithfully. In so doing it must destroy the structures that encase him. These structures are not only ecclesiastical. They are social, economic, and political as well. There are inevitable political implication in the "de-colonizing" of God. if you wish to displace the god of the plantation system, with the Exodus God, or the God who is the Father of Jesus Christ, then the system must go. Thirdly, theology must search out the varied ways in which he has made himself know to our people, and the understanding our people have of him, as these were experienced in their cultural milieu. These may be found in our wisdom sayings, our songs and literature, and the oral tradition. These in turn will have to be subjected to theological inquiry and scrutiny. Fourthly, it must affirm the faithful responses especially those that were once considered unfaithful.

83. Ibid., 17.

84. Qouted in Blount, *Then the Whisper Put on Flesh*, 16–17.

Fifthly, theology must assist in rooting out the foolish supersti-
tions and idolatries that surround so much of Christian life.[85]

Structure of the Book

Theologizing in Black is divided into six chapters that recount a complex
theology of protest, contestation, deconstruction, and reconstruction.
The book provides an analytical framework and intellectual critique
of White Christian theologians who deliberately disengage with and
exclude Black and Africana theologians in their theological writings.
White Christian theology operates on the premise of white supremacy
and theological hegemony. As William R. Jones warned black liberation theologians in his groundbreaking study, *Is God a White Racist?*
Western religions and White Christian theology are built upon and
depended on signs and symbols that may harbor the seeds of the destruction of black and brown people.[86]

From this vantage point, Africana critical theology is said to be a
theology of contestation as it seeks to deconstruct white supremacy in the
theological enterprise. Chapter one considers these vital issues by posit-
ing both religious and theological arguments to ascertain black inclusion
in religious and theological discourse. It responds to the puzzling question: can the African people worship? In other words, do the Africans
know God? Within the intellect trajectories and impulse of the *Africana
Bible*, for example, this book endeavors "to demonstrate awareness of
sociocultural and religious realities in the multiplicity of interlocking
Africana cultural settings as well as of the complex network of African
Diaspora historically."[87]

Moreover, the central objectives of the *Africana Bible* is akin to the
fundamental goals of African critical theology, as narrated in the written
words of this book *Theologizing in Black*; they should be construed as a
tool that

> (1) increases awareness of Black lived experience throughout
> the world; (2) promotes conversation about the history, current
> challenges, and future prospects of peoples of African descent
> internationally; (3) enables Black experience; and (4) can be

---

85. Hamid, "Theology and Caribbean Development," 126.

86. See Gordon, *Existentia Africana*, ix.

87. Page, "The Africana Bible," 6.

used as a literary medium that promotes convergence and community building.[88]

Secondly, this book not only articulates a rhetoric of protest about the misrepresentation and underrepresentation of the humanity of African and Black people in white theological imagination; it also enunciates a positive image of Black humanity and congruently promulgates a constructive representation of blackness. Chapter two gives attention to the moral principles and theological aspect of Ubuntu associating with theological anthropology and ethics in African traditional religion. Ubuntu ethic establishes interconnectedness and relationality between human beings. It provides the theological blueprint to explain black humanity and proclaim the dignity of black people. The moral virtues and ideals associating with Ubuntu are premised on democracy, community, and human solidarity and brotherhood.

Chapter three complements the second chapter by drawing attention to James Cone's theological identity and his argument that Black humanity is grounded on black people's union and identification with Christ, which he also suggested as a solution to cope with the problem of black theodicy. Correspondingly, in Chapter four, Cone also interprets white racism and terrorism (i.e. slavery, lynching) toward black people results in the dehumanization and depreciation of black lives. Cone appeals to the justice of God to vindicate the cause of Black people and to liberate them from white tyranny and violence. Cone posits that Black people's faith in God is the resource that supports them to resist evil in the white world with the hope that God will eventually readjust all things in their original intent and bring restorative healing and transformative renewal in the world.

Moreover, third, Africana critical theology narrates a theology of development and democracy, by considering the living conditions and economic status of Black people in the geographical locations covered in this book (i.e., the United States, Jamaica, Haiti, Trinidad, Kenya). Such theological imagination or project requires the virtue of courage and resistance: courage to conquer the odds of this world and to face the terror and violence in the white world, and resistance to refuse to die, but to remain alive in the midst of cultural alienation, political marginalization, and inequality of opportunity. Chapter five provides a response to these underlying issues within the Caribbean experience

88. Page, "The Africana Bible," 5.

of political corruption, suffering, imperial intervention, famine, hunger, and the violations of their human rights and freedom. According to the Caribbean theologians engaged in this chapter, the most possible solution to bring about the freedom and emancipation of the Caribbean people, both spiritual and natural, is to craft a Caribbean theology of emancipation, decolonization, and hope.

On the issue of development as it pertains to the objective of this present work, I would like to turn to an important discussion in the seminal study (*Emancipation Still Comin'*) by the Caribbean liberation theologian Kortright Davis; this would supply intellectual correlation and support contributing to a more constructive dialogue on Africana theological anthropology and ethics. *Theologizing in Black* shares a similar concern, as articulated in the four major goals of the Caribbean Conference of Churches (CCC), which predicated upon the historic ecumenical meeting on Caribbean development at Chaguaramas, Trinidad, in 1971. As Kortright reports in his book,

> The four major goals the CCC has been pursuing are these: (1) to promote a spirit of self-reliance by helping generate and sustain indigenous development efforts; (2) to provide catalysts for regional development efforts; (3) to contribute to the material well-being of the poorer classes in society; and (4) to promote wider participation in the social and political process, while encouraging greater reconciliation between estranged groups in the region.[89]

In chapter five in his book, Davis assesses each one of the noted objectives in relation to the six crises that mark the Caribbean life: persistent poverty, migration, cultural alienation, dependence, fragmentation, and drug trafficking and narcotics abuse.[90] These existential problems are not just Caribbean problems; they are serious matters deforming and destroying human lives in Africana communities. I strongly believe that Christian communities and religious associations in Africana communities should incorporate or implement these four practices in view that they would help to improve people's living conditions, ameliorate interracial relations, and create a more humane and democratic social order for all people. I will discuss similar issues in the final chapter on

---

89. Davis, *Emancipation Still Comin'*, 48.
90. Ibid., 29–49.

Benjamin Mays's clarion call upon Christians to civic participation and public witness

Finally, Africana critical theology is not only a theology of being, that is, an empowering presence that tutors the marginalized how to fight for existence and instructs the most vulnerable in society what to do to maintain their right to live; it is also a theological discourse of becoming, that is, a massive divine energy that guides the poor to experience change and new birth, and the disinherited to excel and grow in their journey toward faith, wholeness, and shalom. Chapter six addresses these vital concerns in the writings of Benjamin E. Mays who interprets the Christian faith as the only hope for democracy and human flourishing. Like Cone in Chapter four, Mays projects that the prophetic Christian church should be the guiding light to bring all these dreams into fruition. The basic public function of Christian theology and the vocation of the Christian in society is to bring out the emancipative plans and reconciling mission (salvation, healing, hospitality, wholeness, reconciliation, and peace) of God in contemporary societies and in our postcolonial moments. The paramount goal of Africana theological anthropology and ethics is the preservation and promotion of Africana communities in all spheres of life.[91]

---

91. For a detailed study on African social ethics, see Parish, *The Spirituality of African Peoples*, 129–60.

1

Can the African People Worship?

On the Meaning of African Traditional Religion
and African Theological Experience

Introduction

THIS CHAPTER OF THE book locates Jean Price-Mars's religious narrative
within the academic disciplines of Africana Studies and Africana Religious tradition in hope his religious sensibility will help shed light on
Africana theological anthropology and ethics. The chapter explores Price-
Mars's reasonable arguments and propositions for the religious life and
theological experience of the African people. It seeks to demonstrate that
religion pervades every aspect and dimension of the African experience.
In rereading Price-Mars's ideas on the faith of African people, this chapter employs the comparative method used in religion, anthropology, and
ethnology to evaluate the fundamental elements of religious life and experience; particular attention is given to African traditional religion. The
basic argument of this chapter suggests Price-Mars was one of the earliest
pioneers who has offered a scientific study of African traditional religion
in the Black Diaspora, and correspondingly he was one of the precursors
who had laid the intellectual foundations for contemporary scholarship

on African traditional religion. His work anticipated postcolonial religious studies, the academic study of Africana theology and theological ethics—by employing the comparative method.

In the history of Western thought, European and American thinkers and theorists of religion have used religion as a marker to include and exclude certain people and races from the metanarratives of human history and to silence their contributions to universal civilizations and human progress in modernity. Both Western thinkers and anthropologists have reduced the African people to a life of religionless-ness or "heathenism." In certain intellectual circles, from the Enlightenment era to the first half-of the twentieth-century, it was also believed that religion was the ground to assess human morality, and what is deemed the good life or the ethical life; hence, Western thinkers also linked the religious and moral life with the life of reason and progress. Like morality, they associated religion with civilization and modernity. Because religion was interpreted to be the compass that regulates human ethics and behavior, and ultimately facilitated the pathway to civilization and modernity, the religious life of African people was overlooked, as Western scholars have disavowed African history. Consequently, these same theorists, ideologues, and white supremacists have deployed religion as a lens to deny the Black race of human equality; in various unscientific and pseudo-anthropological studies, they advanced the notion that African people were inferior to the white race because of a life devoid of religious commitment and piety.

As a response, the first Black anthropologist, Joseph Auguste Anténor Firmin, in his learned and interdisciplinary work, *De l'égalité des races humaines* (*The Equality of the Human Races*), published in 1885 at the emergence of the new disciplines of anthropology and ethnology, brilliantly dispelled the racial myth and racist ideology of the inferiority of African people because of their inability to rise above fetishism and totemism. Following Firmin's footsteps and beyond Firmin, in the first half of the twentieth-century, the father of Haitian ethnology and religious thinker Jean Price-Mars has employed anthropological knowledge, the cross-disciplinary approach, and the comparative method to showcase the religious life of the African people before European slavery, colonization, and missionary endeavors in Africa.

Although Price-Mars was reared in both the Haitian Protestant and Catholic-Christian traditions, Price-Mars was a religious pluralist and religious modernist; he acknowledged the merits and contributions of all religions to human flourishing. Price-Mars embraced all religions indiscriminately, and did not subscribe to any religious creed, dogma, or confession.[1] Using the pluralist approach to religion promoted by the philosopher of religion John Hick, this chapter is also an attempt to fill in an important gap in the comparative study of religion, Africana Studies, Price-Mars' scholarship, and Haitian studies.

The structure of this chapter consists of three major parts. The first division examines the interpretation of African traditional religion in Western scholarship. The second part of the chapter underscores Price-Mars's historic contributions in the academic study of African traditional religion. Finally, we close the chapter with Price-Mars's interpretation of the moral vision (religious/theological ethics) of African traditional religion.

The Interpretation of African Traditional Religion in Western Scholarship

In the academic study of religion, Western scholars of religion have not given African traditional religion its proper place among other equally important religions in the world. Past scholarship on African traditional religion has deployed various derogatory names and concepts to label not only the religious practices of the African people but also the African religions that are practiced in the Black Diaspora. In his influential book, *African Traditional Religion: A Definition*, published in 1973, Nigerian religious scholar and theologian E. Bolaji Idowu mentions the "errors of terminology" as they apply to the nature and interpretation of African traditional religion and the African experience in general; he provides a thorough analysis of such insulting epithets including "primitive," "savage," "native," "fetishism," "tribe," "paganism," "heathenism," "idolatry," and "animism."[2] Western philosophers such as Immanuel Kant, David Hume, François Marie Arouet Voltaire, Gottfried Wilhelm Friedrich Hegel, and others often described African traditional religion in negative or superficial terms because their understanding of human nature, reason, progress, culture, and civilization influenced their perception of

---

1. For an analysis of Price-Mars' religious worldview and sensibility, see Joseph, "The Religious Philosophy of Jean Price-Mars" and "The Religious Imagination and Ideas of Jean Price-Mars (Part 1)."

2. Idowu, *African Traditional Religion*, 109–34; Hackett, *Art and Religion in Africa*, 10.

Africa and African indigenous religion and spirituality.[3] Idowu is correct to infer that when he pronounces the ignorance of the Other or the unknown that is applicable to African religion, that "The unknown is usually the mysterious and is usually surrounded with dread."[4] African religion became an unknown phenomenon in Western thought not because of its inadequacy or irrelevance; rather, such attitude lies in Western values, and the lack of interest from Western scholars to properly study African traditional religion.

Misconceptions and derogatory appellations about African traditional religion have been proliferated also by Western travelers, missionaries, civil servants, philosophers, ethnologists, and anthropologists as early as in the eighteenth-century to the first-half of the twentieth-century; some of these writers have never visited the Continent, conducted any ethnographic studies on the religious experience of those living in Africa, or engaged in active anthropological fieldwork in any Region of Africa. These thinkers have not only challenged the religious ethos of African people, they doubted any possibility of African people of being monotheists and cogently conceptualized God in theological and metaphysical language. Those who believe in the possibility that African people could worship God quickly clarify that it is not the "Judeo-Christian God" they worship. They speak about the "African gods" with a small "g" and add an "s" at the end of the word god. They also use terms like "false gods" and "idols" to frame the African experience in religion. Others who sustain the idea that African people do worship God would argue the African Supreme Being is a distant Deity, and that he is not near the African people and not actively involved in their affairs. In his interpretation of the misreading of African vision of God in Western scholarship, Idowu's observation is worth noting: "If there is an African concept of God, if African people know God, what or which God? Their own God or "the real God"? This is precisely the predicament in which scholars currently find themselves. The question "You mean, his own God? Not the real God."[5]

Idowu has suggested that the ideas of a "high god" and a "supreme God" are Western inventions to discriminate against the peoples and cultures that might hold contrary opinions about the precise nature of God. The religious sensibilities of the African people are often seen as

---

3. Ludwig and Adogame, "Historiography and European Perceptions," 4.

4. Idowu, *African Traditional Religion,* /8.

5. Ibid., 92.

irreligious, unreasonable, unsystematic, and non-theological as compared to the religious experience of the people in Western societies and the so-called civilized countries. The "Dark Continent" is the common epithet used to depict the spiritual state of continental Africa and to alienate the African people from other people in the world. German-Swiss journalist and writer Emil Ludwig concluded that Black people in Africa had no concept of God and that it is impossible for them to think about God theologically; as he once questioned, "How can the untutored African conceive God? How can this be?"[6] Consequently, for Ludwig, the African mind was not fully developed according to Western standards that it should be engaged in theological speculations or philosophical thinking about the nature and being of God. Ludwig made it plain that "Deity is a philosophical concept which savages are incapable of framing."[7] The nineteenth c[entury] [...]ologist, and geographer Sir Richard Francis [...] [c]omically about African faith and idea o[f] [...] that his hark, eternal De[...] animate and inanimate, [...]d the crocodile, like the [...]e fetish shrub, like the [...]f True Cross, may, by [...] the inscrutable course of

[handwritten annotation: Religion acts as a very vital part of understanding Africa and its presence — it was used as a way to exclude and silence, then to make Black ppl feel inferior. the way many people look at religion in africa is through a derogatory lens, perpetuated by western thinkers. it creates the notion that Black ppl in Africa had no concept of a "true" God]

Compara[...] [B]osman, a merchant originated from the Dutch Republic, tr[aveled] to the Gold Coast (modern day Ghana) in the early eighteenth century, reported in his famous book, *Nauwkeurige beschrijving van de Guinese Goud- Tand- en Slavekust* (1703), that West African people worship inanimate objects as gods and that they were idol worshippers. He describes the religious crisis of the West African people in this language: "It is really to be lamented that the negroes idolize such worthless Nothings by reason that several amongst them have no very unjust idea of the Deity . . . The Devil is annually banished from all their towns with an abundance of Ceremony, at an appointed time set apart for that end."[9] Not only European thinkers accused the African people

---

6. Smith, *African Ideas of God*, 1.
7. Quoted in ibid., 1.
8. Quoted in Parrinder, *African Traditional Religion*, 14.
9. Quoted in ibid., 14.

of practicing idolatry, cannibalism, and superstition, even those who do affirm the religious impulse of African people maintained that African traditional religion was inferior to other religious traditions such as Judaism, Christianity, or Islam; critics who have been influenced by the evolutionary theory of religion would place "fetishism at the bottom, followed by polytheism and then monotheism."[10] African traditional religion would either fall under the first or second category of the evolutionary steps of religion, and the final phase of the evolutionary hierarchy would be granted to non-African religions.

Ugandan thinker and poet Okot P'Bitek, in his excellent work *Decolonizing African Religions*, provides an informative and critical overview of the misrepresentation of African traditional religion in Western scholarship. He emphasizes how Western anthropologists and ethnologists have constructed an unreliable narrative about the religious experience and culture of African people. Based on his research, he reaches two major inferences about methodology and academic interest.

> First, that whereas different schools of social anthropology may quarrel bitterly over *methods*, they may all share the same view that the population of the world is divisible into two: one, their own, *civilized*, and the rest, *primitive*. The second conclusion is that Western scholarships have never been genuinely interested in African religions *per se*. Their works have all been part and parcel of some controversy or debate in the Western world . . . [11]

Because Western thinkers had no genuine interest in African humanity, they described the African way of life as "anarchy, promiscuity, and cruel living."[12] Therefore, P'Bitek could declare this poignant statement about the Western imagination of African people: "One of the most perplexing and amazing phenomena of Western scholarship is its almost morbid fascination and preoccupation with the 'primitive,' and the hostile and arrogant language of the philosophers, historians, theologians, and anthropologists. Like the ogres of the tales of northern Uganda, unprovoked, Western scholars seek out peoples living in peace, and heap insults on their heads."[13] The idea of primitivism or "primitive" has marked Western literary production and intellectual discourse

---

10. Ludwig and Adogame, "Historiography and European Perceptions," 6.

11. p'Bitek, *Decolonizing African Religions*, 1.

12. Ibid., 10.

13. Ibid.

in reference to Africa. Marianna Torgovnick, in her powerful book *Gone Primitive*, offers an insightful analysis of European obsession with the life of the primitives, as communicated in literature and intellectual history books. Torgovnick coined the phrase the "primitivist discourse" to underscore the basic grammar of Western psychological, anthropological, and ethnographic studies:

> To study the primitive is thus to enter the exotic world which is also a familiar world. That world is structured by sets of images and ideas that have slipped from their original metaphoric status to control perceptions of primitives . . . Primitives are like children. Primitives are our untamed selves, our id forces—libidinous, irrational, violent, dangerous. Primitives are mystics, in tune with nature, part of its harmonies. Primitives are free. Primitives exist as the "lowest cultural levels"; we occupy the "highest," in the metaphors of stratification and hierarchy . . . [14]

Furthermore, her remark about the characterization of the primitive in Euro-American history is enlightening:

> The primitive does what we ask it to do. Voiceless, it lets us speak for it. It is our ventriloquist's dummy—or so we like to think . . . The real secret of the primitive in this century has often been the same secret as always: the primitive can be—as has been, will be (?)—whatever Euro-Americans want it to be. It tells us what we want it to tell us . . . Africa is the quintessential locus of the primitive: it tells a tale of "the eternal beginning" and gives "the most intense sentiment of returning to the land of my youth"; it is "the immemorially known." For Euro-Americans, then, to study the primitive brings us always back to ourselves, which we reveal in the act of defining the Other. [15]

The primitivist discourse is pertinent to Western perspective on African traditional religion, which is often depicted as "religious otherness." For example, scholars of religion have proposed three major theories about the beginning of religion and human attitude toward the Divine. In other words, the religious experience can be explained in three different stages: Fetishism, Polytheism, and Monotheism. Interestingly, as early as in the eighteenth century to early twentieth-century, many Western thinkers believed that the religious experience of the African people remained static and unevolved. While some have maintained that polytheism was

14. Torgovnick, *Gone Primitive*, 8.

15. Ibid., 8–11.

the primary religion of the African people; others have projected that fetishism, the bottom of the religious hierarchy, best describes the religious
sensibility of Africa's people. In other words, their primitive state of religious experience never changed from their "eternal beginning." Primitivism is associated with the fetishist stage of (African) religion.

Additionally, P'Bitek writes more lucidly about the ideological inter-
pretation of the essence of African traditional religion in Western thought.
For him, European misapprehension about the religious devotion of the
African people is nothing short of an intellectual crisis in the history of
Africa-European relations. Insightfully, he makes this observation:

> If the missionaries called African deities God because they
> believed that these were the local names of the Supreme God,
> and also because they sought to meet the Africans on their own
> ground, Western anthropologists were confronted with a differ-
> ent problem: that of interpreting African deities and religious
> ideas to the Western world. This they could only do in terms
> of Western concepts. The anthropologists to whom the soul
> and gods had no reality interpreted African religions in terms
> of psychological, biological or sociological theories. Christian
> anthropologists, on the other hand, described African religious
> beliefs in Christian concepts, and called African deities God.[16]

This same P'Bitek, whose religious commitment was probably radical agnosticism, also declares that "'Animism,' 'Fetishism' or belief in a
High God are products of the Western mind. There are no animists' in
Africa."[17] He was also discontent about how trained African religious
scholars and theologians have handled this pivotal issue and equally
responded unsatisfactorily to the "religious charges" against Africa and
African religion.

In the field of religious studies African students have responded
with a vigorous condemnation and rejection of the claims of Western
scholarship which presented their peoples as "primitive pagans." Nonetheless, instead of carrying out systematic studies of the beliefs of their
peoples, and presenting them as African peoples actually know them, the
African scholars, smarting under the insults of the West, claimed that
African people knew the Christian God long before the missionaries told
them about it. African deities were selected and robbed with awkward

16. p'Bitek, *Decolonizing African Religions*, 32.

17. Ibid., 27.

Hellenistic garments by Jomo Kenyatta, J.B. Danquah, K.A. Busia, W. Abraham, E.B. Idowu and others.[18]

P'Bitek has not offered any satisfactory solution to the misconception and misinterpretation of the religion of the African people both by Western scholars and trained African thinkers or religious scholars of African descent. His own vision about African religion seems to be paradoxical, conflicting, and even contradictory. For him, only "African thinkers" can properly interpret the experience of African people in religion. It seems that one had to be born "African" and has lived among the people of Africa ___ an expert opinion on Africa's religious life. On the other ha___ en___fied with the issuing research he has anticipated ___ ative-born African people and those wh___ ___bly, his positive remark is worth___

[handwritten note:] *white people do not care enough about the various nuance in africa, thinking about it as primitive. these western thinkers consider there to be 3 stages of a religious development: fetishism, polytheism, monotheism, "high god," are that a product of a western narcissistic mind. this leads to a fundamental misunderstanding and forces contradictions in African religion.*

___ societies is bound up ___ It is therefore highly ___ understood. The inter- P___ ___he Christian God does no___ ___f the African deities as Afr___

He also ___ ___genous people do not subscribe to a God who is transcendent, supreme, and majestic. To this view, we respond in the following way: if God is not human and physical, and if he is the Creator and Supreme Judge, as affirmed in the language of many African traditional cultures, he must be different from human beings he had created, and must possess essential divine attributes that make him distinctively and supremely "God." The underlying problem with P'Bitek's thesis is not so much about how the African people understand God in their own way; the conundrum lies in P'Bitek's refusal to associate the communicable attributes of African deities or *orisha* with those of the Christian God: "African scholars, trying to interpret the religious ideas of their countrymen in terms of European thought, and also anxious to defend Africa from the intellectual arrogance of the West, presented African deities complete with the attributes of the Christian God."[20] Another equally difficulty with P'Bitek's assessment on this matter pertains

18. Ibid., 21.

19. Ibid., 23.

20. Ibid., 31–32.

to the failure of language to describe "authentically" the religious ideas and vision of the African people. He thus remarks:

> African peoples may describe their deities as "strong" but not "omnipotent"; "wise," not "omniscient"; "old," not "eternal"; "great," not "omnipotent." The greek metaphysical terms are meaningless in African thinking . . . Omnipotence implies infinite power, not merely the power of clearing the forest, as the Ngombe of the Congo describe their deity; the great equatorial forest that once covered most of East Africa has been completely destroyed by man. Nor does the term mean having the power of "bending even majesties," which a political mob or an assassin can easily effect."[21]

As a poet and multilingual speaker, P'Bitek must have had a clear and effective command and understanding of linguistic dynamics. The translation from one language to another and the rendering of one concept from one language to another, however, is a complex phenomenon, and that often could fail human perception and understanding of the world, and about what could be thought, seen, and expressed. This is applicable to any human language or culture—even in the native tongues of African people in which they convey their ideas about God and their articulation about their own religious sensibility. Interestingly, this same P'Bitek, who has defended the authenticity of the religion of the African people, is very pessimistic about its future and the utility of African deities. The radical agnostic predicted the end of African traditional religion because he believed in the primacy of science over religion.

> The belief in these [African] deities provide the explanations as well as the methods of dealing with misfortunes and ill-health. With the advance of medical knowledge, perhaps one day, the people of northern Uganda and other peoples of Africa will tell the diviners, in the words of Voltaire, "You have made ample use of the time of ignorance, superstition and infatuation, to strip us of our inheritance, and strange us under your feet, that you might fatten on the substance of the unfortunate but tremble for fear that the day of reason will arrive."[22]

By implications, for P'Bitek, the religiosity for African people is directly associated with their ignorance of modernity, scientific revolution,

21. Ibid., 52.
22. Ibid., 53.

and the life of progress and reason that often characterized contemporary Western societies. It is doubtful, however, that non-theistic humanism and atheistic secularism will satisfactorily fulfill the spiritual void of the African people or any people in the modern world. On the other hand, British scholar of African traditional religion Geoffrey Parrinder, in various important studies on African religion, has engaged several scholars who have demonized the religious sensibility of the African people.

Nonetheless, Parrinder himself has rejected animism—against Price-Mars' thesis; he used some inappropriate epithets to characterize African indigenous religion and differentiate it from the Abrahamic faiths, especially from Christianity. He describes the historic religious practices of the African people as "paganism" and the religion practiced in West Africa in the regions of Nigeria and Ghana as "polytheism." He also states that the African people practiced "partial worship"[23] in the Christian understanding or interpretation of worship as complete devotion to one God and that the African people also "believe without worship."[24] Hence, the African people are pagans and polytheists. It is unfair to use Christianity as a lens or the only parameter to evaluate the religious character of African people and their piety. For Parrinder, the African people have moved from polytheism to monotheism, from paganism to "standard religion." As he has remarked:

> In West Africa, in particular, men believe in great pantheons of gods which are diverse as the gods of the Greeks or the Hindus. Many of these gods are the expression of forces of nature, which men fear or try to propitiate: These gods generally have their own temples and priests, and their worshippers cannot justify be called Animists, but Polytheists, since they worship a variety of gods.[25]

In addition, Parrinder rejects Father Schmidt's "theory of a general primitive monotheism of Africa . . . that all peoples had once believed in one God from the time of Adam though many of them later fell into polytheism."[26] In response, Parrinder denies the possibility of exclusive African monotheism by pronouncing brazenly: "There is no solid evidence

---

23. Parrinder, *West African Religion*, 17–18.
24. Ibid., 19–22
25. Ibid., 24.
26. Ibid., 14.

to support this in West Africa."[27] Elsewhere, he writes discriminatorily against African traditional faith and from the typical Western ideology about African cultures and religious belief, as compared to the cultures and religious traditions in Western societies; both directly and indirectly, he affirms the sentimental attitude of what other Western thinkers long (dis-) believed about the religion of Africa:

> There are numerous writers on Africa who consider that Africans once worshipped one God alone, and that they have generated into polytheism. A similar view is held by those who believe in the diffusion of culture and religion from a common source, usually thought to be Egypt. Where modern peoples are below of the Egyptians that does not mean, it is contended, that they never attained such heights, but that they have lost their former achievements. So, Africans may not be "primitive" but were, until recently, in a state of degeneration from a former high culture.[28]

Edwin W. Smith, whom Parrinder praises for his terrific writings on African religion, in the 1947 "Foreword" to Parrinder's *West African Religion*, consents that "He (Parrinder) correctly classifies the religion as Polytheism and this immediately puts a new face on it. 'Fetishism' we think of as something brutal, credulous, irrational. We have advanced beyond polytheism, but it is not, I think, inherently absurd."[29] While Smith has erroneously employed polytheism to represent the religious belief of the African people, elsewhere, he introduces the discourteous concept of polydemonism as an appropriate characterization of African faith: "Besides the high and lesser beings who may be dignified by the title 'gods,' there is a multitude of other spirits, which, if taken alone, might warrant us in speaking of polydemonism rather polytheism."[30] Comparatively, in contradiction to Price-Mars' underlying claim, both Smith and Parrinder have rejected animism as a suitable theory for African religion; Smith has suggested "dynamism" as a reference to "the belief in, and the practices associated with the belief in, impersonal, pervasive, mysterious forces acting through charms and amulets, words,

27. Ibid., 14.
28. Ibid., 19.
29. Smith, "Foreword," in Parrinder, *West African Tradition*, xi.
30. Ibid., xii.

spells, divinations."[31] Moreover, Parrinder does not believe that African traditional religion is on par with Christianity nor does it possess equal merit as a religious tradition; according to him, it is the isolation of the Continent from the rest of the world that had contributed much to its backwardness and retardation, as compared to Western civilization or other civilizations in the modern world that had progressed into modernity and transition to the age of reason.

> We come to believe that African religion might "naturally" have developed itself to the heights of Christianity. Infusion of new ideas from the outside has benefited all religions, and one undoubted factor in retarding African religion in the past has been the isolation of tropical Africa from the rest of the world. . . . [As a result] It is important now to treat of African religion separately from the religious beliefs of other parts of the world.[32]

In the closing words of his "Foreword," Smith's allegation about African faith is very ideological like that of Parrinder. He supposes the superiority of Christianity as compared to "the pagan religion" of African polytheists; as he implies, because African paganism is too deep, he doubts the possibility of African redemption and that an African would totally renounce his/her pagan practices even when converted to Christianity. It is important to quote his words in full here:

> [...]rinder, or someone equally compe-[...] of the pagan religion with a study [...] Africans who in various degrees [...]nity. It is not to be expected that [...] complete break with the past, [...]so. What in Christianity most [...] precisely did they react to it? [...]ely set themselves to relate [...]nity may thus be enriched [...]and, it may be debased when [...] are perpetuated.[33]

[handwritten annotation:] all religions & human perception fail to understand the concept of a god of this magnitude, regardless of language or culture. the focus on this has led to demonizing the religious understanding of the african people — put under critique for "other spirits" they might believe in, resulting in the belief that they are not on Christianity

Whi[...] Pa[...] with [...] Christian missionaries and theologians have made conside[...] [...]ributions to our understanding of African traditional religion and cultures, Parrinder, Smith, and Taylor, as one writer

31. Ibid., xii-xiii.
32. Ibid., 19.
33. Ibid., xiii.

has put it, were among the trained theologians and pioneers from the West whose chief objective was to win "the hearts of new African elite for the Christian God by trying to find similarities between Christianity and the traditional religion."[34] In his critical study of the works of European missionaries and theologians in Africa in the twentieth-century, Umar Habila Dadem Danfulani's engaging and incisive criticisms about Parrinder's body of work is worth noting here:

> An Outstanding Christian apologist who not only pioneered but also popularized exploration into the theological interpretation of the West African traditional religions was Parrinder. Parrinder did not use traditional religion as an evangelical tool, but as a systematic and theological presentation, and approach that greatly influenced a number of indigenous West African Christian theologians . . . Parrinder collated in general the *sensus religious or religious universals* found in Yoruba, Ewe, Akan and Igbo religions and those of other kindred peoples, closely following the enumerative approach of Frazier. Through this method, he brought into focus, many religious phenomena from different parts of the continent. He does not only give a descriptive presentation but also a theological explanation of his themes, using his Western Christian theological concepts and formulations. Parrinder did this in order to present the nature of the major beliefs and practices of these deeply religious peoples.[35]

In addition, Danfulani has argued that Geoffrey Parrinder homogenized West African religions as a whole and neglected the historical development of these various religious ideas and concepts in various regions in West Africa; he also undermined the interplays between West African philosophy, cosmology, rituals, and the religious practices and beliefs of the West African people.[36]

The Price-Marsian Turn in the Study of African Religion

Interestingly, Price-Mars, employing the comparative method, who has written insightfully and cogently about West African religions and covered a great deal of scholarly information of the religious experience of

34. Danfulani, "West African Religions," 356.
35. Ibid., 357.
36. Ibid.

Africa, before the publication of Parrinder's major work, *West African Religion*, in 1949, has been ignored in Western Scholarship on the study of African traditional religion. Parrinder's subsequent important works on African indigenous faith include *Religion in an African City*, published in 1953, and correspondingly, *African Traditional Religion*, published in 1954. Price-Mars has written his major work, *Ainsi parla l'Oncle* in 1928—twenty-one years before the publication of Parrinder's very first book on the religious sensibilities of the West African people—on African traditional religions, cultures, and civilizations before Parrinder. Price-Mars, a contemporary of Parrinder, would investigate other dynamics in African traditional religion and cultures and compared them to those in Haiti and the rest of the Black Diaspora in subsequent writings including *Une étape de l'évolution haïtienne*, published in 1929, and *Formation ethnique, folklore et culture du peuple haïtien*, published in 1939.

All of these writings preceded those of Parrinder and other "glorified European thinkers and scholars" who began to write about the West African experience in religion in the second half of the twentieth-century. Unfortunately, Price-Mars's enormous contributions to the study of precolonial African civilizations and African traditional religious beliefs and cosmology have not been acknowledged in Anglophone scholarship. To our great dismay, what remains a historical fact and a scholarly norm in Euro-American scholarship is the intentional disengagement of reputable works published by Black scholars and continental African thinkers.

Nonetheless, trained African scholars and theologians E. Boljai Idowu, John Mbiti, and J. O. Awolalu have made a revolutionary shift in the investigation of African traditional religion; many thinkers have described their work as "representing different shades of what may be called a 'theology of continuity' with its advocacy of the respectability of African religions. Their studies have served as models for the field both in schools, universities and seminaries."[37] Others have proposed that these African thinkers have spread speculate ideology, as noted in this statement: "But they have also been criticized for being 'idealist' and ahistorical for using 'Judeo-Christian spectacles' to view African religions and for constructing homologies between Western Christian and African religious ideas."[38] For example, Idowu has reasoned rightly that while there were some Western scholars who attempted "to write

---

37. Hackett, *Art and Religion in Africa*, 9.

38. Ibid.

off Africa as a spiritual desert, there were, undoubtedly, a few who had the uneasy feeling that the story of a spiritual vacuum for a whole continent of peoples could be entirely true."[39] It was Price-Mars, however, who made the radical turn in the study of African tradition religion in the first half of the twentieth century.

In *Ainsi parla l'Oncle*, Price-Mars has devoted several chapters to the study of pre-colonial African general history and civilizations, and linked the diasporic heritage of the African diaspora with ancestral cultural traditions and practices in Africa. (The chapters were previously delivered as public lectures in various locations in the country.) Price-Mars is also concerned about unearthing and exegeting the thriving African religious traditions that existed in the Continent before the African people encountered the Europeans and were exposed to Western version of missionary Christianity. He relies on "the most advanced references on Africa available in the early twentieth century."[40] His objective was "to establish the map of religious faith of the Negro according to the map of the slave trade."[41] As Antoine affirms, Price-Mars' investigation about Africa "contains a wealth of information which evidences Price-Mars' long and patient research on the various peoples of Africa."[42]

With intellectual brilliance, persuasive rhetoric, Price-Mars chronicles the glorious history of the "Old Continent," and dismiss the stereotypes that Africa was the land of barbarism and savagery. With detailed information and careful interpretation of African history and religious life, Price-Mars has forcefully showcased that "The Dark Continent" was the mother of human civilization and progress.

> He recalled the memory of the theocratic state of the Founta-Djallon in French Guinea where Peuhsl and Mandingos "constantly showed a taste for the study of belles-lettres up to our days." The people of Benin and of Yoruba have made themselves known by their works in bronze as well as in clay, "revealing a remarkable sense of beauty." Then he recalled the memory of the political and social organization of the Kingdom of Dahomey whose civil administration, army and sense of discipline were of the highest order. Thanks to the Kingdom's cohesion it remained

39. Idowu, *African Traditional Religion*, 92.

40. Magloire and Yelvington, "Haiti and the Anthropological Imagination," 15.

41. Antoine, *Jean Price-Mars and Haiti*, 129.

42. Ibid., 128.

> independent under the same dynasty from the sixteenth century
> until the French conquest in 1894.[43]

Through his brilliant and forceful vindicationist discourse, Price-Mars was among the few Black writers in the Diaspora, in the first half of the twentieth-century, who sought to rehabilitate African traditional religion and pre-colonial civilizations in the academic study of religion and world history. In *Thus Spoke for Uncle*, he has devoted three full chapters—which bear the following titles: "Africa, Its Races and Its Civilization," "Africa and the External World," and "African Animism."—to investigate pre-colonial Africa and the study of the religious sentiments of African people. In other complementary chapters in the book where he explains the Haitian life and religious experience—bearing such titles "Popular Beliefs," "The Religious Sentiments of the Haitian Masses;" and the "Appendix"—Price-Mars links Haitian cultural practices and religious traditions to those of ancestral Africa. In other publications such as *Formation ethnique, Folk-lore et culture du peuple haïtien*, and *Une étape de l'évolution haïtienne. Étude de socio-psychologie* (See the chapter titled on "Les Croyances"), Price-Mars has offered compelling propositions and arguments to substantiate this underlying thesis.

Using the comparative methodology, in his discussion on the concept of God in African tradition religion, Price-Mars would anticipate the brilliant studies by Joseph Kwame Kyeretwie Boakye Danquah, *The Akan Doctrine of God: A Fragment of Gold Coast Ethics and Religion* (1944); Bolaji Idowu's *Olódùmarè: God in Yoruba Belief* (1962); and John S. Mbiti's *Concepts of God in Africa* (1970). As a precursor, Price-Mars has laid the foundation for a decolonial turn in the academic study of African history, African traditional religion, and African theology. Price-Mars' postcolonial turn in African scholarship also anticipated important religious works done by African scholars in post-independent Africa such as John Mbiti's *African Religions and Philosophy* (1969); Okot P'Bitek's *African Religions and Western Scholarship* (1970); Idowu's *African Traditional Religion: A Definition* (1973); Kofi Asare Opoku's *West African Traditional Religion* (1978); and J. Ọmọṣade Awolalu's *West African traditional religion* (1979).

Retrospectively, as noted in our previous analysis, African tradition religion has been ostracized in Western scholarship. Western scholars not only rejected the religious life of African people, they also

---

43. Ibid., 137.

challenged the religious sensibility of the Haitian people and stereo-typified their belief as "black magic," "sorcery," "fetish," and "cannibal-ism." Price-Mars has put forth the argument that the descendants of the Dahomeans in Haiti did not continue the animism, the ancestral faith, but created something new:

> Création nouvelle, il n'est ni la reproduction intangible de l'animisme dahoméen, ni la magie noire que les mercantis im-béciles de la plume dénoncent avec tant d'emphase et de malice afin de mieux accuser le peuple haïtien de sorcellerie, de cannibal-isme et de maléfices.[44]

Price-Mars informs us that before 1789, the year of the French Revolution, Western thinkers, colonialists, and enslavers at Saint-Domingue believed that a Black person was incapable of moving forward intellectually. Price-Mars explains the cause of this false belief as reflective of the fact that they ignored the historical past of African civilizations.

> Et d'abord, avant 1789, on pouvait très légitiment supposer, à Saint-Domingue, que le negre était incapable de s'élever au-dessus d'un certain niveau primaire de savoir. Non seulement, on ignorait le passé historique des civilisations, mais ni l'ethnographie com-parée ni l'anthropologie, malgré l'incertitude de leurs méthodes actuelles, n'étaient encore nées. Au demeurant, le negre n'avait de valeur que celle de sa structure et de son endurance.[45].

Price-Mars laments that religious scholars in the Diaspora have been substantially influenced by Western discourse that demonizes African traditional religion; the predicament of Black scholarship is that Black thinkers have also spread these same pseudo beliefs, the European unwarranted claims about Africa's religious system. The mis-interpretation of African tradition religion, according to Price-Mars, is not uplifting and intellectually effective:

---

44. Price-Mars, *Formation ethnique*, 37. "A new creation: it is neither the intangible reproduction of Dahomean animism, nor the black magic that the foolish merchants, with their pen, so denounce maliciously and accuse the Haitian people of witchcraft, cannibalism, and spells."

45. Price-Mars, *Une Etape de l'Evolution haïtienne*, 9. "And first, before 1789, at Saint-Domingue, one could legitimately assume that the negro was incapable of rising above a certain primary level of knowledge. Not only they have ignored the historical past of civilizations, but neither comparative ethnography nor anthropology, despite the uncertainty of their present methods, had yet been invented. Moreover, the negro had no value, but only of his structure and endurance."

Ils ont été obsédés par l'opinion générale très fausse que les Euro-
péens se font ou se sont faite des religions africaines. Pour tous les
auteurs d'Histoire Générale, pour les géographes, les voyageurs, les
explorateurs, pour les premiers essayistes de l'histoire des religions,
l'Afrique est la terre classique du fétichisme.[46]

In the same line of thought, Black Christians who have subscribed
to the European unfounded claims about the religion of African people
repeat, "*Les negres d'Afriques sont fetischistes.*"[47] We should ask at this
juncture of this conversation what is then fetishism?

In a chapter entitled "African Animism," in *Ainsi parla l'Oncle*,
Price-Mars intends to respond to this very question to challenge his
critics. Countering contemporary scholarship on African religion, he
begins the chapter with this introductory words: "A very old tradition
on the misconceptions and on an interpretation that is as superficial as
it is arbitrary, grips most of Africa in the mesh of fetishism."[48] Hence, he
seeks to inquire this same topic: "What is fetishism?"[49] The rhetorical
tone of the initial thought here clearly indicates Price-Mars is enter-
ing in an intellectual battle with his European interlocutors, and in the
process, he seeks to correct an epistemological transgression about the
African experience in religion.

As a result, Price-Mars would cite the definition of fetishism provided by Charles de Brosses, who in a paper delivered in 1787 to the
Académie des Inscriptions, rendered the concept as "*Le culte des objets*
matériels"[50] (The worship or cult of material objects). Price-Mars concurs
that De Brosses employs the term "to characterize the worship in which
Negroes seemed to materialize natural objects . . . I call in general by
this name (fetishism) any religion that has animals or inanimate earthly
beings as the object of worship."[51] Accordingly, Price-Mars explains that

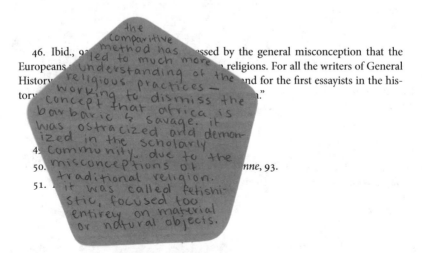

46. Ibid., 9[...] [...]ssed by the general misconception that the
Europeans [...] religions. For all the writers of General
History [...] and for the first essayists in the his-
tory [...]."

4[...]

50. [...]nne, 93.

51. [...]

[handwritten note:] the comparitive method has led to much more understanding of the religious practices — working to dismiss the concept that africa is barbaric & savage. it was ostracized and demonized in the scholarly community. due to the misconceptions of traditional religion. it was called fetishistic, focused too entirely on material or natural objects.

it was this same De Brosses who *"l'a fait entrer dans le langage courant en luis assignant le rôle d'être à l'origine de toutes les religions.* »[52]

This same Price-Mars has contended the concept is not an accurate characteristic of African religion, and that it is a misinterpretation of a poorly observed phenomenon.[53] In other words, Western thinkers have misunderstood this religious phenomenon and as a result, famously appropriated it as fetishism. Nonetheless, the Portuguese sailors, who had first established contact with the Black people of West Africa, wrongly used the word *Feitico*, which is derived from the Latin word *factitius* meaning artificial, to denote the observable religious activity of various African ethnic populations in which African devotees rendered homage or reverence to certain material objects such as shells, stones, or other natural objects; hence, they misconceived the observable African religious ritual as fetishism, and called these symbols of worship "fetishes."[54] The word "juju" was also used to describe the religious experience of West Africans; it is derived from the French word "joujou," which simply translates as "toy" in English. African religion was merely conceived as a form of human entertainment, a playful and humorous phenomenon.

Western critics have consistently put forth the notion that the religion of African people should not be taken as authentic religious experience or genuine spirituality. In summary, the word fetish was used not only to describe the religious activities, the charms and sacred emblems of West Africa, it was also deployed to label the whole of the religion of African people.[55] R. S. Ratray in his highly-esteemed work *Religion & Art in Ashanti*, published in 1923, only five years before the publication of Price-Mars's *Ainsi Parla l'Oncle* in 1928, differentiates fetishism and the worship of God in West Africa:

> Fetishes may form part of an emblem of god, but fetish and god are in themselves distinct, and are so regarded by the Ashanti; the main power, or the most important spirit in a god comes directly or indirectly from Nyame, the Supreme God, whereas the power or spirit in a fetish comes from plants or trees, and sometimes directly or indirectly from fairies, forest monsters,

52. Price-Mars, *Une Etape de l'Evolution haïtienne*, 93. "He introduced it into the everyday (common) language by assigning it the role of being at the origin of all religions."

53. Ibid., 93.

54. Ibid.; Price-Mars, *So Spoke the Uncle*, 84.

55. Idowu, *Olodumare*, 2.

witches, or from sort of unholy contact with death; a god is the god of the many, the family, the clan, or the nation. A fetish is generally personal to its owner.[56]

Price-Mars clarifies that fetishism is not a religion, and that African people do not render homage to material objects. Rather, they revered the Spirit whom they believed incarnated in certain material objects and natural phenomena such as the seas, earth, rivers, forest, trees, etc. It is that which modern science, based on careful research, rightly called animism, he proposes. The original text is as follows :

> L'observation portugaise n'avait marque qu'une partie du phénomène qu'elle prétendait qualifier et expliquer. Le Fétichisme n'est pas une religion. Les noirs d'Afrique ne rendent pas d'hommages as des objets matériels. Ils vénèrent l'esprit qu'ils croient incarnes dans certaines formes de la matière et particulièrement dans les grandes forces cosmiques : La Mer, la Terre, les Fleuves, la Forêt, etc. C'est ce que la science moderne à force de patientes recherches a appelé l'Animisme.[57]

Elsewhere, he writes back to his interlocutors in this strongly apologetic tone:

> The observation as it was established is not only incomplete, it is false because it is the result of misleading appearances. Unfortunately, the doctrine to which it gave birth has sanctioned an error which is now ineradicable. No, it is not the shell, or the stone, or the image of sculptured wood, or even the animals that the indigenous of Africa worship. The most backward of these men can be convinced that an imponderable element, an occult force is sometimes in this body or that animal, just as the Forest, the Thunder, the River, the Sea, the Earth appears to him to be endowed with as will, desires, passions, and likewise are empowered to act as Forces.[58]

---

56. Rattray, *Religion and Art in Ashanti*, 24.

57. Price-Mars, *Une Etape de l'Evolution haïtienne*, 93. "The Portuguese observation was only part of the phenomenon it claimed to qualify and explain. Fetishism is not a religion. Black Africans do not pay homage to material things. They worship the spirit they believe to be embodied in certain forms of matter and especially in the great cosmic forces: The Sea, the Earth, the Rivers, the Forest, etc. This is what modern science, through careful research, has called Animism."

58. Price-Mars, *So Spoke the Uncle*, 84.

Price-Mars rejects the popular thesis among European travel writers, geographers, historians, and anthropologists who describe traditional African religion as superstition and magic. By countering the idea, he suggests that the religious life is the antithesis to magic or superstition for "*La magie n'est que la contrefacon de la religion, la superstition n'en est que la déformation ou la caricature.*"[59] Price-Mars avers the universality of superstition: "It is true that superstition is universal, and one might even venture the aphorism: superstition is the inevitable corollary of religion" ("*Tant il est vrai que la superstition est universelle, on pourrait même hasarder l'aphorisme: la superstition est le corollaire fatal de la religion.*"[60])

The African people make a sharp distinction between religion and magic, the magician and the serviteur of the gods. Price-Mars aptly establishes the dissimilarity between these two phenomena by projecting that sorcery and religion are two different entities. As he observes:

> Should we go back in time to the most distant origins of Africa, we find a distinction between the Magician and the serviteur of the gods, the first being very much feared in these small communities owing to his social evil-doing. Indeed, it is startling to think of the legal offenses being committed every day in these regions by an individual accused of magic. For the protection of the community, in the name of the law which is the expression of social custom and preservation, the accused was subjected to an ordeal which was most often a prompt sentence to death by hanging, or stoning, without burial for the body of the guilt. There was perhaps nothing more tragic than the fate of the individual suspected of sorcery in the African communities.[61]

Price-Mars also links the deliberate rejection of African religiosity and past civilizations by white critics with the race problem in modernity. "*Pendant trois cents ans environ, la race vécut dans cet état de stagnation morale et intellectuelle d'une incomparable bassesse. Il va sans dire que cela s'entend de la grosse masse des esclaves, du monde noir.* »[62] Price-Mars has

59. Price-Mars, *Une Etape de l'Evolution haïtienne*, 106. "Magic is only the counterfeit of religion; superstition is only the distortion or the caricature."

60. Ibid., 109. "As long as it is true that superstition is universal, one could even venture the aphorism: superstition is the fatal corollary of religion."

61. Price-Mars, *So Spoke the Uncle*, 149.

62. Price-Mars, *Une Etape de l'Evolution haïtienne*, 10. "For about three hundred years, the race lived in a state of moral and intellectual stagnation of incomparable baseness. It goes without saying that this means the large population of the enslaved, the black world."

not only questioned the idea of the race concept, he informs us that it does not exist, and that race is categorically a myth. *"La race pure est un mythe an anthropologie. Au contraire, le métissage humain est un fait biologique aussi certain et aussi indélébile que le rattachement de notre organisme a quelque forme plus humble de la série animale. »*[63] He posits that there is only one race : the human race. In an apologetic tone, he declares that God—who is infinitely wise, just and good—in his infinite wisdom has never created the Black people as inferior (*"Dieu . . . qui est infinement sage, juste et bon . . . Dieu dans son infinite sagesse a fait de la race noire une race a jamais inférieure."*[64]) Price-Mars not only affirms the spiritual equality of all people, he is categorically asserting their ontological and social equality before God. Yet, elsewhere, he seems to contradict his own thesis when he converges religion and race; he explains how the world's empires and colonial powers have conquered peoples and civilizations under both the banner of race and religion. Both racial solidarity and common allegiance to a shared faith galvanize nations and peoples toward the fulfillment of their national goals or patriotic zeal.[65]

In Western history of ideas, European thinkers and pro-slavery advocates have distorted African history and the history of the people of African ancestry in the Diaspora because of the crisis of slavery and economic exploitation. Accordingly, "For four hundred years, the white race, without pity or mercy, aroused internecine war in Africa, pitting Negro against Negro, chasing them without respite or mercy, in order to satisfy this ignoble traffic in human flesh and, in so doing, destroying all native civilization and culture."[66] Because of slavery and Western colonization, American-European thinkers also endorsed the idea that African people in general "were the outcasts of humanity, without a history, without morality, without religion, and had to be infused by whatever means available with new moral values, outfitted with a new humanity."[67] Price-Mars laments on the disavowal of African history and the exclusion of African religion in academic study as an intellectual devastation.

63. Ibid., 15. "The pure race is a myth in anthropology. On the contrary, human miscegenation is a biological fact as certain and indelible as the attachment of our organism to some of the more humble type of the animal kingdom."

64. Ibid., 138. "God . . . who is infinitely wise, just and good . . . God, in his infinite wisdom, has not made the black race an inferior race."

65. Ibid., 115.

66. Price-Mars, "From So Uncle Said," 150.

67. Ibid., 145.

The historical amnesia about pre-colonial African civilizations had a profound psychological and spiritual bearing on the people in the African Diaspora as well as on Black Atlantic intellectuals. At that point, everything which was authentically indigenous—language, mores, sentiments, beliefs—became suspect, tarnished with bad taste in the eyes of the elites seized with nostalgia for the lost mother country. As this process occurred, the word "negro," formerly a generic term, acquired a pejorative meaning. As for that of 'African,' it always has been and is the most humiliating term by which a Haitian can be addressed. Strictly speaking, the most distinguished person in this country would rather be that someone found a resemblance between him and an Eskimo or a Samoan or a Tongan rather than to recall his Guinean or Sudanese origins.[68]

The predicament of blackness is further explained against the discourse of hierarchy of values resulting in a crisis of identity and the devaluation of Black humanity. The term Negro becomes a scornful word and a synonym for inferiority. He declares :

> Il en résulta le phénomène suivant à savoir que le type standard ayant été le blanc, plus on s'en rapprochait plus on s'élevait dans la hiérarchie des valeurs, tandis que, à l'inverse le noir ayant été synonyme d'infériorité, le terme negre devint péjoratif. Personne ne voulut être negre et même maintenant personne n'entend être negre, pas même ceux d'entre les hommes dont la carnation en porte l'irrécusable témoignage.[69]

It is this same Price-Mars who would expediently remind his Haitian patriots that "The thread of oral traditions derived from overseas. When one submits these traditions to a comparative examination, they immediately reveal that Africa, for the most part, is their land of origin . . . Well, we only will have the opportunity of being ourselves if we do not repudiate any part of our ancestral heritage. Now, this heritage is eight-tenths a gift of Africa."[70] Price-Mars' commitment to Black consciousness and racial pride in the Black Diaspora has influenced many

68. Ibid., 146.

69. Price-Mars, *La République d'Haïti*, 26. "The result was to find out precisely about the standard of whiteness; the closer we arrived about it associates with the hierarchy of values; whereas black was synonymous with inferiority. Hence, the term negro became pejorative. Nobody wanted to be a black man, and even now nobody desires to be a negro, not even among those of men whose pedigree bears the irrefutable testimony."

70. Price-Mars, "From So Uncle Said," 148.

Black thinkers both in the Caribbean and in Western Europe, including Leopold Sedar Senghor who dubbed Jean Price-Mars "the Father of the Negritude." Price-Mars biographer Jacques Antoine asserts that "Price-Mars' mental courage before the predicament of the Haitian masses and the shortcomings of the Haitian elite has its source, not in despair but in the unswerving faith he had in his race—the Black Race."[71] In an important article, authors Gerarde Magloire and Kevin A. Yelvington add that "Price-Mars avowedly sought to renovate and redeem Haiti precisely by prescribing the place of 'Africa' within the nation."[72]

The mulatto ideology and interpretation of the Haitian History is that Haiti, by the virtue of the Haitian Revolution, is a symbol of Black dignity and proud, "where black and mulatto—all sons of Africa—live in harmony under the leadership of the most enlightened class, which is that group descended from *anciens libres*."[73] While Haitian mulatto historians and intellectuals refuted the doctrine of the inequality of the human races and the ideology that the White race was the superior race, ambivalently, "They believed Africa to be barbarous, or at least relatively backward, and they were generally in favor of rooting out those customs and beliefs in Haiti which derived from Africa"[74] including the Afro-Haitian religion of Vodou, which they condemned and perceived as magic, sorcery, and a superstition. To provide a better historical understanding of the Vodou religion and its role in the Haitian society, it sufficed for Price-Mars to discuss in detail its African origin to his audience. The word "Vodou" (French) or "Vodoun" (Fon) translates as "spirit." Price-Mars sustains the thesis that "*Vodoun e gni Alahounou; Mahou oue do Vodou:* The Spirit is a thing of God; God possesses the Spirit."[75] The Afro-Haitian Vodou has its origin in African religious animism. In the next division of the chapter, we shall consider the essence of African religion considered animistic.

African Traditional Religion as Animism

As previously seen in the second part of the chapter, the precise nature of African traditional religion is a matter of scholarly contestation and

71. Antoine, *Jean Price-Mars and Haïti*, 125.

72. Magloire and Yelvington, "Haiti and the Anthropological Imagination," 7.

73. Nicholls, "A Work of Combat," 34.

74. Ibid., 35.

75. Price-Mars, *So Spoke the Uncle*, 52.

speculation. Scholars of religion have made different propositions concerning the nature of African religion and the religious ideas of the African people. Foremost, unlike the Abrahamic religious traditions and certain Eastern religions, African traditional religion does not have a sacred text, a set of (theological) dogmas, and a foundational historical figure. Price-Mars acknowledges that African animism does not have a codified set of doctrine nor does its adherents subscribe to some rigid sacred texts on African ethics. He has remarked that African animism has tried to purify itself against negative influences and the caricatures of magic and superstition similarly as Christianity has fought for centuries against "*les sectes dissidents, a defender les livres saints contre des surcharges, des falsifications de texte avant de se constituter au corps de doctrine*."[76] George I. K. Tasie puts forth, "It is not a missionary religion per se: there is no messianic expectation or apocalyptic warnings of the end of the world."[77] It is noted that African indigenous religion is largely oral and its belief and practices are preserved in the memory of living persons—cultic functionaries, elders, opinion leaders and other custodians of cultural and religious traditions—and passed on by word of mouth from generation to generation. This feature of African indigenous religion has left it much disadvantaged, exposing most of its doctrines and dogmas to "additions and subtractions, modifications and distortions, exaggerations and confusions, so that it is difficult to separate the truth from the fiction.[78]

The structural elements of African traditional religion include various religious sources: liturgy, songs, myths, stories, legends, proverbs, idioms, prayers, etc. According to Idowu, African songs are closely related to the religious sensibility of African people; they "constitute a rich heritage of all Africa . . . Singing is always a vehicle conveying certain sentiments or truth. When they are connected with rituals, they convey the faith of worshippers from the heart—faith in Deity, belief in and about the divinities, assurance and hopes about the present and with regard to the hereafter."[79] In the same respect, he makes the following observation:

> Every cult has its set liturgy. Liturgy consists of the pattern
> as well as the subject-matter of worship. It is her in fact that

76. Price-Mars, *Une Etape de l'Evolution haïtienne*, 106. "The dissident sects by defending the holy books against exaggerations and falsifications of text before constituting itself into a body of doctrine."

77. Tasie, "The Heritage of the Mouth," 26.

78. Ibid.

79. Idowu, *African Traditional Religion*, 85.

"experiential participation" will be of immense benefit to the researcher. In an unwritten liturgy (or any liturgy), the thing does not sound the same when recited outside the context of actual worship. In fact, experience shows that very often it is either inaccurately said or stumblingly said . . . There is usually a certain body of systematic recitals connected with the cult of the oracle divinity. . . . And finally, we have those pithy sayings, proverbs and adages, which are the sine qua non of African speech. These are to be found in abundance everywhere and it can be astonishing how much they alone could teach us about religion in Africa . . . These are oral traditions constitute the scriptures as well as the breviaries of African traditional religion: therefore, no one can expect to see the religion from the inside unless he proceeds through them. They are, in fact, probably of more value to the student than some printed scriptures and common orders, because they are indeed "living and active."[80]

P. A. Talbot in his investigation of the religion practiced in Southern Nigeria came to this conclusion that African traditional religion is comparable to that of the ancient Egyptians:

On the whole, the religion strongly resembles that of the ancient Egyptians, who combined a belief in the existence of an omnipotent and omniscient Supreme God . . . with that in multitudes of subordinate deities . . . [81]

Similarly, E. Geoffrey Parrinder, having lived in West Africa and studied the religion of the people in Ibadan, comes to this inference, "It would be useful to devise a term which would denote religion that have a supreme God and also worship other gods."[82] Idowu prefers the theoretical concept of "diffused monotheism" or "implicit monotheism" to characterize the totality of the religious experience and practices of African people. As he has remarked in his ethnographic investigation of the Yoruba religion and Yoruba notion of God:

I do not know any of any places in Africa where the intimacy is not accorded to God. That is why, because this is very true of the Yoruba, I conclude that the religion can only be adequately described as monotheistic. I modify this "monotheism" by the adjective "diffused," because here we have a monotheism in which

---

80. Ibid., 84–85.

81. Quoted in Idowu, *African Traditional Religion*, 135.

82. Quoted in ibid., 135.

there exist other powers which derive from Deity such being and authority that they can be treated, for practical purposes, almost as ends in themselves.[83]

Complementarily, he writes with greater precision and clarity in this manner.

African traditional religion cannot be described as polytheistic. Its appropriate description is monotheistic, however modified this may be. The modification is however inevitable because of the presence of other divine beings within the structure of the religion.[84]

Unlike Parrinder and others who have used the idea of "polytheism" to describe the African experience in religion, Idowu is reluctant in using this mischaracterization. According to him, "implicit monotheism" suitably represents the religious practice of African people throughout ages and generations:

We may compare the system among the system among the Yoruba where we have divinities who appear to be completely autonomous, each with his or her own priesthood and set of rituals. A priest will hear, for example, the title of Osogun (the priest of Ogun) or Olobatala (the priest of Obatala). But the unity of the whole is manifested phenomenologically in that the head of the whole community is the Pontifex Maximus of all the cults together. Hence the saying, "Every festival is the king's festival." And, of course, none of the cults have any meaning apart from Oldumare, the Supreme God.[85]

Parrinder, Smith, Mbiti, Danquah, and Idowu have not employed animism as a religious symbolic for the African piety. By comparison, Price-Mars has embraced this representative idea to describe the totality of the religious life of the African people. Nonetheless, before Price-Mars would use the idea of animism to describe the religious experience of Africa, it was Edward Tylor, in 1871, who had coined the word "animism" to theorize the origin of religion, and more precisely that the genesis of religion is rooted in the idea of soul rather than of ghost or the belief in ghosts rather than in souls.[86] Hence, two theories

---

83. Ibid., 135.
84. Ibid., 168.
85. Ibid., 136.
86. Evans-Pritchard, *Theories of Primitive Religion*, 24.

are used to describe the beginning of religion: the ghost theory and the soul theory. Pritchard expounds on the utilization of the concept of animism in the discipline of anthropology:

> Some ambiguity attaches to the term "animism" in anthropological writings, it being sometimes employed in the sense of the belief, ascribed to primitive peoples, that not only creatures but also inanimate objects have life and personality, and sometimes with the further sense that in addition they have souls. Tylor's theory covers both senses.[87]

Pritchard, however, attempts to correct the misconception in anthropological imagination of the religious experience:

> Both the ghost theory and the soul theory might be regarded as two versions of a dream theory of the origin of religion. Primitive man then transferred this idea of soul to other creatures in some ways like himself, and even to inanimate objects which aroused his interest. The soul, being detachable from whatever it lodged in, could be thought of as independent of its material home, whence arose the idea of spiritual beings, whose supposed existence constituted Tylor's minimum definition of religion; and these finally developed into gods, beings vastly superior to man and in control of his destiny.[88]

Although Pritchard's theory had had its heyday, it does not do justice to the so-called revelatory and Abrahamic religions such as Judaism, Christianity, and Islam. According to these religious traditions, it was God himself who had revealed himself to humanity and initiated the first religious experience, in which both men and women were invited to participate in and fellowship with him. Though Price-Mars was quite aware of the scholarly studies on the possible origins of the Abrahamic faiths, theoretically, as a trained anthropologist, he was unorthodox in his religious imagination; his ideas about the nature of religion in general were very close to his contemporary anthropologists and ethnologists. Price-Mars does maintain that African people were not polytheist but animist monotheist. He puts forth unapologetically the idea that animism is the religion universal of Africa: "*L'Animisme, voila la religion de l'Afrique.*"[89]

---

87. Ibid., 25.

88. Ibid.

89. Price-Mars, *Une Etape de l'Evolution haïtienne*, 93. "Animism is the religion of Africa."

He also adds, *"Même lorsqu'il a cédé à des courants de fanatisme qui ont implanté chez lui l'étendard du Prophète ou la croix du Christ, le negre reste fort souvent un animiste."*[90] Hence, the religious sensibility of African people is expressed toward animistic piety. Price-Mars goes on to comment on the different forms of African animism known throughout Africa, under different names such as *Obi* or *Obia*.

In Western Africa, the African people subscribed to an animist religious worldview in which the religion of the Dahomey was *"Le prototype avec son incarnation de l'Etre suprême dans Mahou ou Mawu, dieu adrogyne du ciel, et la multiplicité des puissances intermédiaires qui se manifestent dans les différentes modalités des panthéons dahoméens. Tous ces déités sont autant d'esprits ou Vodou dont les cultes se matérialisent en manifestations diverses."*[91]

African religion is closely bonded with the land, the natural world, and the ancestral hosts, and African deities are concomitant to the object (s) of association or the object (s) of worship. African deities embody and dwell in various natural phenomena.

> *Tous les phénomènes de la nature ont leurs dieux majeurs ou mineurs—dieu du ciel, de la terre, des eaux, du tonnerre, etc. Tous les ancêtres veillent sur les vivants comme des êtres surnaturels et invisibles qui habitent l'espace impalpable. Tous sont objet de culte. Tous sont des esprits ou des Vodou auxquels on doit hommage et respect.* [92]

Because of the complexity of the African religious system and African metaphysics, Price-Mars infers that African religion does not make any logical sense to the Western mind:

> *Celui qui écrit ces lignes de rend bien compte lorsqu'il essaie de pénétrer la complexité de la théogonie dahoméenne, combien il lui*

90. Ibid. "Even when he has yielded to expressions of fanaticism that have been implanted at his home, whether it is the banner of the Prophet or the cross of Christ, the negro forever remains an animist."

91. Price-Mars, *Formation ethnique*, 35. "The prototype, with its incarnation of the Supreme Being in Mahu or Mawu, the androgynous god of the sky, and the multiplicity of the intermediate powers manifest themselves in the different modalities of the Dahomean pantheons. All these deities are spirits or Vodou whose cults are materialized in various manifestations."

92. Ibid., 36. "All natural phenomena have their gods: major or minor, such as the god of the sky, earth, water, thunder, etc. All (the) ancestors as supernatural and invisible beings who inhabit the impalpable space, watch over the living. All are object of worship. All are spirits or Vodou to whom we owe homage and respect."

est difficile de traduire en termes exacts une métaphysique qui se dérobe par ses subtilités et sa fluidité aux « raideurs ambitieuses de la logique » occidentale.[93]

The complexity of African religion is related to the African God who is an intricate Being.

Price-Mars also observes that «*C'est la concrétisation de sa foi en Celui en qu'il reconnait le dispensateur toutes choses et le maître suprême du destin.*"[94] Price-Mars equates the religion of the (African) Spirits with Haitian Vodou, and explains further that religion is intrinsically linked to the social and political life of the Dahomean people. In fact, religion gives order to society and politics : "*La religion des esprits ou des dieux, autrement dit la religion du vodou avec son ritualisme enchevêtre et sa formidable puissance traditionnelle qui est l'ossature même de l'organisation social et politique du Dahomey et particulièrement du royaume de Ouida.*[95]" While Price-Mars has argued that the religion of the Dahomey has substantial import on the popular belief of the Haitian masses, he did not say whether the religion of the spirits has provided both social and political structure in the Haitian society. Perhaps, this is due to the proselytization process of Haitian Christianity and Vodou in the time of slavery in which Christianity has reordered the cultural fabric and the colonial and political order in Saint-Domingue. Elsewhere, he recapitulates his argument that Haiti's ancestral faith is rooted on African soil:

> *Le sentiment et le phénomène religieux chez les Congos comprenant ceux du littoral c'est-à-dire les francs-Congos et ceux d'Angola et du Mozambique appelés Bas-Congo. Eh bien, ceux-là aussi ont été touchés par la propagande islamique . . . En résumé, et au terme de notre analyse, il nous parait possible de tirer cette conclusion légitime que la grande masse des negres arraches de divers points de l'Afrique et amenés à Saint-Domingue furet des gens pieux attaches à la fois musulmane, dahoméenne et même un peu catholique.*[96]

93. Ibid. "Whoever writes these lines does well when he or she tries to penetrate the complexity of the Dahomean theogony; how difficult must it have been for him or her to translate into exact terms a metaphysics that escapes by its subtleties and fluidity the ambitious stiffness of 'Western' logic."

94. Ibid., 35. "It is the concretization of his faith in Him in whom he recognizes as the dispenser of all things and the supreme master of destiny."

95. Ibid., 36.

96. Ibid., 92. "The religious feeling and phenomenon among the Congos including those of the coastline, that is to say the French Congolese and those of Angola

Moreover, he elaborates on the nature of African animism by defining as a viable religion or a complete religious system that constitutes not only of a body of doctrines, but in certain regions in Africa such as in the Sudanese, animism comprises of a genuine hierarchical priesthood that governs or perpetuate the religion. These religious chiefs, known as "Bougho" or "Hogon" –meaning "fire" or the heat of fire—are found especially in the mountainous regions of South-East Sudan.[97] African religious priests, according to Price-Mars' observation, "go through initiation ceremonies and are devoted to an austere life which gives them the great moral authority they enjoy. This animism, which divides the forces of the universe, pays tribute to spiritual geniuses which they embody. African animism, ultimately, renders to the dead ancestors a cult of veneration and implores their blessings and protection."[98] He projects that "in order to assure the perpetuity of the cult, the Sudanese have achieved a half-political, half-religious organization. The treasures of tradition and the defense of the community rest on the authority of a Council formed of all the heads of families whose advanced age constitutes a guarantee vulnerability."[99] One of the responsibilities of this religious-political leader and priest, who lives alone but among the people, is to interpret the will of the deity and to make his will known to the people.

The organization of religious worship among the Sudanese plateau is well organized and a complex system. Sudanese animism comprises various natural forces and energies that are spiritualized such as the sunlight, abundant and energetic; the earth, maternal and protective; the moon, regulator of the seasons, symbol and rhythm of time. If there are other elements near this triad to which the Sudanese imagination lends mysterious and formidable power, it is those responding to the character of Laggan, servant of malevolent divinities. It is probably the dualism of these two dissimilar cults, the one more spiritualistic, the other more

---

and Mozambique called the Lower-Congo. Well, these too have been affected by the Islamic propaganda . . . in summary, and at the end of our analysis, it seems to us that is it possible to draw this legitimate conclusion that the great mass of the negroes torn from various parts of Africa and forcibly brought in Saint-Domingue were a pious people associated with the Muslim, Dahomean, and even (a few) Catholic faith."

97. Ibid., 94.

98. Price-Mars, *Une Etape de l'Evolution haïtienne*, 94.

99. Price-Mars, *So Spoke the Uncle*, 94.

animistic, which reminds people of some strange influence in the religious conception of the Sudanese.[100]

On one hand, Price-Mars remarks that the cult of animism is sometimes materialized in concrete symbols; on the other hand, he posits that animism does not contradict the religion of the unique and sovereign God and the supreme Master of the universe.[101] Price-Mars moves forward to deduce the dynamics between God, the intermediary spirits, and the individual worshippers. In Price-Mars' thought, God is not only a transcendent Being, his relationship with these Spirit-agents at time of their creation is well established. He made them according to the purpose he has designed for each one individually. Price-Mars could remark that African people believe that

> the tutelary divinity has too high a position to be engrossed in the petty affairs of his creatures. Having accomplished his work, this divinity has established between men and himself a class of invisible intermediaries (spirits, names) who alone are accessible and consequently must always be addressed in order to obtain favors and blessings from on high . . . The animism of Negroes is therefore nothing other than a religion of primitive men. I do not know if all primitive peoples in all ages have worshipped the Unknowable in the same ways.[102]

African Traditional Religious Ethics and Critique of Price-Mars theory of African Religious Animism

Price-Mars does not refer to the African God as an "animist deity." As seen in previous analysis, he does characterize African traditional religion as animist. While many African religious scholars have accepted animism to describe the nature of African traditional religion, others have rejected the label altogether. J. Omosade Awolalu argues that we should not label the entirety of the religious experience of African people as animistic; as he pronounces:

> From our own study of the African Traditional Religion, we find there are unmistakably elements of animism . . . We also need

100. Ibid., 96–97.

101. Price-Mars, *Une Etape de l'Evolution haïtienne*, 94–95.

102. Price-Mars, *So Spoke the Uncle*, 85–86.

to add that it would be wrong to categorize the whole religion as animism. Every religion has some belief in the existence of the spirit. Even Christianity sees 'God as Spirit, and they that worship are to worship in spirit and truth. In other words, animism is a part definition of every religion. But to say that African Traditional Religion is animistic would not be correct.[103]

While Price-Mars acknowledges the morphological diversity of African animism, he concurs that its fundamental unity is certain and unwavering. He also confirms the external influence and the incorporation of foreign elements in African animism. In addition, Price-Mars explicates the doctrine of the human nature, and the function of the human soul and body in African religious animism. He also expounds on the doctrine of death and life after death in African religious thought; to these matters, we shall now turn:

> African animism could be summed up in a few very simple propositions: 1st, each man is composed to a double personality, one physical, tangible, material—the body; the other, intangible, immaterial, embodied in the first as its animator—the soul; 2nd, death is the operation by which these two elements are broken apart—the soul is separated from the body.[104]

In a comparative analysis, he explains in detail the concept of death and the view of destiny of the soul after death among various groups of African people including the Loago, the Gabons, and the Mandingo people. In African traditional theology, the soul and the body are two different entities belonging to the individual. While the body may decay and even ceases to be, the soul never dies. The soul, however, after death reincarnates elsewhere. It is clear there are theological differences about the body and soul among the ethnic groups mentioned below.

> What does th [traditional african] eath? According to the Bantus c [religion is deeply] nu (soul or spirit) searches fo [rooted in soul — leading] the cessation of life in the [western thinkers to] a reincarnation, while for [think of it as polytheism,] t randomly or remains [african people are not] [polytheistic, but rather]
> M [just closely bonded with] rinciple, the Mu-Z [the land, so considered] pirit which is att [animist (soul in nature). It's] dependent [spiritualistic, but does] [not contradict their] [sovereign God.]

103. Awolalu,

104. Price-Mars, So

of him. It vanishes from the person at his death and remains invisible although it devotes itself to guarding the group. It is a superior spirit among good spirits. The Mandingo, on their part, establish a difference between the dia, vital breath, and the niama, spirit. Death is the cessation of the vital breath while the niama survives the destruction of the body . . . On the whole, it seems indisputable that the African Negro made a very clear distinction between the body and the soul of humans.[105]

Price-Mars does affirm theological diversity within African traditional religion. By any means, he presents African animism as a homogeneous religious system or tradition. He does affirm the unity within its diversity. As noted, Price-Mars has brilliantly argued that "African animism" is a genuine religion comparable to other religions in the world, and has informed us that the adherent in the bush as the man of the forest has a tutelary deity, thus making personal the religious experience of African people. Price-Mars moves forward to validate the moral value of this belief. Price-Mars admits the relativism of religious morality by stating *"Evidemment, si la morale est en définitive un réseau d'interdits, un code de tabous dont l'observance garanti l'individu contre des infractions préjudiciables à son bonheur personnel et au bonheur de la communauté à laquelle il appartient, il ne peut y avoir de religion sans morale et, également, il ne saurait exister de Société sans une morale publique et privée."*[106]

It is worth nothing at this juncture of the conversation that in Post-Price-Marsian scholarship, both Mbiti and Idowu would expound on these religious ideas and the theology of the body and soul as they are interpreted in African traditional religion. Price-Mars turns to another aspect of African animism: its theological ethics. First of all, he pronounces that *»Dans toute l'étendue de l'Afrique, dans les tribus comme dans les Etas organisés, l'individu obéit à des règles d'autant plus étroites et tatillonnes que ces communautés en tiennent l'observance comme commandement des dieux."*[107] The following ethical and moral principles (theological

---

105. Ibid.

106. Price-Mars, *Une Etape de l'Evolution haïtienne*, 97. "Obviously, if morality is ultimately a network of prohibitions, and a code of taboos that guarantees the individual against prejudicial infractions to his or her personal happiness and the happiness of the community to which he or she belongs, then he or she can not to have religion without morals (morality) and, also, there can be no society without a public and private morality."

107. Ibid. "In all of Africa, in tribes as in organized states, the individual obeys the rules which are all the more narrow and fussy—as these communities hold firmly their

ethics) are, according to Price-Mars, *"the common stock one may find at the base of all the African religions."*[108] Secondly, he proceeds to articulate seven cardinal ethical principles regarding the moral vision of African traditional religion. African people adhere to a rigid moral code, which regulate their life and human relations and social interactions.

"A prohibition on killing, except for an enemy of the tribe" (*"Défense de tuer, si ce n'est un ennemi de la Tribu"*) ;

"A prohibition on stealing, or a ban on casting a bad spell over an individual" (*"Défense de voler, de jeter le mauvais sort"*);

"Interdiction of sexual relations between the spouses during the period of breastfeeding and menstruation" (*"Interdiction de relations matrimoniales entre expoux pendant la période de l'allaitement et de la menstruation"*);

"A ban against women not to participate in religious services during their menstruation" (*"Défense aux femmes de participer au service divin a cette derniere période"*);

"Punishment for adultery" (*"Punition de l'adultere"*);

"Respect for the elderly, to the Spirits and the interpreters of their will, to the sacred places, and in general, to everything consecrated to them" (*"Respect du aux vieillards, aux esprits et aux interpretes de leur volonté, aux lieus reservés a leur rendre le culte, et, en genéral, a tout ce qui leur est consacré*);

"Obedience to those held public places or religious authorities, such as those who have set apart by the will of the Spirits" (*"Obeissance aux chefs detenteurs de la puissance publique, tels qu'ils ont été consacrés par la volonté des esprits"*)[109]

Arguably, these moral codes are on par with those of the Abrahamic religion. Price-Mars asserts that the moral codes and theological doctrines of African traditional religion are not written in a sacred text; rather they are "transmitted from age to age by oral tradition, that it assumes *ipso facto* an esoteric character."[110] He denies the idea that these ethical values are found explicitly or only in African indigenous religion. He insists that these religious-based virtues are shared by all religious

---

observance as the very command of the gods."

108. Ibid.

109. Ibid.

110. Price-Mars, *So Spoke the Uncle*, 99.

traditions, and that these prohibitions constitute all the religious elementary forms—from the simplest to the most complex. He explains further that African religion had "governed their society [African societies] with interdictions similar to those in the law of Moses."[111] For example, he compares the African religious ethical principles to the famous precepts (the 10 Commandments or the "10 words" as it is correctly translated from the Hebrew) of Judaism and Christianity Yahweh revealed to Moses on Mount Sinai. Hence, he could argue that, African (Black) ethics and Jewish ethics, double face of a same coin, have a common divine source or origin, and that it seems that this is an indication of a universal phenomenon that is integral to the very nature of man.

> Je me demande si tous ces interdits ne forment pas l'ossature de toutes les formes religieuses, les plus simples comme les plus complexes. N'est-il pas vrai qu'il suffirait des stéréotypes en formules saisissantes pour qu'elles ressemblent comme des sœurs jumelles aux fameux préceptes que Iaveh dicta à Moise du haut du Sinaï : Tu ne tueras point (probablement l'homme de ta tribu. Tu ne voleras point. Tu ne commettras point d'adultère. Tu n'auras point d'autres dieux devant ma face, etc . . . En définitive, moral negre, moral juive, double face d'une même médaille. Il y a là, ce me semble, un phénomène d'ordre universel qui est inhérent à la qualité d'homme.[112]

Consequently, he could reason as in follows: "If one defines man a religious animal, one can say yet, a gregarious animal subjected to the rule, in a final moral being"[113] ("Si on a définie l'homme un animal religieux, on peut en dire encore, un animal gregaire soumis a la regle, en definitive un etre moral.")

111. Shannon, Price-Mars, 63.

112. Price-Mars, Une Etape de l'Evolution haïtienne, 98. "I wonder if all these prohibitions do not form the backbone of all religious forms, the simplest as the most complex. Is it not true that stereotypes in striking formulas would suffice to make them look like twin sisters to the famous precepts Yahweh dictated to Moses on the mount Sinai: Thou shalt not kill (probably the man of your tribe). You shall not steal. You shall not commit adultery. You shall have no other gods before me, etc. In the end, Negro morality or Jewish morality is the double face of the same coin; it seems to me that this is a phenomenon of universal order that is inherent in the quality of humanity."

113. Ibid.

African Religion in the Haitian Milieu

Price-Mars invites his readers to reason with him in this manner that if the most original primitive African is naturally endowed with a religious status equally to that of other people, isn't it evident that African people of Saint-Domingue have not left their traces in the history of worship in the organized Islam, Dahomean or simply animism?[114] At this juncture in the conversation, Price-Mars is linking the faith of the African descent people in Saint-Domingue-Haiti with the ancestral faith of the West African people. According to him, the enslaved African people never ceased to believe in and pray to the Spirits, Allah, or Mahou. In other words, the enslaved African people at Saint-Domingue assimilated animistic, Islamic, Dahomean, and Christian beliefs in their religious activities and rituals; nonetheless, Price-Mars sustains the idea that it was the Dahomean religion that provided a solid framework of disciplinary traditions, sacerdotal hierarchy, and set of beliefs to the enslaved population.[115] He also clarifies that in the historical milieu of Saint-Domingue

> Non seulement le rite dahoméen n'est pas reste intégral dans ce travail d'absorption, mails le folklore peut en une certaine mesure identifier, dans la mosaïque de croyances parvenus jusqu'à nous sous cette dénomination, les juxtapositions, les apports de plusieurs confessions qui ont contribué à sa formation.[116]

In addition, Price-Mars, in writing *The Vocation of the Elite* in 1919, was not persuaded that the Haitian people of his days were fully and exclusively committed to the Christian faith when they converted from their ancestral religion of Vodou. He maintained that their "conversion to Christianity is only superficial."[117] It is for this same reason he could write the following paragraph about the ambiguity of the Haitian experience in religion and its indecisive rapport between Christianity and ancestral faith.

> For the overwhelming majority of the population, latent animism coexists with belief in the Christian creed. The African gods have not quite surrendered before Jesus of Nazareth.

114. Ibid.

115. Ibid., 104.

116. Ibid., 105. "Not only is the Dahomean rite an integral part of this process of absorption, but the folklore, to a certain degree, can be identified, in the mosaic of beliefs that have come down to us under this name, that is, the juxtapositions, the contributions of several confessions that contributed to its formation."

117. Price-Mars, "The Vocation of the Elite," 23.

> Believe me, for many of us of the elite class, who pride ourselves
> on being devout Christians, the juxtaposition of the two faiths
> and the cooperation between them is something of a double
> insurance against the mysteries of the hereafter.[118]

Price-Mars claims that the evangelization and conversion of enslaved African people to Christianity in colonial Saint-Domingue was
a religious crisis because the enslaved African population was violently
introduced to the Christian faith—against their will. As he observes, "But
this situation is not recent. It flourishes even centuries ago when slaves
newly arrived From Africa rushed in their numbers to be baptized, although the process failed to destroy their fetishism. They simply became
baptized to avoid the mockery and ragging which the *bossales* suffered at
the hand of the creole slaves."[119] The continual practice and devotion to
the African-derived religions—i.e. Vodou, Santeria, Obeah, Candomblé,
Xango, Batuque, Cantimbo, Macumba, etc.) in the Black Diaspora is a
remarkable phenomenon that demonstrates the endurance and resilience
of African traditional religion in the midst of external influences. On the
other hand, if Price-Mars were alive today, he would probably be sur-
prised about the religious diversity in contemporary Haitian society, and
the radical turn of the Haitian people toward Protestant Christianity, and
correspondingly the slow emergence of Islam in the Haitian culture. Sociologists of religion specializing on Haitian religion such as Lewis Ampidu
Clormeus, Terry Rey, and others have estimated that the contemporary
Haitian society is professedly 30 to 40 % Protestant.[120]

Price-Mars, who often equates the religion of the Dahomean with
HaitianVodou reckons that the mystery of the Vodou religion lies in the
fact that Vodou is the origin of all religions. To make such a claim is to
suppose that Vodou is a religious tradition that syncretizes all religious
faiths. In Vodou, the adherents greet the bantou divinities such as the
E gun of the people of Congo; the Sudanese deities such as Mana of the
Mandigues people; and in addition, the adherents equally worship the
Christian God and several Catholic saints.[121] By affirming that African
animism (the religion of the spirits) is the root of all world religions,
Price-Mars is sustaining the notion that African people were the first

118. Ibid.

119. Ibid.

120. See Rey, *Crossing the Water*, 5–7; Clormeus, "L'Église catholique," 155–80.

121. Price-Mars, *Une Etape de l'Evolution haïtienne*, 105.

people in the history of human civilization to articulate a religious consciousness and to worship God the Creator (Mahou). He reiterates the famous statement made by the father of Western history, Herodotus, about ancient Egypt that "The African is the most religious of all people."[122]

In addition to his discussion of African traditional religion (animism), Price-Mars has also argued that Africa is the home of Christianity and Islam. The African people and their descendants in the African diaspora were united by communities of language and religion. The Muslim faith had existed in northern Africa, the Dahomean vodu in the central region, and the Muslim faith mixed with some Catholicism in the south. All of these faiths, Price-Mars emphasized, had rested on the belief of a unitary god, which meant that despite the classic interpretation as a land of fetishism, many African people had not been worshipping physical objects.[123]

What Price-Mars has offered to us in the previous analysis correlates to Idowu's own conclusion about the close links between geography, migration, locality, religious belief, and culture. As one may observe in this informative paragraph:

> When we look at Africa with reference to beliefs, our first impression is of certain objective phenomena which appear to be made up of systems of beliefs and practices which are unrelated except in so far as they are loosely held together by the factors of common localities and languages. But a careful look, through actual observation and comparative discussions with Africans from various parts of the continent, will show, first and foremost, that there is a common factor which the coined word negritude will express aptly. There is a common Africanness about the total culture and religious beliefs and practices of Africa. This common factor may be due either to the fact of diffusion or to the fact that most Africans share common origins with regard to race and customs and religious practices. In certain cases, one could trace specific cultural or religious elements which are common over wide areas which lie proximate to one another; and often there are elements which jump over whole territories to re-appear in several others scattered areas on the continent.[124]

122. Ibid., 109.

123. Shannon, *Price-Mars*, 63.

124. Idowu, *African Traditional Religion*, 103.

Concluding Thoughts

In our analysis in this chapter, we have observed Price-Mars's emphasis on the viability of African traditional religion. Price-Mars's basic argument is a clarion call upon us all to acknowledge the merits of African traditional religion, and pre-colonial African kingdoms and civilizations, and to establish the connective links and the cultural practices and traditions between Africa, Haiti, and the rest of the Black Diaspora. In *Ainsi parla l'Oncle* and other writings he has produced, Price-Mars's overarching goal was to establish direct links between Africa and the Black Diaspora, especially with his country of birth: Haiti. Ultimately, Price-Mars should be regarded as one of the early pioneers who had inaugurated the academic study of African traditional religion in the Black Diaspora.

In summary, through the role of the Spirit-agents of African traditional religion, Price-Mars establishes close intimacy between God and African people. In this way, no one could speak truthfully of the absence of God in Africa and the African way of life. Price-Mars has not discussed the precise manner in which God has disclosed himself in the historic past to African cultures and in African religion. Through the comparative method, he has shown that African people have developed a conception of God that is similar to that of the Abrahamic religions: Judaism, Christian, and Islam. Through the comparative method, he has also demonstrated that African traditional religion also shared a similar ethical system and moral values to those of revelatory religions, and that the African God is not a strange and ethnic deity created by the African mind. As conceived in major religious traditions, God is the Supreme Ruler and Creator of the universe who had not been hidden from his creation and his people. This God is not silent and has not been distant in the African or black way of life.

2

The Logic of Black African Theological Anthropology and Ubuntu Ethics

THE PREVIOUS CHAPTER ESTABLISHED the context for the African experience in religion and the theological impulse that created the desire in the African people to seek for the divine and to be in communication with God. Evidently, the relationship between God (doctrine of God) and humanity (doctrine of humanity) was an important element in this inquiry, that is the African religious life. We have observed in the previous chapter in African traditional religion, not only God is in the search of the African people, thus so revealed himself in their midst, and made his tabernacle among them; correspondingly, because of the deliberate divine self-disclosure (the Christian doctrine of divine revelation), the African people responded to God by attempting to connect with him through various means.

This chapter continues this inquiry by examining the nature of this relationship between God and the African people, particularly in relations to the moral order of the universe and God's ethical demands to the African people as his Creation and image bearers. Thus, this chapter studies the moral values and practical relevance of the South African concept of *Ubuntu* in the process of rethinking Black African theological ethics and Black African theological anthropology. Toward this goal, we examine the invaluable works of three prominent African theologians: Laurenti Magesa, a diocesan priest from Tanzania, John S. Mbiti, an Anglican priest from Kenya, and Bénézet Bujo, a Catholic priest from the Democratic Republic of the Congo.[1] The aim of this comparative analysis is to highlight the importance and implications of Black theological anthropology and ethics to the social and moral life of the individual and the community. This study also aims at articulating a model that is theologically sound and human sensitive and emancipatory. We shall investigate in their ethico-theological writings the intersection of theism, personhood, community, and Ubuntu as an African humanism. The selected African thinkers give the impression that the African perspective on humanity, the social life, and the moral life is more promising, liberating, and dignifying than the Western vision on these issues.

The theological anthropology and ethics of Magesa, Mbiti, and Bujo strongly promote interconnected human relations and interactional social dynamics that are based on the *Ubuntu* moral ethics. This chapter suggests that Black African theological anthropology and theological ethics have a strong foundation on the Ubuntu moral virtues and ethical principles that promotes democracy, human flourishing, and a life in solidarity within the framework of the community and a symbiotic relationship between the individual and the community.

The Question of "Being" or "Person" in African Philosophical Theology

The African thinking on the person or the concept of personhood counters the Western traditional thinking on the notion of being. African Theologian Benezet Bujo explains clearly that "The person is not defined as an ontological act by means of self-realization, but by means of 'relations.' This means that the human person in Africa is from the very beginning in a network of relationships that constitutes his inalienable

---

1. Magesa's most influential works include *African Religion: The Moral Traditions of Abundant Life* (1997), *Anatomy of Inculturation: Transforming the Church in Africa* (2004), *African Religion in the Dialogue Debate: From Intolerance to Coexistence* (2010), and *What Is Not Sacred? African Spirituality* (2013); Mbit's most important works include *African Religions and Philosophy* (1969), *Concepts of God in Africa* (1970), *New Testament Eschatology in an African Background* (1971), and *Introduction to African Religion* (1975); and Bujo's important works include *Foundations of an African Ethic: Beyond the Universal Claims of Western Morality* (2001), *African Theology in the 21st Century* (2003), and *African Theology in Its Social Context* (2006).

dignity."[2] In Black African anthropology, individualism is not favored above the community nor is it that which delimits the telos of life. That does not mean, however, the individual or personal subjectivity is absorbed into the community. It is also from this angle that Laurenti Magesa could write that firmly, the "African worldview is that life, relationships, participation and community are holistic realities, blending the spiritual and the material organically."[3] Accordingly, in the African worldview and religious cosmology, the community plays a substantive role in the life of the individual person. Magesa goes forth to underscore the rewards in living and acting as a corporate person:

> Apart from their community, African people are not fully persons. A person's personality and individuality are guaranteed only insofar as the individual is integrated into the community on the other hand, and the community serves and strengthens the individual on the other. So, the individual does everything in view of assuring the whole community's health and survival. Individuals may not be conscious of this as they work for their family, discipline it, and make sure no taboos are broken; or when they refrain from emotions that might disturb the community . . . The imperative of building relationships and community is instilled in the individual from birth to death.[4]

From a theological standpoint, Magesa sustains that the Christian Gospel "makes explicit the absolute value of the individual person. Created in the image and likeness of God and imbued with divine breath, a person has value in and for him—or herself. One's value and dignity as a human person are not given by nor do they flow from one's community. They originate from God's own self. . . . People cannot begin to grow toward the full stature of their dignity as the image of God unless it leads them to community."[5] The essence of human being derives directly from God with the purpose to establish the God-human fellowship and communion. God himself is the ground of all that exists. Consequently, "from the point of creation, in the very act of creation, the seal of the Maker, the seal of God's self-disclosure, has been stamped all over the face of the created order."[6] Based on an exegetical reading of Genesis

2. Bujo, *Foundations of African Ethics*, 3–4.

3. Magesa, *Anatomy of Inculturation*, 182.

4. Ibid., 193.

5. Ibid., 194.

6. Idowu, *African Traditional Religion*, 54.

1:26 and 2:7, many Christians make the claim that God has equipped man and woman with intelligence, will, reason, a sense of purpose, and a sense of community. This divine presence in people makes them addressable, responsible, and accountable to God. The implication of the divine revelation to human cultures is that it validates and sustains the creation of human communities.

> The significant point here is that revelation presupposes personal communication between the living Being who reveals and the living person to whom revelation is made. It would appear that man is a necessity in this situation; for, without a personal mind to appreciate and apprehend revelation, the whole process would be futile.[7]

David Tracy, in his important study, *Plurality and Ambiguity*, describes phenomenal approach in religious traditions; he establishes a rapport between revelation and interpersonal encounter:

> Authentic religious experience, on the testimony of those all consider clearly religious, seems to be some experience of the whole that is sensed as the self-manifestation of a undeniable power not one's own and is articulated not in the language of certainty and clarity but of scandal and mystery. The religious person does not claim a new control upon reality but speaks of losing former controls and experiencing, not merely affirming, a liberation into a realm of ultimate incomprehensibility and real, fascinating and frightening mystery. When religious persons speak the language of revelation, they mean that something has happened to them that they cannot count as their own achievement.[8]

In his helpful work, *Self and Community in a Change World*, Kenyan philosopher D.A. Masolo puts forth the sharp contrast between "being a person" and "being human" in African philosophical thought. He also elaborates on the interconnecting process by which a human achieves personhood. In other words, in African thought, a human being is not naturally born a person; one becomes a person after undergoing or fulfilling the obligations and rituals of the community. The idea of a person as social construct is similar to the Western postmodernist definition of gender and sexuality. The theory of dependence and interdependence

---

7. Ibid., 55.

8. Quoted in Rodriguez, *Dogmatics After Babel*, 66–67; Tracy, *The Analogical Imagination*, 173.

probably best describes African communitarian philosophical ethics and it is analogous to African theological anthropology. In the paragraph below, Masolo offers rational illumination on this conceptual phenomenon.

> Being a person and being a human being are not the same thing. We are human beings by virtue of the particular biological organism that we are. Our biological type defines us as a species among other living things, and it involves, among other things, having the kind of bring that we possess and all the activities that this kind of brain is naturally endowed to perform . . . This process of depending on others for the tools that enable us to associate with them on a growing scale of competence is the process that makes us into persons. In other words, we become persons through acquiring and participating in the socially generated knowledge of norms and actions that we learn to live by in order to impose humaneness upon our humanness.[9]

The sharp distinction between being a human and being a person is premised on very specific categorical and conceptual notions, as it pertains to human interactions, communal covenant, and reciprocal commitment. The language of participation and collaboration is stressed here as it involves the social obligations of the individual to the community to which he or she is a member. Accordingly, "Being' is a related category in the sense we recognize that the biological constitution of humans as a necessary but not sufficient basis of personhood, because human beings require gradual sociogenic development to become persons. This relational condition circumstantiates not only the physical existence of things and our development into persons but also our cognitive and moral experience of the world."[10] For some thinkers such as Immanuel Kant, the idea of the person is the ultimate question in anthropology and that which underscores or leads to other questions and relations; by contrast, in African anthropology, the community is the starting point of life or human existence. The community underlies everything the person is and will be, and correspondingly, what the individual does and will do. The person is inevitably the product of the community.

Furthermore, in his famous article, "Person and Community in African Traditional Thought," Nigerian Philosopher Ifeanyi A. Menkiti has brilliantly discussed the (processual) nature of being or personhood in

---

9. Masolo, *Self and Community in a Changing World*, 154–55.

10. Ibid., 156.

the African worldview; as he has summed up the logic of this communal ritual in this passage:

> The fact that persons become persons only after a process of incorporation. Without incorporation into this or that community, individuals are considered to be mere dangers to whom the description "person" does not fully apply. For personhood is something which has to be achieved, and is not given simply because of human seed . . . As far as African societies are concerned, personhood is something at which individuals could fail, at which they could be competent or ineffective, better or worse. Hence, the African emphasized the rituals of incorporation and the overarching necessity of learning the social rules by which the community lives, so that what was initially biologically given can come to attain social self-hood, i.e., become a person with all the inbuilt excellencies implied by the term.[11]

As a result, the idea of incorporation (into a community) is what engenders the personhood of an individual. Personhood is premised on a set of communal values and prescriptions the individual must fulfill, and personhood is not natural or automatic. It is always dependent upon fulfilling those promises for the good of the community, which sometimes are contingent upon one's response and attitude toward the community. Consequently, it is apparent that "Human beings are not only individuals belong to the same specifies; they also belong to specific and various groups within which they are born and act."[12] The value and virtues of Ubuntu is communicated through the African system of community.

The Values and Practices of Ubuntu Ethics

Generally, in African worldview, orientation toward life and human and social dynamics is best translated in the South African concept of Ubuntu. Correspondingly, in African cosmology and *weltanschauung*, the idea of human community and the essence of being human is expressed in the African humanism called Ubuntu. It is closely translated as "A person is a person through other persons." In South Africa, when the notion is applied to human beings, the word *abandu/batho* is used; when the reference pertains to the way of life, human values, norms, and traditions,

---

11. Menkiti, "Person and Community," 172–73.

12. Todorov, *On Human Diversity*, 385.

Isi-ntu/sitsu is used. As a linguistic tem, *Ntu* is used in a number of words such as *Unbuntu*, (PI) *Aba-ntu, iSi-ntu, Ubun-tu*. It is equated with the ancient Egyptian word for primordial substance. The Africans peoples, however, developed variants of nu-and gave it the following forms: *du, nbo, -ni ntfu-, -ntu, -nu, -mwu, -so, -tho, -thu, and –tu, e.g. Swazi muntfu; Sotho: motho; Xhosa umntu; Zulu umuntu. Xitsonga vhuthu.*

As a philosophy of African humanism, the triumph of the spirit and demands of Ubuntu make a clarion call to the individual and the collective to foster a life of peace, interdependence, selflessness, and reciprocity towards the preservation of the self and the community. Ubuntu as a way of life provides robust optimistic values and promising ideals to individuals partaking in the harshness and desolation of the modern life:

> Whoever is empowered by the spirit of *Ubuntu*, Black or White, African or foreigner embraces the vision of social inclusion and of a non-racial society. There is no doubt that Ubuntu has its reciprocal concept in other languages. However, a groups that advocate social exclusion and a racial society echo the language of the colonists, regardless of whether this is conscious nor not.[13]

Toward its humanistic orientation, the spirit of Ubuntu tries to rehabilitate the collective self and reinvent the SELF (EGO) and the SUPER EGO that have been victimized and disrupted by the colonial Super Ego. The ideals of Ubuntu are the antithesis of human oppression and exploitation, imperialism and colonization. The thrust of this African philosophy and practical aspect of Ubuntu ethics are effectively articulated in this detailed paragraph.

> Good neighbors live in harmony and are ready to come to the assistance of one another. Despite the caricature of violence so often used against Black people, African and African descendants are essentially peace lovers animated by the shared principle of Ubuntu, the seed for the globalization of solidarity. Impoverished by the globalization of the economy, they shall overcome through the globalization of solidarity. Hence economic growth rooted in human growth. Contrary to the colonial system that secretes a classist neurosis *Ubuntu* inspires concrete expressions of solidarity among literate and illiterate people . . . These concrete expressions of solidarity clearly justify

13. Aristide, "Umoya wamagama," 228.

the claim that Ubuntu generates a social self, or a social love rooted in brotherhood.[14]

This is a call to all people to live together in harmony with each other, to seek the best interest of one's neighbor, and to create more future possibilities for everyone. Ubuntu builds bridges of solidarity and not walls of separation. This particular attitude toward life and people can be construed as a unifying force that helps individuals to cope with and even dispels human anxiety, isolation, and hostility. Ubuntu "is the unifying feauture that generates a social 'self' or a love story rooted in brotherhood . . . The psychology of Ubuntu demonstrates how the concept stands in opposition to the principles of colonialism."[15] Ubuntu provides the empowerment and resources to both Africans and descendants of Africans to create a community of love rooted in African humanistic values and religious traditions.

Moreover, generally, the concept of Ubuntu bears a positive connotation or value; however, some critics have associated it with the patriarchal system in African society that it is responsible for the sustenance of the "deep-seated patriarchy throughout sub-Saharan Africa and its indifference to the insensitivity to gender justice."[16] Other African thinkers such as South African theologian Desmond Tutu defers from this position.

In his excellent work, *God is not a Christian*, Tutu provides a succinct but critical reflection on the nature of *Ubuntu*. He writes, "We need other human beings for us to learn how to be human, for none of us comes fully formed into the world. We would not know how to talk, to walk, to think, to eat as human beings unless we learned how to do these things from other human being is a contradiction in terms."[17] The individual needs other human beings in order to be fully human, and to grow both socially and spiritually. As observed in the paragraph below:

> The completely self-sufficient human being is subhuman. I can be me only if you are fully you. I am because we are, for we are made for togetherness, for family. We are made for complementarity. We are created for a delicate network of relationships, of

14. Ibid., 251–52.
15. Ibid., 258.
16. Magadla and Chitando, "The Self Become God," 12.
17. Tutu, *God Is Not A Christian*, 23.

independence with our fellow human beings, with the rest of creation . . . To be human is to be dependent.[18]

Arguably, there is a link between theology and anthropology in light of the teachings and symbolic meanings of Ubuntu. One can infer that the principles and virtues of Ubuntu have deep roots in African religious traditions. In some degree, one can also construe *Ubuntu* as a theological and moral virtue an individual possesses in the same manner someone can love relationally and be moved by compassion grounded on the virtues of *Ubuntu*. Some of God's immanent virtues are communicated exclusively through the ideals of Ubuntu, as outlined in the subsequent paragraph:

> Ubuntu speaks of spiritual attributes such as generosity, hospitality, compassion, caring, sharing . . . Ubuntu teaches us that our worth is intrinsic to who we are. We matter because we are made in the image of God. Ubuntu reminds us that we belong in one family—God's family, the human family. In our African worldview, the greatest good is communal harmony. Anything that subverts or undermines this greatest good is ipso facto wrong, evil. Anger and a desire for revenge are subversive of this good thing.[19]

While it is possible to appropriate a theistic foundation to this African philosophical tradition, other African thinkers have proposed a non-theistic, but a secular approach to the Ubuntu tradition. As many would consent to this reasoning, Ubuntu occupies a prominent place in traditional African society; conceivably, one can interpret Ubuntu as an ethical system or philosophical worldview that has shaped social interactions, and communal dynamics in the African world. Many African thinkers have sustained this perspective on the value of Ubuntu for human flourishing:

> Ubuntu was coveted more than anything else—more than wealth as measure in cattle and the extent of one's hand. Without this quality a prosperous man, even thought he might have been a chief, was regarded as someone deserving of pity and even contempt. It was seen as what ultimately distinguished people from animals—the quality of being human and so also humane. Those who had Ubuntu were compassionate and gentle, they

18. Ibid., 23.
19. Ibid., 22, 24.

used their strength on behalf of the weak, and they did not take advantage of others—in short, they cared, treating others as what they were: human beings.[20]

The telos of creating a society grounded on the theo-ethical values and socio-philosophical benefits of Ubuntu is promising to lead to communal wholeness and shalom, and to a dynamic fellowship between the individual and the community characterized by harmony and shared interest. Ubuntu virtues, nonetheless, are best cultivated within the camaraderie of the community. The individual is bound to the community and that it is the prize of freedom and mutual accountability that glues the individual to the community. Not only the community has the human resources and potential to sustain the individual, which will eventually contribute to personal or individual growth; the community promotes self-agency and fosters human flourishing toward the common good. This is an important element in both Liberation Theology and Black Liberation Theology, as reflected in the politico-theological narratives of James Cone, the four Caribbean theologians, and Benjamin Mays.

In addition, the freedom of the individual is not the antithesis of the freedom of the community or vice versa; in fact, it is the goal of the community to enrich the freedom and liberty of the individual as long as it does not transgress the good and freedom of the community. One could say that freedom as an essential virtue sustains both the existence and longevity of both the community and the individual. American Ethicist Reinhold Niebuhr alludes to the imperative of freedom as an element that could foster human agency, self-expression, and human maturity.

> Actually, the community requires freedom as much as the individual; and the individual requires order as much as does the community. Both the individual and the community require freedom so that neither communal nor historical restraints may prematurely arrest the potencies which inhere in man's essential freedom and which express themselves collectively as well as individually. It is true that individuals are usually the initiators of new insights and the proponents of novel methods. Yet there are collective forces at work in society which are not the conscious contrivance of individuals.[21]

20. Ibid., 22–23.

21. Niebuhr, *The Children of Light*, 4.

To complement Niebuhr's claim, in the African thought, the freedom of the individual is not prized or proclaimed; rather, if the community is free, it categorically and naturally transmits in the experience of the individual. Black African society puts more emphasis on the group than on the individual, more on group solidarity than on the activity and the desires of the person; the autonomy of the individual is not esteemed apart from the collectivity of the community.[22] The ethics of mutual reciprocity and interdependence is stressed here. The African communitarian tendency can be construed as a way of life that is deeply rooted in the individual's experience of the world: "it is the way a person feels and thinks in union not only with all other people around him but indeed with all other beings in the universe: God, animal, tree, or pebble."[23] The obligations of the individual to the community are designed to enrich the life of the individual; as a corporate person, the life of the individual is dynamically converged in the communal life. Consequently, one can remark that

> The order of a community is, on the other hand, a boon to the individual as well as to the community. The individual cannot be a true self in isolation. Nor can he live within the confines of the community which "nature" establishes in the minimal cohesion of family and herd. His freedom transcends these limits of nature, and therefore makes larger and large social units both possible and necessary. It is precisely because of the essential freedom of man that he requires a contrived order in his community.[24]

To put it this differently, the life of the individual is meaningless apart from his or her experience within the structure of the community:

> The individual is related to the community (in its various levels and extensions) in such a way that the highest reaches of his individuality are dependent upon the social substance out of which they arise and they must find their end and fulfillment in the community. No simple limit can be placed upon the degree of intimacy to the community, and the breadth and extent of community which the individual requires for his life.[25]

22. Quoted in Masolo *Self and Community*, 231.

23. Ibid., 231–32.

24. Niebuhr, *The Children of Light*, 4.

25. Ibid., 48.

As noted in our preceding analysis, we inferred that the idea of community (communitarianism) is the foundational concept in African anthropological ethics; by contrast, in Western worldview, the individual (individualism) is favored. However, what constitutes the African communal system? What is a community? Who are members of the community? In the African way, the community constitutes four entities: God, the ancestors, the community, and the individual. The community includes both the visible (the living) and invisible members—the deceased ancestors. It is possible, however, to construe this African dynamic in the light of the biblical notion of corporate identity and existence:

> This emphasis on the group's role in the formation of the individual is a radical departure from the individualism that has marked European-American theological anthropology since the time of Augustine. However, it should be noted that the corporate understanding of the human person in African traditional thought is very similar to the understanding of the human person in the Hebrew writings of the Bible and may shed some light on why enslaved Africans found the biblical writings both familiar and compelling.[26]

Bujo: On Being Human and Corporate

The corporate unity defines the essence of humanity both in the African and biblical world. What does it mean to be human in the African worldview? According to African theologian Benezet Bujo, "To be human always means sharing life with others in such a way, as Ratzinger puts it, 'the past and the future of humanity are also present in every human being.'"[27] The emphasis is always on the relationship of the individual to the community or the interconnectedness between the community and the person. Consequently, the demise of the individual is contingent to his/her rapport to the community. In Cone, the closest rapport is the notion of Black solidarity which is vital for the survival of the Black community in the United States.

Bujo articulates some key elements pertaining to the Black African theological anthropology and ethics. First, he accentuates the value of the community to the individual and their relationship with God:

26. Evans, *We Have Been Believers*, 102.

27. Bujo, *Foundations of An African Ethic*, 3–4.

It must be recalled that African ethics does not define the person as a process as coming into existence in the reciprocal relatedness of individual and community where the latter included not only the deceased but also God. This means that the individual becomes a person only through active participation in the life of the community. It is not a membership in a community as such that constitutes the identity: only common action makes the human person a human person and keeps him from becoming an "unfettered ego."[28]

Second, he emphasizes the importance for the members of the community to work in solidarity for the preservation of communal life and integrity, as life in the context of the community is foundational in African ethics. Caribbean postcolonial theology accentuates the importance of building a community of faith that valorizes every person and responds to the need of every individual belonging to this community of faith.

The main goal of African ethics is fundamentally life itself. The community must guarantee the promotion and protection of life by specifying or ordaining ethics and morality . . . The life which issues from God becomes a task for all human beings to accomplish: they must ensure that this initial gift of life reaches full maturity, and this is possible only when people act in solidarity.[29]

The actions of the individual member of the community matters, as they could potentially contribute to the success and growth of the community or could hinder human flourishing within that group. Communal solidarity not only sustains the corporate life, it completes each individual member of the respective community. On the contrary, however, when a member of a community transgresses or commits an evil act, the entire community suffers leading "to the lost or reduction of its life." [30] As Bujo also underscores:

Life in the community demands alertness and the maintenance of one's own individuality . . . The individual can enrich in the community only when he is made a person by its individual members, so that he is in his turn can share in the process by

28. Ibid., 87.
29. Ibid., 88.
30. Ibid.

which others become persons. No one is dispensable in this process; the individuals are not exchangeable.[31]

Ghanaian philosopher Kwame Gyekye strengthens the preceding passage about the communitarian nature of African societies when he asserts forthrightly, "A harmonious cooperative social life requires that individuals demonstrate sensitivity to the needs and interest of others, if that society is to be a moral society. The reason is that the plight or distress of some individuals in the society is likely to affect others in some substantial ways."[32] Within this framework, the goal of social arrangement is to maximize life and the welfare of every member of the community, and that "arrangement will have to include rules the pursuit of which will conduce to the attainment of communal welfare. In this connection, such moral virtues as love, mercy, and compassion will have to be regarded as intrinsic to satisfactory moral practice in the communitarian society.[33]

Arguably, as previously noted in our analysis, the African communitarian society is linked to its religious ethos. This view on theological anthropology is also accentuated in the writings of JoLaurenti Magesa and John S. Mbiti, who have demonstrated cogently what African American liberation theology Dwidght Hopkins called "the dynamic and interdependent relationship between the individual and the community."[34]

God and the Human Community

Laurenti Magesa:

In the thought of Magesa, the central themes of African cosmology coincide with the religious sensibility and values of the African people:

> [The] African view of the universe contains the following major themes: the sacrality of life; respect for the spiritual and mystical nature of creation, and, especially, of the human person; the sense of the family, community, solidarity and participation; and an emphasis of fecundity and sharing in life, friendship, healing and hospitality. Created order other than humanity must be approached with care and awe as well, not only because of its

31. Ibid., 90, 93.
32. Gyekye, *Tradition and Modernity*, 72.
33. Ibid.
34. Hopkins, *Shoes That Fit Our Feet*, 95.

communion with God, but also because of its own vital forces
and its mystical connection with the ancestors and other spirits.[35]

African moral theology or religious ethics are community—oriented which involve primarily four entities: God, the individual, the ancestor, and the community. The ultimate objective of these moral codes
is to safeguard the community and to hinder individual transgression
that could jeopardize the welfare and fellowship of the community. More
importantly, the preservation of life is the *raison d'etre* of these censored
principles and social mores. Consequently, when someone sins or transgresses against a particular tradition, he/she acts against the will of the
community, and therefore, damages communal fellowship and shalom.
As Magesa has pointed out:

> In African Religion, wrongdoing relates to the contravention of
> specific codes of community expectations, including taboos. In-
> dividuals and the whole community must observe these forms
> of behavior to preserve order and assure the continuation of
> life and its fullness. To threaten in any way to break any of the
> community codes of behavior, which are in fact moral codes,
> endangers life; it is bad, wrong or "sinful."[36]

While some individuals have suggested that the moral vision of the
peoples of Africa is predicated upon the taboos, beliefs, and the narratives
or stories the people had created, their sense of sin or transgression ultimately orients them toward the one God who sees and knows everything.
In the passage below, E.A. Adegbola presents God as the ultimate source
of morality, and implies that God keeps a record of human conduct, and
that he is also a vigilant watcher of evildoers

> Everywhere in Africa, morality is hinged on many sanctions.
> The most fundamental sanction is the fact that God's all seeing
> eyes scan the total areas of human behavior and personal rela-
> tionships. God is spoken of as having eyes all over "like a sieve"
> (*Al'oju-k'ara bi-ajere*). Those who do evil in the dark are con-
> stantly warned to remember that God's gaze can pierce through
> the darkness of human action and motive.[37]

Consequently, a possible aim of traditional African religion is to reconcile the transgressor with God, as well with the ancestors, the spirits,

35. Megesa, *African Religion*, 52–53.
36. Ibid., 166.
37. Adegbola, "The Theological Basis of Ethics," 116.

and the community. One must always remember that "Existence-in-re-lation sums the pattern of the African way of life. And this encompasses within it a great deal, practically the whole universe . . . The African is full conscious of the wholeness and cohesiveness of the whole creation of God, within which interaction is the only way to exist."[38]

In the context of theological ethics or the moral vision of African religion, in the words of Magesa, "God stands as the ultimate guard-ian of the moral order of the universe for the sole, ultimate purpose of benefitting humanity. Humanity, being central in the universal order, is morally bound to sustain the work of God by which humanity itself is, in turn, sustained. Humanity is the primary and most important benefi-ciary of God's action."[39] The idea that a powerful Creator-God voluntarily chooses to safeguard human beings is almost akin to Black theology's idea that God has voluntarily taken side with the oppressed and margin-alized people in society to liberate them and cause them to flourish in the world. The function of ethics is thus to assess a way of life on the basis of certain guided theological, religious, and moral principles.[40]

Because religion pervades every dimension or aspect of the Af-rican, therefore, there is no contradiction between the secular and the religious. All is executed within the boundary of the community. Mag-esa has contended that any system—secular and/or religion—should be able to provide a plausible response to the purpose of human existence and the meaning of life in this world. In the African world, the human experience and the purpose of human existence are integral to the life of the community.

> For any religious orientation, the most important principles that determine the system of ethics revolve around the purpose or goal of human life. Within this horizon African communities shape and direct their manner of living in terms of what is or is not acceptable to them. Human experience and responsibility are judged in light of this goal, which does not change. From the dialectic between the established goal and human responsibil-ity to realize it existentially and experientially arise values and norms of behavior, what Africans would general call "customs," in the most morally-laden sense of the word. These customs help the community and individuals within it to keep the goal

38. Sidhom, "The Theological Estimate of Man," 102, 104.

39. Magesa, *African Religion*, 46.

40. Ibid., 29.

of life in sight, to strive toward it, and to have a basis with to deal their shortcomings in this endeavor. For African Religion, all principles of morality and ethics are to be sought within the context of preserving human life and its "power" or "force."[41]

On one hand, Magesa posits that the transformative aspect of the Christian Gospel "makes explicit the absolute value of the individual person. Created in the image and likeness of God and imbued with divine breath, a person has value in and for him—or herself. One's value and dignity as a human person are not given by nor do they flow from one's community. They originate from God's own self. . . . People cannot begin to grow toward the full stature of their dignity as the image of God unless it leads them to community."[42] On the other hand, Swailem Sidhom helpfully explains that human conduct is patterned after invented social norms. There is a sense to say that like religion, human morality is a human invention or social construct:

> There is no doubt that the pattern of life within any given society is an expression of a particular view of man held by that society. The shape of political life, for instance, rests on a particular view of man. The practices of religion are as much the outcome of its doctrine of God as of its estimate of man. There is a sense in which the doctrine of God can be viewed as an expression of a certain view of man. Evidently, wherever we may turn, the question of who man is cannot be avoided.[43]

What is undeniably clear in Magesa's theological anthropology is his focus on the sanctity of life and the urgency placed upon us to uphold the dignity of the person within the life and context of the community. Magesa's emphasis on the imperative of the community in defining the life and well-being of the individual is shared by other African theologians, such as John S. Mbiti. Mbiti develops this central thesis about African theological ethics and theological anthropology in two important volumes: *African Religions & Philosophy*, and *Introduction to African Religion*.

41. Magesa, *African Religion*, 31–32.

42. Magesa, *Anatomy of Inculturation*, 194.

43. Sidhom, "The Theological Estimate of Man," 113.

John S. Mbiti: God as the Ground for Communal Life and Harmony

In the writings of John S. Mbiti, the critical reader may arrive at the conclusion that that the African understanding of humanity is more promising and dignified than the Western perspective of man. The understanding of humanity in the African cosmology is linked to the religious sensibility of the African people and their theological viewpoint about the God-human- relationship. African anthropology is deeply rooted in the theological premise that God created both man and woman, male and female for relationship, community, and mutuality. While Africans believe that God is Creator of everything including the universe, nonetheless, "of all that created things man is the most important and the most privileged."[44] The belief of the supremacy of man over everything else is by virtue that God has created him/her as the pinnacle of creation. Mbiti has lucidly reasoned that man (both the male and female gender) "was the perfection of God's work of creation, since nothing else better than man was created afterwards."[45] Therefore, man is the center of the universe and the link between earth and heaven. Mbiti writes informatively about the religious universe and the place of man in it:

> Man, who lives on the earth, is the centre of the universe. He is also the priest of the universe, linking the universe with God its Creator. Man awakens the universe, he speaks to it, he listens to it, he tries to create a harmony with the universe. It is man who turns parts of the universe into sacred objects, and who uses other things for sacrifices and offerings. These are constant reminders to people that they regard it as a religious universe.[46]

This passage is critical because it provides a better interpretation of African theological anthropology, and the dignity of humanity as God's special creation according to this tradition. This notion is important as it counters any form of human oppression, degradation, and demonization, as clearly articulated in constructive theologies (i.e postcolonial, liberation, black liberation).The doctrine of humanity in African cosmology is associated with the special function or role of man and woman in the universe, as so ordained by God himself.

---

44. Mbiti, *Introduction to African Religion*, 32.

45. Ibid., 79.

46. Ibid., 36.

In the African view, the universe is both visible and invisible, unending and without limits. Since it was created by God it is subsequently dependent on him for its continuity. God is the sustainer, the keeper and upholder of the universe . . . As the Creator of the universe, God is outside and beyond it. At the same time, since he is also its sustainer and upholder, he is very close to it. Man, on the other hand, is at the very centre of the universe.[47]

The idea that the universe is both "unending and without limits" is comparable to the notion of the "openness of the world," as found in the work of the German phenomenologist philosopher Max Scheler. In his groundbreaking study *Die Stellung des Meschen im Komos* (1928), translated in English as *Man's Place In Nature* (1961), Scheler employed the phrase "openness to the world" to recognize the unique place of human beings in the domain of animal life, and to encapsulate the relationship between humans and the universe, and their place in the cosmos; openness to the world means to expound on "the unique freedom of man to inquire and to move beyond every regulation of his existence."[48] Wolfhart Pannenberg, using logical reasoning, explains with great clarity the philosophical implications and the theological underpinnings of the concept:

This relation is implicit in the awareness of the contingency, conditionedness, and transcendibility of all finite contents . . . This means that the relation of human exocentric existence to the infinite unconditioned is always given only through the mediation of a finite content. But it may be said conversely that every human relation to finite objects implies a relation to the infinite and therefore has in the final analysis a religious foundation and that from the transcending of all finite realities it always return to the reality given in each instance . . . It is also true that this infinite is always given in the context of the moment's experience of finite reality, whether it is given merely implicitly or in explicit religious thematization but then always in relation to contents derived from finite experience. The way of human beings to the (divine) reality in which they can ultimately ground their exocentric existence and thereby attain to their own identity is thus always mediated through the experience of the external world. This is especially true of the relationship with the other human

---

47. Ibid., 35, 38–39.
48. Panenberg, *What is Man?*, 3.

beings, that is, with beings whose lives are characterized by the same question and experience.[49]

Like Mbiti in his referenced passage above, Pannenberg presupposes this web of relations, which characterizes the human experience in the world, has a divine origin. Complementarily, Stanley Grenz stresses the theological significance of the openness to the world concept and the spirit of interdependence that mark the relationship of the human spirit and life to God and other individuals. He deploys the idea of "infinite dependence" to make sense of this viable bond; hence, he could write the following stunning words:

> The connection between "openness to the world" and "infinite dependency is obvious. Because we have no niche in the biological framework, we simply can find no ultimate fulfillment in any one "world" or environment we create for ourselves. This human incapability to be fulfilled by any structure of the world, in turn, drives us beyond the finitude of our experience in a never-ending quest for fulfillment. We are, therefore, dependent creatures. But our dependency is greater than the finite world can ever satisfy.[50]

He goes on to underscore the centrality of God in human quest for meaning, joy, dignity, and satisfaction in this world of uncertainty:

> Infinite dependency readily points in the direction of God as the final answer to the human quest. . . . In short, anthropology itself suggests that our existence as humans presupposes an entity beyond the world upon whom we are dependent and toward whom we directed for ultimate fulfillment . . . We are designed to find our meaning and identity in relation to, and only in relation, God.[51]

As could be pointed out, both Mbiti and Magesa advance the notion that God is the telos of human existence, and it is he who gives human life meaning and makes life in this world of anguish worth living. "The affirmation that God is the origin of our essential humanity means that God is the source of value for all creation. Neither other human beings nor the human community has the ultimate prerogative to determine

---

49. Pannenberg, *Anthropology in Theological Perspective*, 70.

50. Grenz, *Theology for the Community of God*, 131.

51. Ibid., 132.

the value of anyone or anything that God has made."[52] At face value, it appears in that claim that theocentrism undermines the value and important role of the community. God is the primary giver and architect of human hope, grace, and faith; yet, through the community serving as the divine tangible venue, God willingly dispenses these virtues so that both the individual and the community could achieve fulfillment and foster meaning in this life.

Furthermore, God created the human community through which human goodness and dignity, values and virtues could be cultivated socially and channeled relationally. Observably, the belief is that it is God's design for the individual to experience life in fullness within the context of the community; the community completes the individual as God has intended it to be. In other words, to refuse to do life together within the community of faith is to reject God's plan and underlying goal for the individual and the (Christian) community.

> God designed us to enter into relations with others—to participate in the community of God. This divine intention is that we live in harmony with creation, that we enjoy fellowship with one another, and that we participate in the divine life. Through community, we in turn find our identity as children of God . . . As we live in love—that is, as we give expression to true community—we reflect the love which characterizes the divine essence. And as we reflect the divine essence which is love, we live in accordance with our own essential nature, with that for which God created us. In this manner, we find our true identity—that form of the "world" toward which our "openness to the world" is intended to point us.[53]

Hence, African theological anthropology is best understood in terms of being in close proximity with the universe, God, and the ancestors, leading to a better appreciation for the human life and to the community in the world. It also compels us to treat the land with gentleness and sensibility, and to care for the environment in which we live. As Mbiti explains, "Because man thinks of himself as being at the centre, he consequently sees the universe from that perspective. It is as if the whole world exists for man's sake. Therefore, African people look for the usefulness (or otherwise) for the universe to man. This means both what the world can do for man, and how man can use the world for his own

52. Ibid., 142–43.
53. Ibid., 207, 180.

good."[54] Caribbean Liberation theologian Kortright Davis reflects on the significant impact of African cosmology on Afro-Caribbean based religions. He argues brilliantly that the Caribbean religion is not only a carrier of culture, it embodies the "African soul."

> Caribbean religion itself could not have survived without its African soul . . . The African soul has been nurtured and sustained not only one the mother continent but also in the New World, where it has taken root . . . Africa is both a physical reality and a spiritual reality in the New World. African forms, styles, tastes, and substance may vary, because of cultural and historical factors, but there is an African soul, a life force, a vitality, a heartbeat, a spiritual substream that runs through this portion of the human family.[55]

Alluding to the moral ideals of Ubuntu discussed above, Davis proceeds by parsing the contribution of Africa to human solidarity and interconnectedness in the African diaspora:

> The African life force underlines the African people's deep sense of communalism . . . The African life force creates a strong need to memorialize these ancestors through family story and tradition., so that the past provides continuity with the present and assurance for future. African people believe strongly in the immediacy of supernatural beings who share with ordinary persons a common existence and who must be appropriately addressed for the welfare of the whole community. This belief gives a concreteness to religion, a historical foundation to spirituality, and an integrated approach to the dominant view of the world, so that there is hardly any distinction between sacred and secular, or between matter and spirit, or even between consecrated and unconsecrated medicine.[56]

In our previous conversation, we have already pointed out the idea that the universe is deeply religious—from the perspective of the African people. We have also illustrated that in the African worldview, there is no division between the religious and the secular, the profane and the sacred. Everything is relational and integrated. The bond between the African and the universe may be construed as a relationship of reciprocity and interdependence. Giving the religious or theological motif that

54. Mbiti, *Introduction to African Religion*, 38.

55. Davis, *Emancipation Still Comin'*, 50, 63.

56. Ibid., 59.

undergirds his rapport to the universe, the African exploits the universe and makes use of it "in physical, mystical, and supernatural ways."[57] Mbiti expounds further on this dynamic by asserting:

> He sees the universe in terms of himself, and endeavor to live in harmony with it . . . The visible and invisible parts of the universe are at man's disposal through physical, mystical, and religious means. Man is not the master in the universe; he is only the centre, the friend, the beneficiary, the user. For that reason, he has to live in harmony with the universe, obeying the laws of natural, moral and mystical order. If these are unduly disturbed, it is man who suffers most. African peoples have come to these conclusions through long experience, observation and reflection.[58]

This African anthropocentric perspective on life and about man's place in the world is grounded on a theocentric explanation of humanity and the cosmos as a religious entity. It is in this context, Mbiti could make this valiant declaration: "Man is at the very centre of existence, and African peoples see everything else in its relation to this central position of man. God is the explanation of man's origin and sustenance: it is as if God exists for the sake of man."[59] He rectifies his idea about God's providence, divine nurturing, and the mothering function of the first created individuals (Adam and Eve) in this language: "He [God] was the parent to them and they were his children. He supplied them with all the things they needed, like food, shelter and the knowledge of how to live . . . God supplied them with cattle, or other domestic animals, fire and implements for hunting, fishing or cultivating the land. God allowed or told them to do certain things but forbade other things."[60]

God's presence among his people is what constitutes the good and happy life in African traditional theology.[61] African theological anthropology begins with God and ends with God; without excluding God's other creations, man is primarily the recipient of divine blessings since the African people "believe that even though individuals are born and die, human life as such as no ending since God is its Protector and Preserver."[62] Stanley

57. Mbiti, *Introduction to African Religion*, 39.

58. Ibid.

59. Ibid, 90.

60. Mbiti, *African Religion and Philosophy*, 79–80.

61. Ibid, 96.

62. Mbiti, *Introduction to African Religion*, 44.

Grenz supports Mbiti's conviction when he writes: "At its core the human identity problem is religious [and theological] in nature."[63] Moreover, in African theology, the doctrine of God lies in the absolute sovereignty and lordship of God over all things and human history.

> God rules over the universe. In this aspect he has names like King, Governor, Ruler, Chief, Master, Lord, Judge and Distribu-tor. In their prayers people acknowledge God to be the Ruler and Governor of the universe . . . To speak of God as the Ruler of the universe means that there is no spot which is not under his control; nothing can successfully rebel against him or run away from him.[64]

John Mbiti's view of God has been criticized by both Western and African thinkers. His critics have contended that he has imposed Western categories and concepts into African indigenous theology and African doctrine of God. For Mbiti, the theological categories have previously existed in the oral stories and languages of the African people before they made their way into Western theological texts.

Moreover, another equally important feature of black African an-thropology is the idea that God created the community for individuals to belong and share life together. As we have observed in our previous conversation, the nature of the African community is essentially linked to the human nature as defined by God; in African theological view of humanity, it is also true that the role and destiny of the individual is within the structured life and framework of the community. Mbiti admits that the life of the individual becomes meaningful and worth living only within the life of the community he or she belongs. The individual exists corporately, and "owes existence to other people, including those of past generations and his contemporaries. He is simply part of the whole. The community therefore make, create or produce the individual; for the individual de-pends on the corporate group."[65] The notion of "social man" or "corporate individual" can be applied implicitly and efficiently here as the individual recognizes whose he/she is, and fulfills his or her responsibilities to the community. It is only in this manner can he or she be deemed a genuine and living being in the African outlook of the corporate person.

---

63. Grenz, *Theology for the Community of God*, 127.

64. Mbiti, *African Religion and Philosophy*, 46.

65. Ibid., 106.

> Only in terms of other people does the individual becomes conscious of his own being, his own duties, his privileges and responsibilities towards himself and towards other people . . . Whatever happens to the individual happens to the whole group, and whatever happens to the whole group happens to the individual. The individual can only say: "I am, because we are; and since we are, therefore I am." This is a cardinal point in the understanding of the African view of man.[66]

Mbiti summarizes this mysterious phenomenon in two dependent clauses: "I am, because we are; and since we are, therefore I am."[67] The concept of the "collective person" is also convenient here. It bears the notion of human solidarity and the responsibilities and duties due from the individual toward the community. This philosophical perspective on social anthropology is grounded on the concept of solidarity and sharing. This supportive statement on the dynamic between the collective person and his role in advancing the cause of the community is further developed in the detailed paragraph below:

> "Collective Person" is the deepest and the most profound level of community. To a certain extent, it is the evolutionary outcome of both the life-community and society. What most distinctively characterizes the collective person is its sense of solidarity. Each member of the community is not only fully responsible for his or her actions but is also co-responsible for the actions of others and of the community. In contrast to the life-community, each member is self-aware of him or herself as an individual, as a fully realized person. Yet, in contrast to society, the individual is caught up in a network of relations with others. The sense of solidarity in the collective person is that of an "unrepresentable" solidarity. Every member of the collective person is absolutely unique. No one can stand in for anyone else and each bears responsibility for others and for the group.[68]

Solidarity is a pivotal characteristic and virtue of the communal life, which the collective person must sustain for the best interest of every member of the community:

> Solidarity assumes two distinct types of responsibility: a responsibility for one's own actions and a co-responsibility for the

66. Ibid.
67. Ibid.
68. Davis and Steinbock, "Max Scheler."

actions of others. Co-responsibility does not compromise the autonomy of the individual. Every person is fully responsible for his or her actions . . . Solidarity assumes the manner in which we have shared our lives and feelings with one another in a community, but also the necessity for a person to act to end evil and injustice. The presence of evil in one's community demonstrates that every member ought to love more fully and act so that evil is not possible. At the level of the collective person, this call to responsibility is felt uniquely by each person, revealing the uniqueness of one's role in and for the community . . . Sharing a community with others and sharing the responsibility for the community with others is the context in which the person is formed and realized.[69]

Liberation theologians contend for the necessity of communal solidarity and especially camaraderie with the oppressed and the disinherited contributing to the happiness, growth, and joy of the entire community. In *Things Fall Apart*, brilliant Nigerian novelist Chinua Achebe chronicles the fall of the ambiguous protagonist Okonkwo, a member of the Umuofia village, who acts outside of the will and design of the community. As a result, he has isolated himself from the fellowship and life of the community, and his life has become empty and ineffective. He even challenges what is deemed sacred and religious by his clan members; as the narrator reports:

His life had been ruled by a great passion—to become one of the lords of the clan. That had been his life-spring. And he had all but achieved it. Then everything had been broken. He had been cast out of his clan like a fish onto a dry, sandy beach, panting. Clearly his personal god or *chi* was not made for great things. A man could not rise beyond the destiny of his *chi* . . . Okonkwo had yielded to despair and he was greatly troubled . . . Okonkwo's gun had exploded and a piece of iron had pierced the boy's heart. The confusion that followed was without parallel in the tradition of Umuofia. Violent deaths were frequent, but nothing like this had ever happened.[70]

The religious sensibility of the community is put in perspective against the crime of Okonkwo. The violation of the moral and ethical codes of the community is accentuated in this passage in the novel:

69. Ibid.

70. Achebe, *Things Fall Apart*, 124, 131.

> The only course open to Okonkwo was to flee from the clan. It was a crime against the earth goddess to kill a clansman, and a man who committed it must flee from the land. . . . That night he collected his most valuable belongings into head-loads. His wives wept bitterly, and their children wept with them without knowing why . . . And before the cock crowed Okonkwo and his family were fleeing to his motherland.[71]

As seen in both passages above, in the African worldview, a life of solitude and isolation is not a fulfilled life. The religious and communal significance of the life of the individual to the community is stretched and desirable. It is from the vantage point of the religious tradition and the communal life we should grasp Mbiti's important thesis about the vital connection between the individual, the community, and God: "Just as God made the first man, as God's man, so now man himself makes the individual who becomes the corporate or social man. It is a deeply religious transaction."[72] On a complementary note, African American theologian James Evans explains nicely the correlation between God, the ancestors, the community, and the individual; together these entities prioritize existential solidarity and interconnectedness:

> The cultural matrix of the African tended to affirm the infinite worth of the African as a human being in relation to other human beings and under the auspices of a benevolent creator God. The community (the no longer living, the living, and the yet to be born) was affirmed as the basic social unit and the social framework in which the individual was defined. All creation, including nature, was seen as infused with the spiritual presence of God.[73]

Conclusion

Africana theological anthropology and theological ethics is grounded on the Ubuntu philosophy and moral virtues. The spirit of Ubuntu is a spirit of liberation that empowers the oppressed community to effectual shalom and freedom. What remains true about the philosophy of Ubuntu is its theological foundation and its stress on the divine desire and God's ultimate goal to establish relational community with human beings whom he had created leading both to individual and collective

71. Ibid., 124.

72. Mbiti, *African Religion and Philosophy*, 106.

73. Evans, *We Have Been Believers*, 5.

flourishing; through the community, the individual will find fulfillment and satisfaction in God.

In his fascinating text, *Theology for the Community of God*, theologian Stanley J. Grenz makes an insightful observation about the theological understanding of humanity in relationship with God the Creator:

> Christian anthropology is an extension of the doctrine of God. In our doctrine of humanity we speak about human beings as creatures of God. We may encapsulate our human identity as God's creatures in three postulates: We are the good creation of God, we are marred through our fall into sin, but we are the object of God's redemptive activity . . . God created us with great value, for he designed us for community. And he desires we reflect his own image.[74]

Complementarily, both Christian ethicist David Tracy and liberation theologian Hopkins assert that the telos of the individual or human being is the search of a "common good, a common interest in emancipatory reason and a common commitment to the ideal of authentic conversation within a commonly affirmed pluralism and a commonly experienced conflictual situation."[75] In his reflection on the doctrine of God, Paul Tillich accentuates relational love as the underlying virtue that defines God, and man to man relationship; as Tillich has further remarked:

> We are, we know that we are, and we love this our being and knowing. This means we are self-related and self-affirming. We affirm ourselves in knowledge and in will. On the other hand, love and knowledge transcend ourselves and go to the other beings. Love participates in the eternal; this is its own eternity. The soul has transtemporal dimensions. This participation is not what is usually called immortality, but it is the participation in the divine life, in the divine loving ground of being.[76]

Black African theological anthropology and theological ethics constitute a value-based system grounded on the theology of love conceived as relationality and interdependence; within the moral framework and ethical vision of the South African concept of Ubuntu, both the individual and the community will achieve harmony, peace, and solidarity. At the closing page on his chapter on ethics and eschatology, African American

74. Grenz, *Theology for the Community of God*, 125.
75. Quoted in Hopkins, *Being Human*, 17.
76. Tillich, *History of Christian Thought*, 121.

liberation theology J. Deotis Roberts (A first generation of Black liberation theologian along with James Cone and Gayraud S. Wilmore) not only affirms the "African contribution to socialism or to peoplehood;"[77] he affectionately asserts that it is "precious" to Black people outside of continental Africa. He provides some key practical reasons why Black people and Black churches in the Diaspora should embrace and practice the ethical values of Ubuntu and the moral principles embedded in traditional African theological ethics and anthropology:

> We need to recover a sense of "familyhood" in our churches and communities. Reverence for ancestors among African people is clearly bound up with the understanding of the common life. What happens beyond death is not separated from social relations here and now. All of life is a unity and death is an experience within life. Thus ethics and eschatology come together in a way that brings enrichment and fulfillment to the present form the vantage point of a frame of reference beyond this life, including a fellowship between the living and the living dead.[78]

77. Roberts, *A Black Political Theology*, 187.
78. Ibid.

3

American Christian Theology and the Meaning of James Cone and Black Liberation Theology

My God is a rock in a weary land,

My God is a rock in a weary land,

Shelter in time of storm.

—NEGRO SPIRITUAL

ARGUABLY, BLACK LIBERATION THEOLOGY could be construed as a theological discourse that promotes the African principle of Ubuntu. The central thesis of Black liberation theology is to care for the needy, empower the most neglected, inspire the racialized and minoritized human groups in society (i.e. black and brown people), and correspondingly, advocates of Black liberation theology argue for the defense of their humanity and dignity in the world. As previously discussed, the concept of Ubuntu has a theological value that alludes to the moral virtues and ethical attributes of God, which human beings are called to emulate. Whenever an individual, a group, or a race fails to incorporate these divine ideals and standards in their lives or fail to treat others according to the ideals of Ubuntu, God's image in that person, group, or race is challenged and could potentially result in human oppression and exploitation.

Black liberation theology of James Cone is an attempt to counter human oppression, exploitation, and abuse by interrogating any human force that dehumanizes black and brown people and questions their role in the world as emissaries of God. It is from this complex and important perspective in this chapter we assess the meaning and relevance of the politico-theological discourse of James Cone in the grand intellectual narrative of Africana theological anthropology and ethics.

On April 28, 2018, students of Christian theology and Black religion around the world lost one of the most brilliant theological minds the United States has ever produced in the history of American Christianity. Arguably, James H. Cone was America's most important and controversial theologian in the twentieth-century. Cone was born in August 5, 1938 in Fordyce, Arkansas. He grew up in a segregated and racist society that dehumanized black people, demonized black women, and robbed them of political justice and human rights. As a result, Cone would construct distinctively a theological discourse about the black experience and freedom struggle in the United States and concurrently transform America's theological landscape and enterprise, especially Christian theology.

Within the narrative of Africana theological tradition, this chapter is an attempt to reflect critically, theologically, and historically on the meaning and legacy of James Cone and accentuate the relevance of Black Liberation theology for our current moments of crisis as well as within the intellectual tradition of African critical theology. The chapter is an effort to reassess and bring greater clarity to the theological ideas and writings of Cone in respect to three significant interconnected and inseparable themes in his theology: (1) Theological identity, (2) Theological anthropology, and (3) Cone's theodicy. The essay suggests a threefold argument: (1) While Cone's Black Liberation theology has its main sources in the Bible and the Black experience, Cone did not find the Black sources adequate to solve the problem of black theodicy.

Therefore, Cone had to construct a Christology of appropriation and relationality to establish symbolically the rapport between the historic suffering and pain of Black people and the historic suffering and pain of Jesus Christ. The mystery of black theodicy is resolved in Cone's (Black) Christology; (2) hence, Cone's critical Black theological anthropology became a theology of union and identification with Christ. While Christ was hung on the wooden cross as a form of substitutionary atonement for the world's sin, Black people were also hung on the lynching tree to appease white fear and atone for the wrath of the white world; both events had cosmic significance. The first reason is that white supremacy as a universal and global phenomenon is the leading cause of human suffering and death—through white conquest and hegemonic domination over the vulnerable people and developing nations—in the contemporary world. White supremacy was also the principal source of colonization and the enslavement of Africans in the Americas and the lynching of black bodies on American soil. The second reason is that the cross of Christ had an ultimate value for Cone and his people; from a theological perspective, Cone interpreted the cross as a means for God to extend justice to Black people, eradicate white oppression, and to effect redemptive suffering on behalf of the black race.

Nonetheless, this position does not undermine Cone's urgent call for the liberation of black people from white oppression and white racism. In fact, Cone's symbolic triple references and pillars of Black Liberation theology include the Exodus, the prophets, and Jesus. Cone contended that they are the center of black religion and as a unified theme, they provide liberation event in black theology.[1] Finally, (3) Cone's theory of knowledge about black lives is a categorical denunciation of white epistemology and white reason to define black values and black dignity. Rather, Cone argued that Black people have intrinsic value because they also are created as Image of God for freedom; therefore, the meaning of black life is secured in God who had purposed black existence and integrated the black race into his inclusive and global human family. Cone's quest for black dignity and liberation was an intellectual crusade that challenged anti-black racism and white supremacy.[2]

The three major forces that contributed to the historical context and the advent of Black Liberation theology in the American society included the Civil Rights movement of the 1950s and 1960s, associated with the

1. Cone, *Said I Wasn't Gonna Tell Nobody*, 66–68, 81, 125.

2. In 2011, I published my first article on James H. Cone, "The Rhetoric of Prayer: Dutty Boukman, The Discourse of 'Freedom from Below,' and the Politics of God," *Journal of Race, Ethnicity, and Religion* 2/9 (June 2011) 1–33. The article explores the interconnecting interplays of freedom and God's preferential option for the poor and the oppressed within the backdrop of the historical-religious context of the Haitian Revolution as a grand political event in world history and human emancipation.

revolutionary political theology and activism of Martin Luther King Jr., the publication of Joseph Washington's ground-breaking and controversial text, *Black Religion*, in 1964; and the emergence of Black Power movement, connected with the radical political philosophy of black nationalism and social activism of Malcolm X.[3] Within these historical trajectories and revolutionary times, in the words of Gary Dorrien, "Cone was the apostle of the revolutionary turn in American theology that privileged liberationist questions."[4]

Childhood in Bearden and Theological Identity

Cone spent his childhood in Bearden, Arkansas, where his religious conviction, black identity, and early intellectual pilgrimage were shaped by his social environment and the Black Church. In his book, *My Soul looks Back* (1999), he discussed the importance of Bearden to his intellectual and theological development:

> The importance of Bearden is the way it enters my thinking, controlling my theoretical analysis, almost forcing me to answer questions about faith and life as found in the experience of my early years. It is as if the people of Bearden are present, around my desk as I think and write. Their voices are clear and inconsistent: "All right, James Hal, speak for your people."[5]

Cone developed an early consciousness about his identity as a black person and associated with the plot of the poor and oppressed blacks in Bearden. Later in his writings, he would portray himself as their conscience, their spokesperson, and their ambassador in the American society. In his theological writings, Cone interpreted his underlying role as the voice of reason in the interconnecting fields of Black religion, race, ethics, and Black anthropology. His described his connection to the Black community in this sentence: "I had to give voice to the feelings of rage in the Negro community, and especially the rage inside of me . . . I was too obsessed with my calling to be a theological witness to the black freedom struggle."[6] On one hand, as a young black man growing up in

3. Cone has devoted the first chapter of his book, *For My People*, 5–52, to analyzing and assessing these three major influences and forces.

4. Dorrien, *Breaking White Supremacy*, 457.

5. Cone, *My Soul Looks Back*, 17.

6. Cone, *Said I Wasn't Gonna Tell Nobody*, 8, 21.

Bearden, anti-black racism, white supremacy, and white violence toward blacks psychologically changed his perspective about white people and the American society. On the other hand, in Bearden, he witnessed the burden of blackness and the history of suffering and pain characterized the black experience in the United States. Growing up in a racist society, he reflects painfully on the conundrum of black people:

> Two things happened to me in Bearden: I encountered the harsh realities of white injustice that was inflicted upon the black community; and I was given a faith that sustained my personhood and dignity in spite of white people's brutality. The dual reality of white injustice and black faith, as a part of the structure of life, created a tension in my being that has not been resolved.[7]

As a result, in all of his work, Cone would seek to find both a theological solution and moral response to the problem of evil and suffering in the black community, what we may phrase "theodicy in black." His ardent quest was motivated by the desire to find meaning in black suffering, if that was even a possibility. Cone, however, believed that the liberation of black people and their holistic freedom from the white world was non-negotiable, especially if the American nation was going to atone for its racial sins and transgressions toward the African American population. Cone also maintained the idea that if white people in America were going to be healed from their racist wound and past transgressions, they would have to treat black citizens like human beings who are their equal—not like their enemies and strangers—and have dignity. James Baldwin, Cone's intellectual mentor, contended that white people would have to change their "antihuman attitudes which have ruled in this country for so long and which have effectively prevented the Negro"[8] from enjoying political rights and the benefits of American democratic system. Another conundrum confronts the Black experience, according to Baldwin, is that exclusion of Black people from the American narrative: "The whole American in terms of reality is based on the necessity of keeping black people out of it. We are nonexistent. Except according to their terms, and their terms are unacceptable."[9] Cone urged white America to include black people in its story because the history of America is the history of Black people. James Baldwin remarked that Black people

7. Cone, *My Soul Looks Back*, 18.
8. Baldwin, "The Last Interview (1987)," 140.
9. Baldwin, "Dialogue in Black and White," 210.

have been here since the beginning of the American Republic. Yet for Cone, the omission of Black people in America's story is intentional and has become a theological problem, as religion and race in the American experience are always intertwined.

Therefore, Cone sought to inquire energetically about the existential question (coupled with the potential meaning of God for black people and their suffering): "If God is good, and also powerful, as black church folk say, why do blacks get treated so badly?"[10] Cone's version of *theodicy in black* would underline the theological grammar and radical rhetoric of his three epoch-making and seminal texts, *Black Theology & Black Power* (1969), *A Black Theology of Liberation* (1970), and *God of the Oppressed* (1975). The quest for the meaning of black suffering and the indifference of white Christianity toward black pain have become both a theological inquiry and moral concern for Cone. Cone struggled to accept the silence of white churches and white theologians on the suffering and dehumanization of black people in the American society.

Nonetheless, Cone was not alone in thinking both theologically and intellectually about the predicament of black people in their own land. For example, in early years of their teenage life as well as during their adulthood, Cone and his brother Cecil Cone have been reasoning about the meaning of black existence in America and attempting to make sense about the structural inequality and systemic racial oppression that characterize black life in the land of their birth. Often, they engaged in stimulating conversations about "the problem of suffering in the context of the Christian faith."[11] Cone, for instance, concluded that the white people of Bearden not only contributed to the problem of black pain and suffering, "they regarded the social and political arrangements that they maintained as an expression of the natural orders of creation."[12]

Eventually, his childhood experience in Bearden would contribute to a series of self-discoveries about race relations between black and white Americans, the problem of economic inequality and black poverty, the question of race and American Christianity, the relationship between black freedom and the doctrine of God, the rapport between the justice of God and America's justice system. While some of these findings were scandalous for Cone, others were both (potentially) liberative and

10. Cone, *My Soul Looks Back*, 18.

11. Ibid.

12. Ibid.

comforting. These major social and moral factors would shape Cone's theological methodology and discourse, make him to question the validity and relevance of European and White American theology in regard to the suffering black population in the United States. Cone would actively engage in a long revolutionary theological campaign, an incessant quest for a constructive theology of justice, freedom, and redemption on behalf of the oppressed African American population—until the day he resigned his last breath on April 28, 2018, in the land that cursed his people. Not only Cone wanted to craft a theology of liberation for Black people, he enthusiastically labored to liberate Christian theology from White supremacy and White theological hegemony.

Notably, James Cone progressed to intellectual maturity and articulated a theological difference that challenged his formative academic theological training and ideas (i.e. Barthian, Tillichian). This intellectual self-retrospective also marked his early theological diction and methodology. He explained the process in this paragraph:

> The fourth and last weakness that I wish to comment on was my inordinate methodological dependence upon the neo-orthodox theology of Karl Barth. Many of my critics (black and white) have emphasized this point. It is a legitimate criticism, and I can offer no explanation except that to say that neo-orthodoxy was to me what liberal theology was to Martin Luther King, Jr.—the only theological system with which I was intellectually comfortable and which seemed compatible with the centrality of Jesus Christ in the black church community. I knew then as I know now that neo-orthodoxy was inadequate for my purposes, and that most American theologians who claimed that theological identity would vehemently reject my use of Karl Barth to interpret black theology. However, I did not have the time to develop a completely new perspective in doing theology. I had to use what I regarded as the best of my graduate education.[13]

For Cone, the Gospel of Jesus simply and categorically means the total liberation of the poor and the oppressed people from all human oppressive forces in society. Cone contended that the message of the Gospel was not embedded in sophisticated theological abstraction and theorization. The teachings of Jesus were liberative and brought about the ultimate victory, concrete hope, and practical emancipation for those who were suffering and subjugation to human victimization and subjectivity.

---

13. Ibid., xvii.

Cone also believed that the Gospel has called all people to a definitive decision about life and moral issues; the Gospel summons us to take sides, that is, to be in solidarity with the abused, the dispossessed, and the economically-disadvantaged. Cone maintained the individuals in society who choose the side of the oppressor and abuser are not only the enemy of the Gospel, they are antichrists and antagonists to the welfare of the poor and the disinherited. With rhetorical balance and intellectual precision, he made this pronouncement:

> Christian theology is a theology of liberation. It is *a rational study of the being of God in the world in light of the existential situation of an oppressed community, relating the forces of liberation to the essence of the gospel, which is Jesus Christ.* This means that its sole reason for existence is to put into ordered speech the meaning of God's activity in the world, so that the community of the oppressed will recognize that its inner thrust for liberation is not only *consistent with* the gospel but *is* the gospel of Jesus Christ. There can be no Christian theology that is not identified unreservedly with those who are humiliated and abused. In fact, theology ceases to be a theology of the gospel when it fails to arise out of the community of the oppressed. For it is impossible to speak of the God of Israelite history, who is the God revealed in Jesus Christ, without recognizing that God is the God *of* and *for* those who labor and are over laden.[14]

Yet for Cone to be able to make his landmark contribution to the freedom of Black people and to deliver America from its racial wound, he had to exegete both the dominant-white culture and to find sources of inspiration from the marginalized-black culture. For example, he learned from his father that "the survivable for black people requires constant struggles and that no black should ever expect justice from whites."[15] Second, Cone came to realize that America's race problem was linked to white Christian practice and antihuman attitude toward black and brown people. He sustained this belief by asserting that "The extermination of Amerindians, the persecution of Jews, the oppression of Mexican-Americans, and every other conceivable inhumanity done in the name of God and country—these brutalities can be analyzed in terms of the white American inability to recognize humanity in persons of color."[16]

14. Cone, *A Black Theology of Liberation*, 1.
15. Cone, *My Soul Looks Back*, 20.
16. Cone, *A Black Theology of Liberation*, 8.

Third, through his careful reading of the Biblical narrative, especially the writings of the Prophets and the teachings of Jesus, he became convinced that God was for the freedom of the oppressed black masses and all the world's poor: "All blacks seemed to think that God was on our side and against the satanic force of white supremacy. We did not need approval of white theologians and preachers to know that whites were in the wrong both morally and legally."[17] There is a sense to infer that the Bible was the moral compass for Cone to weigh the moral character and ethical actions of the white world and assess the role of American White Christianity in society and its regard toward the blacks.

Fourth, another pivotal force of enlightenment for Cone, manifesting as a "theological shock," was the contradiction of faith and injustice in White churches and White Christian institutions in America.[18] During the height of the Civil Rights movement in the 1960s, White churches failed to participate in justice and equality conversations and support liberation movements on behalf of black citizens. White Christians were equally culpable in delaying legal, civil, and human rights to blacks. Finally, after Cone obtained his Ph.D. degree in Systematic theology from Garett-Northwestern University in 1965, he began to question the relevance of the white theological education he received for the progress and future of Black people. He also contemplated whether the white theological curriculum was adequate to contribute to the ensuing deliverance and political rights of his people in the American society.

> I returned to Philander Smith with added enthusiasm. But what did Barth, Tillich, and Brunner have to do with young black girls and boys coming from the cotton fields of Arkansas, Tennessee, and Mississippi seeking to make a new future for themselves? This was the major question for me. And it was further intensified by the civil rights struggle. The contradiction between theology as a discipline and the struggle for black freedom in the streets was experienced at the deepest level of my being. How was I going to resolve it?[19]

White theological formulations and approaches to human ethics, as expressed in the writings of Cone's first theological mentors (Barth, Tillich, and Burner) failed the test to respond satisfactorily to the existential

---

17. Cone, *My Soul Looks Back*, 25.

18. Ibid., 27, 30.

19. Ibid., 38–39.

needs and quandary of Black people. By contrast, Cone affirmed that above all it was the Black church in his hometown that was the catalyst of his identity formation and the source of survival for the black masses; correspondingly, the Black Church was the antithesis of white supremacy and white version of the Gospel. The Black church, such as the Macedonian African Methodist Episcopal Church where Cone and his family were members, provided the resources for the sociopolitical struggle and relief of black people. The Black church was a symbol of black resistance to white injustice and racial terror. The Black church and Black Radical Tradition (i.e. the Black Power Movement, Black Consciousness Movement) provided to Cone socio-political consciousness and theological awakening. Black hope in God's righteousness and justice was also the catalyst for black people to endure the evil of the white world—toward an ethics of black optimism and emancipative future.[20]

Cone's intellectual activism through his politico-theological writings would supply to many generations of black thinkers and scholars of black religion and black theology a new black consciousness rooted in his defining claim that theology is always political, particular, and contextual. Theology is also sexist, racial, and hegemonic. His work has also contributed to the validity of black people thinking theologically and to many thinkers of Black liberation theology and Womanist, Cone has armed them with a theological consciousness, activist mindfulness, and a rhetoric of rage. Such an intellectual impact would radically shape the content of their scholarship and mark their thinking process toward the blending of scholarship and service in the best interest of the black masses. Like Cone, they promote the unnegotiable liberation, defense, rights, and dignity of black people and black women and they proclaim and defend forcefully the motto that "Black lives matter"[21] and the intrinsic worth and dignity of Black women.

Moreover, like his contemporary eminent theologian J. Deotis Roberts, Cone would contribute distinctively a "theology to make human life

---

20. Ibid., 22.

21. See for example the interdisciplinary works: Christopher J. Lebron, *The Making of Black Lives Matter: A Brief History of an Idea* (2018); Kelly Brown Douglas, *Stand Your Ground: Black Bodies and the Justice of God* (2015); Leah Gunning Francis Ferguson, *Faith: Sparking Leadership and Awakening Community* (2015), and *Faith Following Ferguson: Five Years of Resilience and Wisdom* (2019); Keeanga-Yamahtta Taylor, *From #BlackLivesMatter to Black Liberation* (2016).

human for the American Negro."[22] In the same pattern of thought like Cone, Roberts was convinced that "Black Theology must be radical and militant. It must move men to act upon the ethical imperatives of their faith. To the assertion that 'Black is beautiful,' it must answer *Amen*, but to the call for violence it must say *No*."[23] In a nutshell, for Cone, the basic goal of Black theology coupled with the rhetoric of the Black Power movement is the recognition and validation of black life and the non-negotiable demand of the rights of Black people to be free in their homeland. Through his activist-theological work, Cone crusaded on behalf of Black and oppressed American citizens to be accepted as human beings and equal to their white American counterparts. This twin demand was inseparable in the objectives two Black liberation projects: The Black Power movement and the Black Liberation movement, correspondingly, in the 1960s.

Sources and Origins

Black theology constitutes many sources and historical trajectories that predate the Civil Rights movement of the 1950s and the 1960s or the Black Power movement of the 1960s. In his creative and brilliant work, *Shoes that fit our Feet*, Black liberation theologian Dwight N. Hopkins establishes the emergence of Black theology in the very religious culture of the enslaved African population as they theorized and theologized through songs and folktales their understanding of God, humanity, sin, and Jesus, and their inherent desire for freedom, which was compatible with God's pursuit of the liberation of the enslaved.[24] As Hopkins writes with conviction:

> White theological proscriptions served as a negative incentive for slaves to pursue their independent religious thinking. On the positive side, blacks felt the powerful living presence of divinity in the midst of their daily burdens and concentrated in the Invisible Institution. These radical religious experiences colored their biblical interpretation; and, thus, they produced a theology of liberation. Given the contours of the Invisible Institution as backdrop, the slaves' liberation faith in the divine burst through in their own theological perspectives on God, Jesus Christ, and human purpose . . . American slaves discovered the nature of

22. Quoted in Dorrien, *Breaking White Supremacy*, 446.

23. Ibid., 445–46.

24. For a careful study of these three topics, see Hopkins, *Shoes That Fit Our Feet*, 13–48.

God as the One who sees the afflictions of the oppressed, hears their cries, and delivers them to freedom.[25]

In various studies and especially in *The Spirituals and the Blues*, Cone examines the content, language, and theology of slave religion or religious worldview to find historical sources in the development of a theology of liberation. Cone traced the origin of Black theology to the aesthetics of the spirituals and the blues. He proposed that the Black spirituals, as a source for Black theology, articulates the collective experience of the enslaved black population in the United States, and their longing to be relieved from chattel slavery and white terrorism. In the Spirituals, Cone remarked, the slaves interpreted God as (their) Liberator and Jesus Christ as "the King, the deliverer of humanity from unjust suffering."[26] They sung about black suffering, death, sin, faith, freedom, and the conviction that ultimately God will act justly on their behalf. Cone cogently summarized the slaves' conception of freedom; the slaves associated freedom with a particular and historical event in which God's liberating intervention and power will graciously bring about consolation to their misery:

> Freedom, for black slaves, was not a theological idea about being delivered from the oppression of sin. It was a historical reality that had transcendent implications. Freedom meant the end of "driber's dribin," "Massa's hollerin," and "missus' scolding,'—"Roll, Jordan, roll." It meant that there would be "no more peck o'corn," "no more driver's lash," "no more pint o'salt," "no more hundred lash," and "no more mistress's call for me, Many thousand gone." The slaves' view of God embraced the whole of life—their joys and hopes, their sorrows and disappointments; and their basic belief was that God had not left them alone, and that God would set them free from human bondage. That is the central theological idea in black slave religion as reflected in the spirituals.[27]

In his classic work on *The Books of American Negro Spirituals*, James Weldon Johnson and J. Rosamond Johnson attributed the beginning of the Negro spirituals to the context of American slavery, in which African slaves developed many thematic topics that would inform the historical development and background to Black theology in the 1960s. Johnson

25. Ibid., 22–23.
26. Cone, *The Spirituals and the Blues*, 43.
27. Ibid., 53.

inferred that the Negro spirituals "was a body of songs voicing all the cardinal virtues of Christianity—patience—forbearance—love—faith— and hope—through a necessarily modified form of primitive African music. The Negro took complete refuge in Christianity, and the Spirituals were literally forged of sorrow in the heat of religious fervor."[28] For the slaves, "To speak of faith was to speak of politics, and to speak of politics was to draw the God of one's faith into the conversation. It was for this reason that a longing for spiritual liberation and heavenly redemption. connected with hope for social and political salvation."[29]

Moreover, in his admirable work, *God of the Oppressed,* Cone surveyed the African ancestral cosmology and slave culture that served as valuable resources to the slaves in the attainment of two united objectives: the democratization of America's institutions and systems and the realization of America's progressive ideals in the best intent for the country's darker population. These ancestral religious and secular sources served as mechanisms of survival and existential hope in the era of slavery, lynching, and Jim Crow (racial segregation) for the black population. As Cone explained with lucidity and rationality in this paragraph:

> That American black people have a tradition of their own that stretches back to Africa and its traditional religions. We are an African people, at least to the degree that our
> Grandparents came from Africa and not from Europe. They brought with them their stories and combined them with the Christian story, thereby creating a black religious tradition unique to North America. African culture informed black people's perspective on Christianity and made it impossible for many slaves to accept an interpretation of Jesus story that violated their will for freedom. The passive Christ of white Christianity when combined with African culture became the Liberator of the oppressed from sociopolitical oppression.[30]

According to Cone, the rich elements of black culture provided the viable resources for oppressed blacks to reconfigure their identity and remake their fragmented lives. African ancestral cultural practices and religious traditions assisted the oppressed slaves to reject the God of their masters; through the optimistic content of Black religion, they reaffirmed their humanity and believed that God was a God of justice and on their

28. Johnson and Johnson, *The Books of American Negro Spirituals,* 20.

29. Blount, *Then the Whisper Put on Flesh,* 39.

30. Cone, *God of the Oppressed,* 105.

side. Cone asserted that the suffering African population during the era of slavery believed in a God who was not their oppressor but their Liberator. Ostensibly, the slaves believed that the end of slavery was linked to God's emancipative turn in history on the behalf of the abused, the terrorized, and exploited population in the United States. This collective understanding of divine deliverance was substantially shaped by the slaves' doctrine of God and theology of liberation. They believed that God was fighting for them and against their white oppressors and Christian slave masters.

Yet after the proclamation of general emancipation from slavery in 1865, the former slave population during the Reconstruction era would experience others forms of enslavement and terrorism: the ritual and public performance of lynching, the enforcement of Jim Crow laws, and mass incarceration. Antiguan Black theologian Kortright Davis reflects on the shared history of racial humiliation, violence, and dehumanization among the people of African descent in the Diaspora:

> The Black story is thus a most powerful framework through which Caribbeans and Americans, especially those of African descent, can move forward in an intercultural theological process in the struggle for Christian solidarity and the search for more concreted expressions of human freedom. We can contribute to each other's freedom by the collective engagement in the common discovery of our rich heritage . . . The common experience of oppression and slavery, the common struggle for full humanity and economic self-reliance, and the common fight against racism and other forms of social and systemic injustice are all too compelling to engender tensions of mistrust and hostility between Afro-Caribbeans and African-Americans.[31]

The Dilemma of American Slavery and Lynching

Not only slavery was the institution that tortured the African population in the United States and the rest of the American continent, it was also the system that led them to find solace and freedom through their own religious worldview and political activism. (As will be seen in our subsequent analysis on Caribbean theology, Caribbean thinkers critically discuss the problem of divine intervention and the theological crisis of God's absence in the time of slavery. The pivotal questions these Caribbean theologians ask: what did God abandon the Caribbean

31. Davis, *Emancipation Still Comin'*, 127.

people and allow them to be enslaved, exploited, raped, and abused by white colonists and slave masters? Where was God during the time of slavery?) Their collective belief was in a warrior-God who would crush down mightily their white foes and colonizers.

It is good to note here, nonetheless, in the historical context of America's colonial society, characterized by racial violence and death, colonial savagery, and anti-black racism, white colonists and slave owners undermined the culture of enslaved Africans because according to Cone, they "demeaned black people's sacred tales, ridiculing their myths and defining their sacred rites. Their intention was to define humanity according to European definitions so that their brutality against Africans could be characterized as civilizing the savages."[32] Many historians such W. E. B. Du Bois, C. L. R. James, Eric Williams, John Hope Franklin, Lerone Bennett Jr., David Brion Davis, Robin Blackburn, Eric Foner, Ira Berlin, Marcus Rediker, and Edward E. Baptist have attested that slavery in the American continent as a system was both racial and economic, sexual and political, producing damaging mental and psychological effects on the slaves and slave masters.[33]

Evidently, the enslavement of the Africans was determined by economic factors, which also legitimized the transatlantic slave trade and the birth of Western capitalism. The need for large and cheap labor in the agricultural fields (i.e., sugarcane, coffee, tobacco, indigo, rice, cotton plantations) in the Americas contributed to the booming of the institution of slavery and financial wealth of the American and European countries and their allies. Paradoxically, the complexity of slavery led to its ultimate destruction in the Americas (thanks to the Haitian Revolution, 1791–1804) and the emancipation of the enslaved population. The

32. Cone, *God of the Oppressed*, 23–24.

33. For further studies on slavery as a system in the Americas, see Du Bois, *The Black Reconstruction*; Franklin, *From Slavery to Freedom*; Bennett, *Before The Mayflower*; Baptist, *The Half Has Never Been Told: Slavery and the Making of American Capitalism*; Williams, *Slavery and Capitalism*; James, *The Black Jacobins*; Davis, *Inhuman Bondage: The Rise and Fall of Slavery in the New World*, Davis, *The Problem of Slavery in Western Culture, Slavery and Human Progress*, and Davis, *Problem of Slavery in the Age of Revolution, 1770–1823*; Blackburn, *The Making of New World Slavery: From the Baroque to the Modern, 1492–1800*, Blackburn, *The American Crucible: Slavery, Emancipation And Human Rights*, and Blackburn, *The Overthrow of Colonial Slavery: 1776–1848*; Rediker, *The Slave Ship: A Human History*, and Rediker, *The Many-Headed Hydra: Sailors, Slaves, Commoners, and the Hidden History of the Revolutionary Atlantic*; Berlin, *Many Thousands Gone: The First Two Centuries of Slavery in North America*; Foner, *The Fiery Trial: Abraham Lincoln and American Slavery*.

degradation of the black body during the era of slavery was associated with the commercialization and objectification of both African male and female slaves. To put it another way, the system of slavery and its inhuman economic demands made them both slaves and objects. The racial attitude attached to slavery led to slave suicide, mass murder, sexual rape, and all forms of contaminated diseases in slave societies. Western writers who wrote about the African population during the era of slavery also confirmed that the enslavement of the Africans was predicated on racial/color prejudice and the strict doctrine of white supremacy and black inferiority. Further, nineteenth-century scientific racism legitimized that the Africans and people of African descent belonged to the lowest racial hierarchy, and that their culture, language, and tradition were inferior to those of the white Americans and Europeans.

Consequently, Cone could concur that "The black experience in America is a history of servitude and resistance, of survival in the land of death. It is the story of black life in chains and of what that meant for the souls and bodies of black people."[34] To put it simply, the possibility for white people to affirm the value of black people and that they were equal human beings to whites was unthinkable. African American theologian J. Kameron Carter adds that the modern nation-state was based "on a new type of anthropology, which had at its core a discourse of race (replete with a logic of racism) that was itself tied to how Christianity came to be 'rationally' repositioned within the framework of modernity's political economy."[35] Not only white supremacists and slave masters denied the inherent human elements, which black slaves shared with them, white colonialists and the (post-) colonial government in the American continent used the legal system to contest the full humanity of the slaves and denied the human virtue of dignity. Baldwin explains that "one must justify the appalling action of turning a man into a thing. To turn a human being into a moneymaking beast of burden and, by this action, believe—or make oneself believe—that one is "civilizing" this creature is to have surrendered one's morality and imperiled one's sense of reality."[36]

The denial of black subjectivity would lead to another form of excruciating white terror performed on the black flesh: the public lynching of black people on American soil. Cone, in his stimulating work *The Cross*

34. Cone, *God of the Oppressed*, 20.
35. Carter, *Race*, 80.
36. Baldwin, "The Fire This Time," 217.

and the Lynching Tree, expressed righteous black rage about the intimate rapport between American slavery and America's lynching practices—as the most terrified moments in American history. Cone interpreted the lynching of black people historically and theologically, as white terrorists publicly exhibited black flesh as a form of substitution and atonement akin to the manner Roman soldiers shamed Jesus, the Jewish Messiah, and displayed openly his body on the cross. While the Roman Empire hanged the body of Jesus on the cross, the American Empire hanged the body of black people on the lynching tree.

> The sufferings of black people during slavery are too deep for words. That suffering did not end with emancipation. The violence and oppression of white supremacy took different forms and employed different means to achieve the same end: the subjugation of black people . . . At no time was the struggle to keep such hope alive more difficult than during the lynching era (1889–1940). The lynching tree is the most potent symbol of the trouble nobody knows that blacks have seen but do not talk about because the pain of remembering—visions of black bodies dangling from southern trees, surrounded by jeering white mobs—is almost too excruciating to recall.[37]

The brutal death of African Americans through the method of lynching was to be understood as an example of social salvation and a ritual of racial cleansing. Many white people in that era believed that the purification of the American soil lied in the total elimination of black lives through the instrumentalization of pre-arranged lynching ceremonies. Hence, the lynching of black people as a sacrificial atonement brought about the redemption of white folk from the presence of black folk in the land. Paradoxically, the brutalization of black bodies and annihilation of black lives in the American society created an exclusive white identity, and the denial and demonization of black humanity established the racial difference between black and white Americans. Hence, the American form of whiteness articulates a strong rationale for racial inequality and uncommon humanity, and as James Baldwin tells us, "Whiteness entails a moral choice—a choice to justify black oppression and also to include certain positive aspects of human experience in one's life and to exclude other negative things, which are subsequently, relegated to the racial

---

37. Cone, *The Cross and the Lynching Tree*, 2–3.

Other."[38] The history of Black death through lynching is an intricate narrative of American atonement.

However, in Christian theology of atonement, unlike the atoning death of Christ that bears a universal application and salvific effect for the redemption of all people, the lynching of black—a particular racial group or people—Americans as a form of racial atonement, in the Calvinistic logic, is particular and limited. Black lynching as a ritual of reference was a cultural crisis because white Americans misapprehended the (human) nature of black people and refused to coexist in the same land with them. The victims of America's lynching system, as it were in the time of slavery, suffered a form of substitutionary death to appease the white fear of the Negroes, as well as to placate the wrath of America's white population. Thus, lynching has become a (theological) heresy that highlights America's great moral dilemma. Cone's remarkable observation is worth noting below:

> Lynching was the white community's way of forcibly reminding blacks of their inferiority and powerlessness. To be black meant that whites could no anything to you and your people, and that neither you nor anyone else could do anything about it . . .
> It was a family affair, a ritual celebration of white supremacy, where women and children were often given the first opportunity to torture black victims—burning black flesh and cutting off genitals, fingers, toes, and ears as souvenirs.[39]

The memory of (Black) lynching in the Black psyche is cogently expressed in Cone's uneasy language: "The possibly of violent death was always imminent. African Americans knew what it means to make the best of a bad situation—to live 'under a kind of sentence of death,' not know [ing] when [their] time will come, it may never come, but it may also be any time."[40] The lynching of black American citizens established an ambiguous relationship between memory, citizenship, and race in American social history and historical theology. It also reveals significantly the history of American white Christianity and the exclusive nature of white theological discourse altogether deliberately erased the history of lynching in theological textbooks and religious curriculum. In addition, white churches were also silent about the degradation, hanging,

38. McKinney, *Being White*, 11.

39. Cone, *The Cross and the Lynching Tree*, 9.

40. Ibid.

suffocation, and burning of black bodies on the lynching tree. As a result, both white theologians and white churches were culpable in this grave American evil, which continues to haunt them today. Cone was correct that the Gospel of Jesus Christ cannot coexist comfortably with white supremacy and that biblical Christianity could not endorse or be silent on white terrorism and anti-black racism.

The history of American lynching invites us to consider whiteness as a collective imagination and the shared participation of American citizens in white wickedness. It also indicates that lynching, as a public expression of white power and white mechanic of controlling black visibility, is a hate and universal crime toward blacks and a destructive force in the American society. Ultimately, the lynching of black Americans was a devastating demonstration of America's "sick soul." In the paragraph below, Cone penned one of the most painful statements about the history of this American tragedy:

> Postcards were made from the photographs taken of black victims with white lynchers and onlookers smiling as they struck a pose for the camera. They were sold for ten to twenty-five cents to members of the crowd, who then mailed them to relatives and friends, often with a note saying something like this: "This is the barbeque we had last night." Spectacle lynchings attracted people from nearby cities and towns. They could not have happened without widespread knowledge and the explicit sanction of local and state authorities with tacit approval from the federal government, members of the white media, churches, and universities.[41]

The Problem of Black Theodicy:
How Long, O Lord?

Furthermore, Cone construed black lynching as a serious theological problem rooted in a distorted theological narrative and biblical worldview about the doctrine of divine providence and doctrine of humanity (theological anthropology):

> The claim that whites had the right to control the black population through lynching and other extralegal forms of mob violence was grounded in the religious belief that America is a white nation by God to bear witness to the superiority of "white over

41. Ibid.

> black." Even prominent religious scholars in the North, like the highly regarded Swiss-born church historian Philip Schaff . . . believed that "The Anglo-Saxon and Anglo-American, all modern races, possess the strongest national character and the one best fitted for universal dominion . . . Cole Blease, the two-time governor and U.S. senator from South Carolina, proclaimed that lynching is a "divine right of the Caucasian race to dispose of the offending blackamoor without the benefit of jury.[42]

It is good to note here that the colonial system, the institution of slavery (i.e. slave auctions), and the practice of lynching have contributed incalculable suffering and pain to the people of African and people of African ancestry in the modern world. These historical events and moments have resulted in the crisis of black theodicy, which had impacted Christian (moral) theology and the discourse of black theological anthropology and ethics. Accordingly, black theological anthropology must respond critically and responsibility to the calamity of black theodicy (The phrase "black theodicy" here pertains to God's seemingly absence in black anguish and the persistent problem of evil in the black world[43]), the pain of black history, and the Calvary of black suffering in the modern world. James Cone himself has deliberately acknowledged the uneasiness of black conscience and black faith in the midst of black suffering and the perceived invisibility and inaction of God in the plight of his (Black) people:

> The cross places God in the midst of the crucified people [black people], in the midst of people who are hung, shot, burned, and tortured . . . No historical situation was more challenging than the lynching era, when God the liberator seemed nowhere to be found . . . Throughout the twentieth century, African Americans continued to struggle to reconcile their faith in God's justice and love with the persistence of black suffering.[44]

Cone's restlessness to make sense of the supposedly divine absence in black suffering and the lack of God's redeeming interference in black lives is troublesome. Beyond Cone's solution to the problem of black theodicy, according to Anthony Pinn, the moral evils in this world are expressed in "oppression, injustice, inequality, and the resulting psychological and

42. Ibid., 7.

43. For a critical study on the theme of black theodicy, see Jones, *Is God a White Racist?*

44. Cone, *The Cross and the Lynching Tree*, 27–28.

physical damage," [45] and the "tridimensional oppressions"[46] are channeled through the dynamics of race, class, and gender. Womanist theologian Stephanie Mitchem interrogates the very possibility and the promise of salvation and redemptive suffering in Christian theology:

> Suffering in itself is not salvific. It is redemptive only in that it may lead to critical rethinking of meaning or purpose, as might nay life crisis. Such reexamination is part of the process of human maturation. However, suffering is a distinctive staring place for thinking about salvation as it brings into sharp focus humane experience with God.[47]

Like Pinn, Mitchem denies the possibility of redemptive suffering in divine providence in history, and in the same manner Womanist theologian Emilie Townes engages the question of the commodification of black women's body, and the problem of evil and suffering in society. On the other hand, for Cone, black suffering can be redemptive. Townes, in her dazzling study, *Womanist Ethics and the Cultural Production of Evil,* offers an engaging and insightful commentary on black theological anthropology with a special attention to the various forms of structural evil and constructed cultural stereotypes about black womanhood.[48] She underscores five representational stereotypes of black women which embody the manifestation of evil as a cultural production in the American society. These negative labels not only deprecate the black woman's body, defame black womanhood, they also identify the black female as property and commodity, and the subject of white gaze—as it were in the time of black lynching and slave auction.

> New interest in blackface stereotypes involves historical, political, and aesthetic implications that are more complex than allowed by the debates over positive and negative images. Every stereotype emerges in the wake of pre-existing ideology that deforms it, appropriates it, and naturalizes it. The blackface stereotype, by deforming the body, silences it and leaves room for white supremacy to speak through it . . . Black identity has been made property and it should leave a sickening weariness in the pit of our collective stomach for property means things owned, possession.[49]

45. Pinn, *Why Lord?*, 13.

46. Ibid.

47. Quoted in Whitted, *A God of Justice?*, 10.

48. Townes, *Womanist Ethics*, 6.

49. Ibid., 42–43.

Townes correlates the notion of property/commodity with black lives resulting in the selling of black flesh as part of the Western capitalist order and economic exploitation of black bodies in New World slave marketplaces.

> The modern conception of property considers it an economic resource, deems it friendly to money making, and regards the demands of the state as a drain on resources and a threat to a person's right to do as he or she will with their property. Implicit in this is an understanding of liberty as noninterference from the state. Ownership, then, means rights over resources that the individual can exercise without interference. [50]

In addition, Townes' evocative rhetoric of the commodification of black flesh can be construed as the process of devaluing black humanity. This remark is on par with Cone's candid observation about the lynching and dehumanization of black people. As pointed out earlier, the misrepresentation of black flesh as a non-human value was a shared ecstatic moment between white families and their friends; it also functioned as an economic transaction in Southern United States:

> The commodification of bodies mutated into the commodification of identity—Black history, Black culture, Black life—Black identity. Black identity as property means that a community of people has been reduced to exchange values that can be manipulated for economic gain—but rarely by the members of the community themselves. This manipulation includes merging race with myth and memory to create history. It includes caricaturing Black life, and in some cases Black agony, to sell the product.[51]

Complementarily, prominent African theologian John Mbiti could elaborate on the intersections of the origin of black liberation theology, black theodicy, American history, and white violence toward black people in America:

> The roots of Black Theology must in fact be traced to a much earlier period of American history, the arrival of the first African slaves in the seventeenth century. The subsequent history of Americans of African origin—of exploitation, segregation and general injustice—is the raw material of what we now call Black

50. Ibid., 43–44.
51. Ibid., 44.

Theology. Insofar as Black Theology is a response to this history of humiliation and oppression it is a severe judgment and an embarrassment to Christianity, especially in America.[52]

Thus, the subject of black theodicy is not just a theological concern. It is an interdisciplinary dialogue in Black Atlantic Intellectual Tradition as well as in Africana Critical Studies. Black thinkers in the African diaspora congruently and those in continental Africa have written voluminously on the topic of black suffering as a global problem in human history and cosmic effect of global white supremacy. For example, Lewis Gordon contends that "The racial problematic for Africana people is twofold. One the one hand, it is the question of exclusion in the face of an ethos of assimilation. On the other hand, there is the complex confrontation with the fact of such exclusion in a world that portends commitment to rational resolutions of evil."[53] Race, black suffering, and theodicy inevitably converge to shape the content of black religion and black theological anthropology and ethics—which are evident in the theological writings of James Cone. In a different passage, Gordon explains more clearly that the predicament of blackness and black existence in the modern world is tied to the institution of slavery and anti-black racism:

> U.S. slavery was a concerted dehumanizing project. It is this dimension that gardened its peculiarily *antiblack, racist* characteristic. The tale itself reveals much about racism. Racism, properly understood, is a denial of the humanity of a group of human beings either on the basis of race or color. This denial, properly executed, requires denying the presence of other human beings in such relations. It makes such beings a form of presence that is an absence, paradoxically, an absence of human presence.[54]

Not only slavery had deformed black lives, divided African families, altered African retentions in the Black diaspora, as historical records verify, both African women and men were sexually harassed and raped. The horrors of white slavery and colonization forced the African slaves to experience social alienation and physical death in large number.[55] While slave masters and colonizers used the power of Christianity to pacify the slaves, black slaves in the Americas turned to the religious resources to

---

52. Mbiti, "An African Views American Black Theology," 379.

53. Gordon, *Existentia Africana*, 9.

54. Ibid., 61.

55. For a good reference on this subject, see Patterson, *Slavery and Social Death*.

rescue themselves from this abyss of white supremacy. By consequence, the quest to reconstruct a positive black image/theological anthropology within the theological grammar of black liberation theology has been an intellectual journey and for James Cone and other black thinkers. Cone began this long journey in 1969 with the publication of his inaugural text of Black Liberation theology. In his posthumorous autobiography, Cone reflected on the quandary of black humanity and his courageous drive to uphold the dignity of black people:

> As a theologian, I felt compelled to write a manifesto to white churches announcing that Negroes could no longer tolerate the violation of their dignity. I had to give voice to the feelings of rage in the Negro community and especially the rage inside of me . . . It was an *existential* issue about black dignity—the political liberation of black people from white oppression.[56]

Cone's Black (Positive) Anthropology

Cone's black theological anthropology can be summarized in four major points. First, it is premised on the general race concept linking black humanity to what Victor Anderson phrases "ontological blackness." His race-based theological inclination and hermeneutics influence his understanding of the human nature and black existence in the United States and in the modern world. He affirmed unapologetically that "Black theology emphasizes the right of blacks to be black and by so doing to participate in the image of God."[57] Cone's assertion about the essence of blackness as a racial category is plainly conveyed in this language: "To ask them to assume a 'higher' identity by denying their blackness is to require them to accept a false identity and to reject reality as they know it to be;"[58] Cone's audacious affirmation that "black is beautiful" is reminiscent to what the Negritude writers believed about the aesthetics of blackness and conceptual beauty of the black world. The phrase attests to the belief that the black race has inherent worth and intelligence; this was a consensus among the radical thinkers of the Black Power movement. Charles Long interprets the "Black is beautiful" pronouncement in Cone as a way to deny the authority of the white world to define black

---

56. Cone, *Said I Wasn't Gonna Tell Nobody*, 13.
57. Cone, *A Black Theology of Liberation*, 92.
58. Cone, *Black Theology and Black Power*, 117.

reality and the black experience as a metaphor for a theory of knowl-edge.[59] In other words, Cone dismissed white epistemology and reason as viable ingredients to direct black thought and inform black action in the world. Cone's unequivocal conviction about the essential humanity of both black male and female is probably grounded on the theological aesthetic of the creation story in Genesis:

> So, God created mankind in his own image, in the image of God he created them; male and female he created them . . . Then God formed a man from the dust of the ground and breathe into his nostrils and the breath of life, and the man became a living being . . . So, the Lord God caused the man to fall into a deep sleep; and while he was sleeping, he took one of the man's ribs and then closed up the place with flesh. Then the Lord God made a woman from the rib he had taken out of the man, and he brought her to the man (Genesis 1:27; 2:7, 21–22)

Having argued that the black humanity bears the divine imprint, Cone emphasized the value of freedom as a ground of being. For Cone, freedom is the most fundamental virtue associating with human nature and agency; he advanced the idea that God has not withheld freedom, the "most cherished ideal"[60] in Western civilization, from black people.

> The biblical concept of image means that human beings are created in such a way that they cannot obey oppressive laws and still be human. To be human is to be in the image of God—that is, to be creative: revolting against everything that is opposed to humanity . . . The image of God refers to the way in which God intends human beings to live in the world. The image of God is thus more than rationality, more than what so-called neo-orthodox theologians call divine-human encounter. In a world in which persons are oppressed, the image is human nature in rebellion against the structures of oppression. It is humanity involved in the liberation struggle against the forces of inhumanity.[61]

Cone rejected the traditional theological definitions of the "image of God" as God's bestowing upon all people (1) reason or rationality, (2)

---

59. Long, *Significations*, 206.

60. Patterson, *Freedom in the Making of Western Culture*, 48. Patterson insists that in the origins of Western culture, freedom was not "founded upon a rock of human virtue, but upon the degraded time fill of man's vilest inhumanity to man."

61. Cone *A Black Theology of Liberation*, 93–94.

human responsibility, and (3) human rulership over the natural order. He creatively contextualized the biblical concept non-theologically and non-theoretically to address the historical suffering and the imperative of practical freedom for black people. By emphasizing the idea that the divine image means existential and practical freedom from human oppression and control, Cone was not questioning the ability of black people to reason and assume their God-given responsibility of being good stewards of the created order.

Further, by proposing this alternative view, Cone corrected a theological misstep in Euro-American Christian theology and contended that both American and European theologians have failed to link existential freedom (of blacks) with the divine image in (black) humanity. As he declared, "The inability of American theology to define human nature in the light of the Oppressed One and of particular oppressed peoples stems from its identity with the structures of white power."[62] He also elaborated this theological shortcoming in the history of Western biblical and theological scholarship with greater clarity and precision in the paragraph below:

> Modern theology, following Schleiermacher's unhappy clue to the relationship of theology and anthropology, forgot about Luther's emphasis on human depravity and proceeded once again to make appeals to human goodness. The nineteenth century is known for its confidence in the rational person, who not only knew what was right but was capable of responding to it. The image of God in human nature was the guarantee that the world was moving in desirable direction. It never occurred to these "Christian" thinkers that they had missed some contrary evidence: this was the period of black enslavement and Amerindian extermination, as well as European colonial conquests in Africa and Asia.[63]

European thinkers attributed reason, morality, and the leadership role to conquer and dominate to the Aryan race/white people, thus leading to their global conquest and hegemonic domination of dark and brown people. From this perspective, Cone's postulation was that Western thinkers have never attributed rationality to black folk. Immanuel Kant, for example, has argued that rationality or reason is a mark of genuine humanity, and that to be human means to be a rational being. In

62. Ibid., 86.
63. Ibid., 91.

his attempt to explain Cone's relationship between freedom and human existence, African American theologian James H. Evans claims that "This image is essential to humanity because it is the image of God pressed upon the human being in the moment of creation. When God set out to make humanity in God's own image, freedom became the guiding in human existence."[64] Cone argued that the teachings of Jesus provide liberation for black people from white oppression.

The meaning of the Gospel entails the categorical emancipation of the oppressed and the marginalized, and the radical transformation of society from systems of oppression and structural racism, such as white oppression and racism toward black people. Cone could pronounce that "If the content of the gospel is liberation, human existence must be explained as 'being in freedom,' which means rebellion against every form of slavery of everything creative."[65] In the words of Lewis R. Gordon, "Problems of existence address the human confrontation with freedom and degradation."[66] It is apparent that in our analysis we noted that the history of the people of African ancestry has been a search for holistic/emancipative freedom and cathartic healing—both at the personal and collective level—from the catastrophic phenomena of "alienation, crisis, struggle, resistance, and survival—not thriving, flourishing, or fulfillment. Its self-identity is always bound by white racism and the culture of survival."[67]

In response to the plight of black people in modernity, Cornell West has identified three dimensions of freedom in the Black expression of Christianity: the existential, the social, and the eschatological. They are also consistent with Cone's black theological anthropology:

1. Existential freedom is a mode of being-in-the-world which resists dread and despair. It embodies an ecstatic celebration of human existence without affirming prevailing reality;

2. The social dimension of the freedom predominant in black Christianity does not primarily concern political struggle but rather cultural solidarity . . . Yet the cultural practices of the black church embody a basic reality: sustained black solidarity in the midst of a hostile society;" and

---

64. Evans, *We Have Been Believers*, 110.

65. Cone *A Black Theology of Liberation*, 87.

66. Gordon, *Existentia Africana*, 7.

67. Anderson, *Ontological Blackness in Theology*, 87.

3. The eschatological aspect of freedom in black Christianity is the most difficult to grasp. It is neither a glib hope for a pie-in-the-sky heaven nor an apocalyptic aspiration which awaits world destruction. Rather, it is a hope-laden articulation of the tragic quality of everyday life of a culturally degraded, politically oppressed, and racially coerced labor force.[68]

Correspondingly, Cone has detected the threefold manifestations of black freedom linked to black anthropology: black religious texts channeled through the spirituals, secular songs such as the blues, and the writings of the Old Testament Prophets and teachings of Jesus. As already reported in our previous analysis, through the message and theology of The Spirituals, African slaves anticipated freedom as a practical reality in their lifetime. They also projected freedom as a future-eschatological event, which they will inherit in the afterlife when they leave this world for a better world: heaven. Black blues musicians protest against the hard life of black people and challenge the political system that hinder the progress of the black population.

The second aspect of Cone's black theological anthropology relates to God's decision to give the gift of existence and the gift of stewardship to the black race. Cone sustained the theological position that black people like other people in God's creation are protagonists and collaborative agents with God in the world. Accordingly, all human individuals and races are various manifestations of the divine image, energy, and grace. In other words, the black race exists out of the divine will and that God created black people so that they could participate in his life and like other races could enjoy life in the world through the divine endowment of gifts of (cosmic) rulership, administration, and pioneership. Cone did not believe that black people were destined for failure and tragedy. He challenged the racist theological view that God has ordained the descendants of the Hamites to become the servants of the white race. Yet racial tragedy during the time of chattel slavery was designed to alter the black (human) condition in America.

In the Reconstruction era, the enactment of racial segregation through Jim Crow laws was designed to break the black soul, to limit the future and potential of black citizens, and to debase their humanity. Cone believed in the power of protest and rhetoric to challenge the assumptions of his interlocutors, chiefly white theologians, the white church, and

68. West, *Prophesy Deliverance!*, 162–64.

the American government; specifically, he used theology as a rhetoric of protest to speak on behalf of the black masses and galvanize them toward racial consciousness and to become aware of their socio-economic condition. In relation to this observation, Cone could argue that the function of Black theology is to restore the black image and to articulate theologically a positive representation of the black life. Therefore, Cone's doctrine of black theological anthropology is a weapon against global

white supremacy, racial violence, and the triumph of global whiteness in modern history:

> Black Theology must take seriously the reality of black people—their life of suffering and humiliation. This must be the point of departure of all God-talk which seeks to be Black-talk. When that man is black and lives in a society permeated with white racist power, he can speak of God only from the perspective of the socio-economic and political conditions unique to black people. Though the Christian doctrine of God must logically precede the doctrine of man, Black Theology knows that black people can view God only through black eyes that behold the brutalities of white racism.[69]

Evidently, a proper belief in black identity must lead to the recognition of black humanity in the white world. This belief is also predicated upon God's positive thought about black people and his definition of what they are and should be in the world. Accordingly, Cone called black people to reject white values and how whites define them and the functions they ascribe to Black people in society. Here, Cone explored what constitutes the human nature and the ontology of being:

> The question about the human person is not answered by enumerating a list of properties; a person is not a collection of properties that can be scientifically analyzed. Rather to speak of the human being is to speak about its being-in-the-world-of-human oppression with the reality of human suffering as our starting point.[70]

As already mentioned above, the idea of black humanity is derivative from God as life giver. According to Cone, God is the one who determines black personhood; therefore, Cone appropriated the third aspect of black theological anthropology to the doctrine of the fatherhood of God and

69. Cone, *Black Theology and Black Power*, 117.
70. Ibid., 87.

basic belief that God has purposed the black race to be included in the one universal human race that he created. Black people of all times are human beings because they belong to God's global community and inclusive human family. This belief was a non-negotiable theological fact and a sustainable intellectual reality for James H. Cone. Yet Cone inferred that the personhood of Jesus is what gives black people dignity and worth. It is from this angle Cone would establish a bond between the essence of black humanity and the meaning of Jesus Christ for black people.

Therefore, the final aspect of Cone's constructive black theological anthropology is situated within the doctrine of union with Christ. On the lynching tree, black people became united with Christ as he himself also suffered, hanged, and died on the wooden cross. An important thought about Cone's anthropology establishes its roots in the doctrine of divine disclosure in the person and deeds of Jesus Christ. Cone construed the incarnation of God in the historical Jesus of Nazareth as an important event in human history that legitimized black humanity; through the incarnation, God's intention and provision for the welfare and emancipation of black people and the world's oppressed was made known. In the paragraph below, he explained in great detail:

> The task of Black Theology is to analyze the black man's condition in the light of God's revelation in Jesus Christ with the purpose of creating a new understanding of black dignity among black people, and providing the necessary soul in that people, to destroy white racism . . . Because Black Theology has its starting point the black condition, this does not mean that it denies the absolute revelation of God in Christ. Rather, it means that Black Theology firmly believes that God's revelation in Christ can be made supreme only by affirming Christ as he is alive in black people today.[71]

To put it simply, Jesus Christ is for the oppressed and the world's poor. Since black people are marginalized and oppressed in the United States, Jesus is for them. He is the defender of their rights and dignity. The emancipative intent of the divine incarnation—as a radical act of divine freedom and love—was to set free those who have been subject to human tyranny, acts of evil, and acts of dehumanization. Since black people in America have faced these troubles and continue to experience similar things in the present, the benefits of the incarnation are still relevant to them. God has

71. Ibid., 117–18.

distinctively revealed himself in Christ in order to emancipate black people from mental, physical, and psychological enslavement and oppression. In the incarnation, God's love became relentless and a restorative force to heal the wound of the oppressed. In this way, Cone could converge the doctrine of divine providence, divine revelation in the incarnation, black existence, and the meaning of Christ's birth and life (Christology) for the marginalized communities and exploited peoples in the world. The incarnation has a universal and cross-cultural aspect.

We already noted above that Cone's Christ is Black and therefore he suffers and is marginalized. To be black in the white world is to experience suffering, demonization, and alienation in the same way Jesus the "Black Messiah" was suffered in the Roman world, demonized by his enemies, and alienated by those who despised him. It is at this point Cone articulated a Christology of symbolic appropriation and "symbolic blackness," to borrow the expression from Victor Anderson. Therefore, Cone could say that black theology calls black people to exercise faith in God and the Christ of redemptive suffering and sustaining hope:

> [Black Theology] it calls upon black people to affirm God because he has affirmed us. His affirmation of black people is made known not only in his election of the oppressed Israel, but more especially in his coming to us and being rejected in Christ for us. The event of Christ tells us that the oppressed blacks are his people because, and only because, they represent who he is.[72]

Cone appropriated (black) critical theological anthropology within the framework of a Christology of symbolic representation and relationality. Jesus' humanity is very selective, meaningfully, and meaningfully racial and class-based. God took the form of a human flesh in order that he could be in solidarity with the poor and relate to them as his children in their suffering and liberation:

> Jesus is not a human being for all persons; he is a human being for oppressed persons, whose identity is made known in and through their liberation. Therefore, our definition of the human being must be limited to what it means to be liberated from human oppression. Any other approach fails to recognize the reality of suffering in an inhuman society.[73]

72. Ibid., 118.
73. Cone, *God of the Oppressed*, 85–86.

Cone's Christ is actively working to deliver his impoverished children from their socio-economic woes and structural poverty. Cone's "Black Christ" affirmed brazenly the humanity and dignity of black people and the poor; as he pronounced affirmatively, "In every case, Christ is the otherness in the black experience that makes possible the affirmation of black humanity in an inhumane situation."[74] Even though Christ accompanies the poor in his/her daily struggle and suffering, the existential challenges and threats about his/her self-respect and personhood do not go away. Cone himself confessed, "The crucial question, then, for the black man is, 'How should I respond to a world which defines me as a nonperson?'"[75] The dilemma of blackness is excruciating, relentless, and existential: "But when he attempts to relate as a person, the world demands that he respond as a thing. In this existential absurdity, what should he do? Should he respond as he knows himself to be, or as the world defines him?"[76] His only hope is to turn to the Black Christ for soul-comforting and mental rehabilitation.

Therefore, one can infer that Cone accentuated the meaning of Christ the Liberator and his redeeming power to reconstruct a hopeful Black theological anthropology. (Some critics have argued that Cone was not optimistic, but he did have hope on the basis of his faith in God.) Based on this premise, he could declare that "The essence of the gospel of Christ stands or falls on the question of black humanity, and there is no way that a church or institution can be related to the gospel of Christ if it sponsors or tolerates racism in any form."[77] A Christology rooted in the ways of the white world and the logic of whiteness is inadequate for black redemption and nor could it fully liberate the economically-disadvantaged brown and black populations. For Cone, the Christology of the white church is not a Christology of hope for black people. In fact, white Christology disregards the Christian message of peace, reconciliation, and hospitality as it pertains to the welfare of the black population in society. The challenging message of James Cone for white supremacist Christians and American racists in general is expressive in this one sentence: "Blackness is the image of God in Black people." As Jacques Grant interprets Cone's Christology of black hope and renaissance, "The condition of Black people today

74. Ibid., 105.
75. Cone, *Black Theology and Black Power*, 11.
76. Ibid.
77. Cone, *A Black Theology of Liberation*, 14.

reflects the cross of Jesus. Yet the resurrection brings the hope that libera-tion from oppression is immanent. The resurrected Black Christ signifies this hope."[78] In other words, Cone attempted to solve the mysterious of theodicy, and more specifically black theodicy in the Christ-event as the exaltation-liberation event for those who suffer, including black people. In a nutshell, Cone's Christology provides "the internal answer to the theod-icy question in Black Theology."[79]

The Meaning of Cone, or Cone in the Construction of Meaning in Theology

It is the divine image of God in Black people that gives them significance and their reason to resist white oppression and racism. Cone believed that black agency or autonomy is necessary in black people's quest for meaning and freedom. He insisted that black theological expression mat-ters and that the voice of the black masses is significant to God. Hence, black theologians and thinkers must challenge any force or racial power in society that seeks to silence the collective optic and autonomy of black people. This attitude entails both a practical task and intellectual respon-sibility to publicly denounce the sin of racism, global white supremacy, and white hegemonic control in the world.

For Cone, racism is not just systemic and structural. It is America's first transgression and a great sin this nation committed at its birth. Yet racism is a product of white supremacy and white supremacy is identified with the making of the United States; the Christian religion has been foundational in the construction of the narrative of whiteness. Cone stated, "White supremacy is America's original sin. It is found in every aspect of American life."[80] America was founded on the geno-cide of the "First Nation" (the Native Americans) and the progressive annihilation of Black people through forced labor (slavery), substanti-ated by Jim Crow segregation and the mass incarceration of its black population. America's first transgression has fourfold dimension: ra-cial, political, theological, and moral. America's white Christianity did

78. Grant, "Womanist Theology," 284.

79. Cone, "Epilogue," 437. For a comprehensive exploration of the issue of theod-icy in Black Theology, see chapter 8, "Divine Liberation and Black Suffering," in Cone's *God of the Oppressed.*

80. Cone, *Said I Wasn't Gonna Tell Nobody,* 54.

not condemn its government but cheered for the nation in all of these transactions. Since Cone is primarily a theologian and not a political scientist, he emphasized the sin of racism as America's first theological problem; thus, race is a theological conundrum. Cone could say that "For a black person who was born in the South and whose church came into being because of racism, the failure to discuss it as a central prob lem in theology appeared strange and racist to me."[81] The thesis that racism is a theological problem is also a core matter in Washington's influential book, *Black Religion*. Washington established a distinction between Black religion and White Protestantism and contended that the birth of Black religion occurred within the historical context of American slavery and American religious segregation in white church- es. Black Christians were excluded from the practice of Christianity in white churches, hence resulting in the creation of the Black church. The emergence of Black religion or the Black church was the consequence of a historic theological problem in white American Christianity.[82] Hence, the demands of Black liberation theology consider the various aspects of the nation and from its dominant white Christian religion including moral, ethical, legal, economic, and theological reparations.

James H. Cone advanced the idea that white Christians should be proponents of divine justice and love in the American society and em- body a biblical faith consistent to the teachings of Christ and inseparable from the notion of divine justice and fatherhood of God. The denial of justice to black people in America is a categorical attack on their human- ity and an unqualified act of disobedience to God. Cone never divorced the causes of social justice and civil rights for blacks and the economi- cally-disadvantaged American population to the central message of the Christian gospel. He identified the gospel with the struggle (of blacks) for justice in society and accentuated that white Christianity must address with social justice and civil rights issues.[83] To put it simply, Cone did not separate Christianity and politics, theology and moral or ethical issues. Cone alleged that "Christian ethics was the natural link for the connec- tion of the problem of racism."[84]

81. Cone, *My Soul Looks Back*, 37.

82. For Cone's critical analysis of Washington's work, see Cone, *For My People*, 8–10.

83. Cone, *My Soul Looks Back*, 39.

84. Ibid.

Additionally, Cone conceptualized his politico-theological ideas and moral demands as a corrective rejoinder to the triumph of American-based white supremacy, white violence against Black citizens, and the culpability of white American churches and theologians. Black people continue to undergo the terror of Police brutality and mass incarceration, what Michelle Alexander called the "New Jim Crow" in America's twenty-first century culture. In an article entitled, "Black Theology and the Black Church: Where Do We Go from Here?" published in 2004, Cone defined his Black theological discourse as a "radical response from the underside of American religious history to the mainstream of white Christianity." One can safely infer that Black liberation theology is an urgent call to racist white American Christians and white churches to exercise their power and influence to construct a new American society and to radically change their racist behavior, attitude, and actions toward the oppressed blacks and the marginalized populations in this nation.

Consequently, the goal of Black liberation theology is to fight against all forms of human oppression and assault, and all forces of alienation and destruction against the underrepresented black and downgraded populations—toward their full emancipation, human flourishing, and the realization of their human potential and the creation of a new human community. Correspondingly, in his second seminal work, *A Black Theology of Liberation*, Cone argued that Christian "theology cannot be separated from the community it represents. It assumes that truth has been given to the community at the moment of its birth. Its task is to analyze the implications of that truth, in order to make sure that the community remains committed to that which defines its existence."[85] Cone's theology is a theological discourse that predicates on the collective responsibility and the sacred task of Christian churches to uphold justice, to fight evil, and to promote human dignity. Its premise is grounded on truth-telling and public witness in the rhetorical mannerism of James Baldwin and the Black Radical Tradition.

On the other hand, both Black theologians and Black Womanist theologians and ethicists, in and outside of the Black Liberation Theological Tradition, have criticized Cone. Those criticisms engage his earliest writings in the 1960s and some in the 1970s. There are five general complaints raised about Cone's theology. First, critics have remarked that in his theological discourse, he gave primacy to white racism as a form

---

85. Cone, *A Black Theology of Liberation*, 9.

of oppression toward blacks. Second, some of Cone's critics have argued that Cone held to a fixed, unchanged, and essential concept of race (i.e. whiteness, blackness). Third, Cone's former (Black women) students have accused him for underrepresenting the black woman and her suffering in his theological account. They also remarked that Cone has undermined the issue of gender oppression/sexism as another form of male oppres sion directed toward women. Black womanist theologians and ethicists (i.e. Jacquelyn Grant, Delores S. Williams, Kelly Brown Douglas, Katie G. Cannon, Cheryl Townsend Gilkes) have argued that the issues of class, race, and sexism are all interconnected and contribute to the oppression of black women. Fourth, other critics have said that Cone's Black liberation is reverse racism toward white people and Western theological models to construct a black theology of liberation; one cannot dismantle the master with his own tool.

For example, Anderson uses the concept "ontological blackness" and "symbolic blackness" to brand Cone's theological narrative. Carter explains, "Anderson sees in ontological blackness a claim that makes race, though always present, the exhaustive principle of identity, its thoroughgoing index."[86] Anderson's criticisms of Cone's theology highlight several important shortcomings about Cone's idea on race and blackness:

> Blackness has become a totality of meaning. It cannot point to any transcendent meaning beyond itself without fragmenting . . . Existentially, the new black being remains bound by whiteness. Politically, it remains unfulfilled because blackness is ontologically defined as the experience of suffering and survival . . . The essential theological meaning of black experience, black history, and black culture—all of which represent the black collective consciousness.[87]

In his further appraisal of Cone's theology, he posits that their internal contradictions and conceptual problems in Cone's theological analysis:

> (a) Blackness is a signification of ontology and corresponds to black experience. (b) Black experience is defined as the experience of suffering and rebellion against whiteness. Yet (c) both black suffering and rebellion are ontologically created and provoked by whiteness as a necessary condition of blackness. (d)

86. Carter, *Race*, 159.
87. Anderson, *Beyond Ontological Blackness*, 89–90.

> Whiteness appears to be the ground of black experience, and
> hence of black theology justifies itself as radically oppositional
> to whiteness, it nevertheless requires whiteness, white racism,
> and white theology for the self-disclosure of its new black being
> and its legitimacy.[88]

Furthermore, both Black Womanist theologians Kelly Brown
Douglas and Jacquelyn Grant protested because of the failure of Black
theology to address sexism in theology, the American culture, and the
Black Church. According to Grant, although Black liberation theologians
claimed that they wrote about the totality of the black American experience, the collective experience of Black women was not discussed and
even ignored in black theological discourse. Grant posited that Black
women in Black Theology are "invisible." She presumed there were two
reasons for this theological shortcoming. First, perhaps, Black women
had no place in Black theological enterprise. Second, Black male theologians believed that they were also capable of speaking for Black women
and their life trajectories and experiences. Beyond the deficiencies of
Black theology in not affirming Black Women subjectivity and agency in
theological discourse, Grant underscored a general concern in the field
of Theological Studies that it was a male-dominated discipline and is representative of the patriarchal culture.

> Black women have been invisible in theology because theo-
> logical scholarship has not been a part of the woman's sphere
> . . . from the historical orientation of the dominant culture. If
> women have no place in theology it becomes the natural pre-
> rogative of men to monopolize theological concerns, including
> those relating specifically to women . . . Racism and sexism are
> interrelated just as all forms of oppression are interrelated. Sex-
> ism, however, has a reality and significance of its own because
> it represents the peculiar form of oppression suffered by Black
> women at the hands of black men.[89]

Consequently, Douglas could declare that "Womanist theology has
emerged partly because of Black theology's failure to address the concerns
of Black women." Yet she acknowledged that "Black theology gave Black
women access to systematic theological reflection."[90] On the other hand,

---

88. Ibid., 91.

89. Grant, "Black Theology and The Black Woman," 326–27.

90. Douglas, "Womanist Theology," 292.

William R. Jones, one of the most influential critics of Black theology, wrote about the inability of Black theology to provide a plausible response to the problem of black theodicy or the question of black suffering and the goodness and sovereignty of God. Provocatively, he pondered:

> If black liberation is the goal of black theology, black suffering, in the final analysis, is its starting point. To regard liberation as the *summon bonum* necessitates that its opposite, suffering as oppression, is an aspect of the *summum malum*. The precondition for black liberation as the objective for black theology is the prior affirmation of black suffering as oppressive.[91]

Jones suggested that Cone has avoided to deal with the issue of theodicy with rigor because it implies "the perpetuity of black suffering."[92] According to Jones, Cone's theodicy did not explain adequately why black people suffer. Yet Cone "is content to see white racism as the cause,"[93] he inferred. Further, Jones reasoned that there was no empirical evidence to justify that God, in essence, is for the liberation of the oppressed black population in the United States, and there is no eschatological hope that God will deliver specifically black people from white oppression and racism in the United States. As Cone recapitulated Jones' concern, "If God is involved in history, then there should be some empirical evidence of that involvement. Where then is the proof of your assertion that God is the God of oppressed Blacks, liberating them from bondage? Without an exaltation-liberating event, there is no basis for the theological claim."[94]

As could be noted in our previous analysis, Cone, in fact, in his latter writings, beginning in the 1970s to the year he died (2018), has responded both directly and indirectly to many criticisms and claims raised by his critics. Nonetheless, the topic of black theodicy is the inescapable problem in black liberation theology; generally, theodicy has been one of the most theological and philosophical questions in the Humanities and Social Sciences. The paragraph below articulates Cone's attempt in 1993 to engage the subject of theodicy, from an ontological, salvific, and Christological perspective:

> First, suffering is the source of faith. That is, without human suffering, there would be no need for the Christian gospel in

91. Jones, "Theodicy and Methodology," 142.
92. Ibid., 146.
93. Ibid.
94. Cone, "Epilogue," 437.

particular or religion generally. Ludwig Feuerbach was right: "Thought is preceded by suffering." There would be no need for a Christian doctrine of salvation if there were no evil in the world. Therefore, the gospel is the Christian answer to human misery. Second, the Christian faith arises out of suffering, suffering is the most serious contradiction of faith. That is the paradox. If the gospel of God is the answer to human misery, why do people still continue to suffer? There is no easy answer to this question.[95]

Black Liberation Theology and (Black) Liberal Theology

Finally, those of the "Evangelical Camp," especially White Evangelical theologians have accused Black liberation theology as being a "liberal theology" and James Cone as being a theological heretic. To bring some clarity about these two theological traditions and opposing poles (Black Liberation Theology and Liberal Theology), in the subsequent paragraphs, I would like to provide a brief comparative analysis.

While there are many confluences and converges between Black liberation theology and liberation theology, Black theology is a contextual theological discourse that is grounded on the history, culture, life, and experience of black people in the United States. For example, the theological writings of James Cone demonstrate substantial marks of influence from white liberal theologians such as Paul Tillich and Reinhold Niebuhr, and concurrently, Cone is indebted to slave religion and African cosmology, black history, black literature, and the Black Power and Consciousness movements in his theological formulation. A network of black intellectuals such as James Baldwin, Richard Wright, Leroi Jones (a.k.a. Amiri Baraka), Malcolm X, Martin Luther King, and others have supplied to him the intellectual platform and cultural tools that he needed to articulate a theology of liberation from below and from an interdisciplinary and cross-disciplinary perspective. As he affirmed:

> I needed more help with the actual content of black history. For the first time, I began to read Frederick Douglass, Booker T. Washington, W. E. B. DuBois, and Carter G. Woodson. Reading black thinkers, most historians, I encountered the various ways that black people have struggled against white racism. I

95. Ibid.

learned that black people have never been as passive as whites had suggested in their history books. Therefore, my contemporary rebellious spirit had its roots in earlier black generations. This knowledge was quite liberating.[96]

Black liberation theology is also linked to Black Radical Tradition, and Africana Critical Tradition. Black Liberation Theology seeks to reinterpret the Bible and the black experience in the light of black struggle for freedom, political rights, and social justice in the American society. In addition, Cone's black liberation theology is also related to the Liberal Theology[97] and the revolutionary Black Social Gospel movement, which Gary Dorrien has brilliantly chronicled in his two well-researched and excellent books, *The New Abolition: W. E. B. Du Bois* and *the Black Social Gospel* (2015) and *Breaking White Supremacy: Martin Luther King Jr. and the Black Social Gospel* (2018). The summary below offers a few propositions differentiating Black liberation theology and Liberal theology, distilling from the work of Cone.

While Black liberation theology emphasizes the black experience in theological inquiry and thought, Liberal theology rejects some of the cardinal doctrines of Orthodox Christianity—such as the virgin birth of Jesus, the deity Jesus Christ, etc. Liberation theology and Liberal theology are two different theological systems that do not share the same methodology. They have different sources of origin, address different (theological) issues or (practical) concerns, and speak to different audiences or people. Liberal theology is a Eurocentric theological model that is written for a white audience, chiefly the educated white intellectuals. Like any European theological systems, Liberal theology is concerned about theological abstracts and the fundamental doctrinal concerns. (Of course, one can speak of various segments of liberal theology that is not concerned with theological formulas and theological dogmas.) By contrast, Black liberation theology is the theology of and for the black masses, its primary audience, and speaks directly to their struggles and predicament in the American society. It is not written for the bourgeoisie class, but for the economically-disadvantaged blacks who confront

---

96. Cone, *My Soul Looks Back*, 28–29.

97. For an excellent evaluation of Liberal Theology within the American theological landscape, see Garry Dorrien's trilogy, *The Making of American Liberal Theology: Imagining Progressive Religion, 1805–1900* (2001), *The Making of American Liberal Theology: Idealism, Realism, and Modernity, 1900–1950* (2003), and *The Making of American Liberal Theology: Crisis, Irony, and Postmodernity, 1950–2005* (2006).

daily the burden of American racism, white oppression, and the reality of political alienation and social injustice. While anti-black racism and the question of black justice are fundamental and existential concerns of black theology, classical liberation theology in the European tradition does not engage social justice and human rights issues in the best interest of the powerless, those on the margins, and the world's oppressed black and brown populations.

Black liberation theology seeks to interpret the plight of Black people and the most vulnerable in society from a theological and political vantage point of view and within a very specific social system and cultural milieu. Cone asserted that the Black liberation theologian examines the Christian Scripture and other sources of inspiration carefully to discover what God has to say about the black experience in the world and its rapport to black freedom in a society controlled by whites. Three fundamental questions Black liberation theology attempts to answer when considering the plot of the black and brown populations:

1. What does it mean to be black (Black existence) and oppressed (Black oppression)?

2. Is God on the side of the oppressed? Or is God in solidarity with "black people" and the poor in their suffering and oppression?

3. Will the oppressed find justice or will God vindicate the oppressed and judge the oppressor?

As already examined in previous analysis, Cone believed that the God of the Bible is the God of the oppressed and as a relational Being, he is totally committed to the welfare and safety of his people and his creation. God is for the weak and the most vulnerable individuals and degraded groups in society. Any human phenomenon or activity that causes suffering and pain is a theological matter that demands moral reckoning. Sin of any form or expression (i.e. structural, systemic, cultural, political, racial, economic, sexual) is worth examining through the lens of the liberative message of the Christian Gospel and America's social justice democratic politics.

Furthermore, as in any theological worldview, there are many good things one can learn from (Black) theological liberalism. First, (Black) theological liberalism in the contemporary intellectual enterprise accentuates the imperative of black freedom and black agency in a society that constantly undermines the value of black life and black dignity. Second, this theological category or system seeks to promote the holistic welfare of black people. It sustains the notion that black life in the modern American society is worth safeguarding and that black people are individuals who have worth, autonomy, agency, desires, dreams, and a future. Third, black theologians, operating within the tradition of black theological liberalism, embrace the promises of the Social Gospel movement to envision an alternative life for black people in America. Black Theological Liberation and its allied Black Womanist theology campaigned for equal opportunity and access to better employment and housing opportunity, better education, healthcare, job promotion, and economic mobility for black people and black women.

Fourth, Black liberation theology draws from a wealth of sources and traditions for theological reflection and imagination. The Bible is not its sole authority in matters of faith and practice. Finally, Black liberation theology supports non-European theological scholarship and biblical exegesis toward better and more inclusive ecumenical, transnational, transcultural, and interdisciplinary dialogues. Not only James H. Cone is the father of Black Liberation theology, Black liberation theology created Cone. Theological liberalism provided both the theological language and the intellectual force for him to develop a truly-empowering theological discourse to respond to the existential needs and conundrum of America's most humiliated group and race.

Concluding Thoughts

James H. Cone has helped an entire generation of black and brown scholars in America, Africa, and elsewhere in the world to take seriously the biblical portrayal of God as a God of justice and as a relational Deity whose ultimate mission involves (1) the deliverance of the world's oppressed from human-inflicted oppression and pain, and (2) God's decisive commitment to holistic justice and the radical transformation of unjust societal systems and oppressive structures that are detrimental to the welfare of the world's poor and the economically-marginalized people. A similar theological attitude is found in the politico-theological works of the Caribbean theologians to be examined later in this book. In his work, Cone accentuated the urgency of theological praxis and insisted that followers of Jesus must embody and showcase the emancipative teachings of Jesus Christ in their lives. Cone declared that "God was Black" because God has deliberately chosen to be in solidarity with the powerless, those on the margins, and the "historical oppressed," especially the black victims, of white racism and white oppression in the United States.

James Cone and Benjamin E. Mays (to be discussed later) also believed that in order for American Christianity to be a truly liberative faith for the black and brown people in America, it must be the antagonist of whiteness and dissociate itself from the white world. Both Cone and Mays argued that white churches in America must reject the racist structures that are inherent to the birth and practices of white American Christianity. Until the day he died, Cone maintained the idea that Christianity and racism are antitheses and cannot coexist. In other words, one cannot be a genuine Christian and practice anti-black racism and cannot be a true follower of the God of justice and remains silent in the faces of oppression and injustice toward the black and brown communities in the American society. Cone believed that a committed follower of Jesus is a friend of the oppressed and the poor, the black neighbor.

Cone's enormous contribution to Africana critical theology, Black Liberation theology, Christian theology, and Human Rights studies constitute another pivotal facet of his ongoing legacy: he always challenged those in position of power and influence and theologians about the ongoing threats and disastrous effects of white supremacy and white racism in the American society. Likewise, Cone was also critical of America's military interventions in the world and America's hostile xenophobic attitude toward the immigrants and political refugees. Similarly, Mays was very critical of America's unjust war in Vietnam and was criticized by the American Conservative group and enthusiastic patriots.

Moreover, Cone maintained theological thinking is a performance that is rooted in the theologian's values, attitude, imagination, and worldview. No one does Christian Theology without assuming a worldview. For him, Christian theology is not a set of abstracts and principles the theologian articulates, promotes, and defends. Biblical Christianity does not divorce theology and ethics, or belief and action.

While we must always pursue theological truths that are rooted in God's revelation to humanity, we should not undermine the milieu and human environment in which God communicated his will, plan, and message to humanity. Cone argued in God of the Oppressed that God's revelation came to us in a contextualized form, the world and experience of the poor and oppressed; hence, all theologies and theological systems are contextualized forms and expressions of the individual who created them. God always speaks in the context of the human experience and the culture of the people who are the recipients of his gracious revelation. God has indeed spoken to black people within the parameters of their own culture. God is not (has not been) absent in any culture in the world. He has indeed revealed himself specifically to the poor and oppressed— as we also learned from Latin American Liberation theology.

Finally, for Cone, a theological system that emphasizes academic theology while undermining practical theology and God's passion for justice and his command to care for the poor, the oppressed, the orphan, the widow, and to show compassion and hospitality toward strangers and the needy is inadequate and insufficient. The theological system that is silent on human suffering, pain, and oppression, as well as human hunger, and the exploitation of workers, and sex slave trafficking in the world is also a rigged system. Cone has taught us that these are "Gospel issues," not merely "social issues"; they are equally human concerns that touch the deepest part of the divine heart and mind.

One could infer that Cone was conscious about his manifold functions: his vocation as a public black theologian and intellectual, his role as a passionate interpreter of the black experience, and his public function as a fierce critic of white supremacy and white American Christianity. If there are key words to recapitulate the whole of Cone's theological vocation, the following ones are suggestive: bearing witness, truth-telling, black dignity, protest, rage, liberation, and passion.

4

The Relevance of James Cone for Africana Critical Theology

Rethinking Christian Theology and the Plot of the Poor and the Marginalized

Men were not created for separation, and color is not the essence of man's humanity.

—JAMES H. CONE, *BLACK THEOLOGY, BLACK POWER*

Introduction

THIS PRESENT CHAPTER IS a reinforcement of the thesis articulated in the previous chapter. As previously observed, Cone articulates a Black theology of liberation in the context of the history of black suffering and white domination in the United States and frames it as a corrective response to American (white) theology that is silent on black pain and suffering and the alienation of Black people from white theological account about God's involvement in human history. He defines Black Theology as a "radical response from the underside of American religious history to the mainstream of white Christianity."[1] In his second and seminal work, *A Black Theology of Liberation* (1970), Cone argues that Christian "theology cannot be separated from the community it represents. It assumes that truth has been given to the community at the moment of its birth. Its task is to analyze the implications of that truth, in order to make sure that the community remains committed to that which defines its existence."[2] The relationship between theology and ecclesiology is intertwined in Cone's theological language and reasoning, as it is also a central theme in Benjamin Mays and J. Deotis Roberts's ecclesiology. The concerns and experiences of the people of God in the church are the raw material for theological hermeneutics and the reading of God's liberating actions among his people.

While Cone prioritizes God's revelation as the beginning point of theological inquiry, correspondingly, he contends that the culture of a people is another fundamentally adequate source to think theologically about the redemptive movement of God in the world—through the agency of his church, his emissary in the local culture. Consequently, Cone establishes that theology has both a communal function and public vocation in relations to the needs of the Christian community, and the needs of the people in society that contextualize and inform theological imagination and hermeneutics. Because of the complexity of human relations in society and the multifaceted functions of the church in culture, if Christian theology and the Christian church are going to be faithful witnesses to God's active involvement in human affairs, they must contribute to the wholistic transformation of the human condition in society and the reconciliation of all things through Christ the Liberator. Christian theology as an academic discipline and the Christian church as God's chosen agent in the world must not remain unresponsive to the plot of the oppressed and the vulnerable in society.

The objective of this chapter is to investigate the interplay between Christian theology and the Christian church and their engagement or disengagement in society in the (politico-) theological writings and ecclesiological hermeneutics of James H. Cone. In Cone's work, Christian theology is expressed as a public discourse and testimony of God's

1. Wilmore, "A Revolution Unfulfilled," 147.
2. Cone, *A Black Theology of Liberation*, 9.

continuing emancipative movements and empowering presence in society with the goal (1) to set the oppressed and the vulnerable free, (2) to readjust the things of the world toward divine justice and peace, and (3) to bring healing and restoration to the places in which volitional (human) agents have inflicted pain, suffering, oppression, and all forms of evil. This essay is an attempt to imagine creatively with new hermeneutical lenses and approaches—liberative, postcolonial, and decolonial—both the task of Christian theology and the vocation of the church as public witnesses to carry out the emancipative agenda and reconciling mission (salvation, healing, hospitality, wholeness, reconciliation, and peace) of God in contemporary societies and in our postcolonial moments. As will be observed subsequently in the politico-theological work of Benjamin Mays, Mays believed that the American church should be a "prophetic church" that could contribute to the transformation of the civil and political societies. For the church to obtain this significant objective in society, Christians must engage actively in civic participation and public witness toward the common good and the holistic welfare of society.

The basic argument of this chapter is twofold. First, it contends for the essential role of liberation theology in redefining Christian theology and ecclesiology in general. Rather than being a "special interest" or merely political theme in theology, it suggests that black liberation theology has a special role to play in "freeing" Christian theology and ecclesiology (globally) from racism, oppression, and imperialism. Second, by promoting some new understanding of Cone's work and applying it in some new context, this chapter is deploying Cone's theology to critique or awaken dominant white theology to a new way of thinking about the whole field of theology and church in the twenty-first century.

Broadly, the chapter is divided in five parts. Briefly, the first part discusses the complexity of race in the history of American Christianity; particularly, it provides some historical examples of how white supremacy completely distorts theology and race relations in America. By providing three main examples, the second part of the essay demonstrates the bankruptcy of white American theology and Cone's constructive criticisms to white theological discourse. Particularly, it showcases how an "other worldly" Christianity consistently dehumanizes the black other, but also mangles Christian theology itself into a mere cover for human oppression. The third part discusses the task of Christian theology in the quest for human flourishing. It demonstrates how Cone's project of black liberation affirms the humanity and agency of the oppressed and has the potential to redefine Christianity for ALL people as this-worldly, engaged, situated, and attuned to the healing of suffering in the present, rather than Christianity as other worldly ideology covering racism, oppression, and i~ ~~~~~lism.

While the fourth part of the char___ ___ ___ about the true vocation of the Christian c___ ___ ___ essay provides some suggestions on how ___ ___ ___ tices of the church. Cone's rich ecclesi___ ___ ___ rces and practical examples about t___ ___ ___ rch in contributing to a prophetic ___ ___ ___ rst century. As we learn in Cone ___ ___ ___ ch "spiritualize" sinfulness and o___ ___ ___ e depredations of racism and expl___ ___ ___ of their humanity. We look to Cone for ___ ___ ___ ...istian theology and the Christian church in our ___ ___ ...ients.

[Handwritten annotation overlaid: "this chapter first talks of the race — how religion can be used for a direction in life, or the purpose of religion at all. if we consider oppression of Christianity, the exploitation of those oppressed under the radar goes as intentional in god's plan."]

Fragments of American History: Theology and Race in "Christian America"

The introductory article of The Universal Declaration of Human Rights (1948) that bears considerable political ideologies and linguistic parallels with The Constitution of the United States and The Bill of Rights (1791) and France's Declaration of the Rights of the Man and of the Citizen (1789) begins with the following declaration: "Whereas recognition of the inherent dignity and of the equal and inalienable rights of all members of the human family is the foundation of freedom."[3] Both historical documents were written in the blossoming era of the transatlantic slave trade and the flourishing of the institution of slavery in the slaveholding North America and French Caribbean colonies. The practice of racial slavery in the newly-independent and republic of the United States violated the very inalienable rights of the enslaved African population the U.S. Constitution and its Bill of Rights promised to all people.

Not only the systemic oppression of blacks through the institution of slavery robbed the enslaved of their honor and humanity, anti-black racism equally demoralized and culturally alienated them in the American society. Unquestionably, racism is a question of human

3. Universal Declarations of Human Rights, http://www.un.org/en/udhrbook/pdf/udhr_booklet_en_web.pdf.

respect and honor. Ghanaian-born philosopher Kwame Anthony Appiah interprets the American racial slavery as "the subordination of one race by another and it entailed the systematic subjection of black people to dishonor."[4] Unfortunately, the history of racism as America's great moral failure and the dishonor of black lives is linked to America's theological conviction and religious habitus.

The American experience is captured within five central "American ideologies" that tell a distinctive story of American Christian expression, the country's theological development, and the interplay between Americans' attitude toward race and the triumph of American freedom and unfreedom. These ideologies also explain the history of internal wars, oppression, violence, and dehumanization that have marked the life of America's people of color and the disfranchised poor. The complex relations between black and white Americans, and the people of European descent and those of non-European ancestry living in America correspondingly provide an important window to make sense of the triumph of white supremacy, racial segregation in American churches and society, and the economic injustice toward the poor and the mistreatment of racialized Americans. Below, I highlight the five cardinal American ideals and beliefs already signaled above:

1. Election of God: The idea that America is a Christian nation distinctively chosen and called by God to protect and bring American freedom to the developing nations, and to bear witness of God's blessings in America to the world.

2. Racial Purity: The concept that America is a white nation, and for many white Americans, it entails the natural separation of the two major races, the black and white races, and the maintenance of the supremacy of the white race in all human affairs and transactions.

3. Slavery: for many white Christian Americans and non-Christian white racists, the enslavement of Africans in the country of America was a divine sanction and the institution of slavery should be construed as God's predestining choice of the Africans to be brought to America, so they could be exposed to the light of the Gospel and receive the grace of Christ's forgiveness and salvation.

4. White Christianity and White Theology: the belief in the white version of Christianity and white articulation of Christian theology

4. Appiah, *The Honor Code*, 104.

is prominent among both white American Christians and white American theologians; it is connected to the ideology of the divine election of America as a white and Christian nation, and that the "white church" and the theological reflections done by white religious thinkers are the best models to imitate and to think theologically and Christianly.

5. Jim Crow segregation (the 1896 Supreme Court doctrine of "separate but equal"): the American legal system of racial segregation, similar to the South African apartheid, was a means to purify the white race and control the black race, and to keep each race in its God-ordaining roles and functions in public spaces; racial segregation flourished through various invented systems and institutions including(1) the legal prohibition of interracial relationships and marriage between white and black Americans, (2) the lynching era (1889–1940) in which black bodies were publicly and unashamedly displayed in Southern trees, and (3) the separation of black and white Christian churches in worship and other religious activity, and the defense of this religious attitude through the reproduction and dissemination of an idiosyncratically-American white theology framed by the race question, and the disfranchisement of America's black population.

As a result, historically, white supremacy in the American life has manifested itself in three broad traumatic events: the harshness of slavery, Jim Crow segregation, and the public lynching of black people. The five underlying factors outlined above would lead to a web of complex relations: the emergence of various protest and cultural-political movements throughout American history, from the eighteenth to the first-half of the twentieth-century, the creation of African American Christianity ("The Black Church"), what we may call "Black religious tradition," as a counter-religious movement to White Christian hegemony during the time of slavery; subsequently, the development of the Civil Rights Movement, the social-political and moral activism of Martin Luther King, Jr., the emergence of Black Power Movement, and the birth of Black Theology could be traced historically to the 1960s—an era in which Blacks proclaimed their humanity in the midst of cultural despair, white terror, and existential alienation.

These major events and ideologies are watershed moments in Black theology and American history. They represent very specific historical contexts to understand the politico-theology and intellectual ideas of James H. Cone, and the fortification of American Christianity and White American theology. Because of our limitation in this essay, we will not develop these five topics, but will concentrate on Cone's interaction with American theology and the American church in these fragile moments. Yet Black religious tradition, and Black liberation theology would modify the content and contours of American religious thought and social history.

Blackness as Symbolic Curse and Emptiness in the American Society

People, who live in the United States and who do not share a European lineage, have also experienced immensely the oppression and evil of the American empire, which historically changed their relationships with the American state. For example, the Native American people were tragically tortured and dehumanized in the era of the Trails of Tears (1831–1850); those from China bravely endured The Chinese Exclusion Act (1882); the Japanese were brutalized and tortured in the Japanese internment camps (1942 to 1945). The American empire is an empire of death and human annihilation. Not only "Empire is life denying,"[5] according to South African Liberation Theologian Vuyani Vellem; for the victims of the American and European empires, "Living against the logic of Empire is rebellion against the life killing order of Empire."[6]

The validity and worth of black life in America have always been a matter of cultural curiosity, contestation, and intellectual uncertainty. The racial structure of the nation and the anti-black narrative inherent in the American psyche make black identity as a curse and a symbolic void. Working within the rhetoric of existential philosophy (i.e. Sartre, Camus, and Fanon), James Cone describes the dialectics of blackness and whiteness in this powerful language:

> The structure of white society attempts to make "black being" into "nonbeing" or "nothingness." In existential philosophy, nonbeing is usually identified as that which threatens being; it is that ever-present possibility of the inability to affirm one's existence. The

5. Vellem, "Black Theology of Liberation," 2.
6. Ibid., 1.

courage to be, then, is the courage to affirm one's being by striking out at the dehumanizing forces which threaten being.[7]

The fundamental binary opposition between black and white can be traced to the history of the early Republic. In 1706, the influential New England Puritan Minister Cotton Mather published an ambivalent pro-slavery pamphlet entitled *The Negro Christianized*, a Christian pedagogy on the spiritualization of American racial slavery. Although he published the religious essay anonymously, it was well known among the people in the colony that Mather has authored the work; Mather and many Christians in his New England congregation were slave merchants and slave owners. One of the central propositions he makes in this evangelistic work was for Christian masters to educate their slaves in the Christian religion and to treat them kindly as their spiritual brethren.[8] Nonetheless, Mather's central argument is that the Christian master has "a moral responsibility for the souls of those in danger, and the Christianized servant is more profitable to his master."[9]

The puzzling issue about Mather's pro-slavery Christian ideology was his belief that it was God who had sovereignly ordained the servitude of the Africans in the newly-conquered land of the Native Americans. Second, it was also God who had appointed freely the enslaved African population, whom he termed humorously "Rational Creatures," to be the "Servants" of white (Christian) masters.[10] Having established a close rapport between American Christianity and American slavery, Mather instructed Christian masters in these well-crafted religious precepts:

> The greatest Kindness that can be done to any Man is to make a Christian of him. Your Negroes are immediately Raised unto an astonishing Felicity, when you have Christianized them. They are become amiable spectacles, & such as the Angels of God would gladly repair unto the Windows of Heaven to look upon. Tho' they remain your Servants, yet they are become the Children of God. Tho' they are to enjoy no Earthly Goods, but the small Allowance that your Justice and Bounty shall see proper

7. Cone, *Black Theology and Black Power*, 7.

8. Mather, *The Negro Christianized*, 2. Prior to this publication, in 1702, Mather wrote the seminal text and perhaps the greatest literary articulation of New England's intellectualism *Magnalia Christi Americana*.

9. Mather, *The Negro Christianized*, 2–3.

10. Ibid., 3.

for them, yet they are become Heirs of God, and Joint-Heirs with the Lord Jesus Christ. [11]

For Mather, to be a Christian and an owner of slaves was not a theological tension. He also reminds the Christian slave owners in the colony of their role as masters, and of the unfreedom and constraints of their enslaved as servants.

> Tho' they are your Vassals, and must with a profound subjection wait upon you, yet the Angels of God now take them under their Guardianship, and vouchsafe to tend upon them. Oh! what have you done for them ! Happy Masters, who are Instrumental to raise their Servants thus from the Dust, and make them objects for the Nobles of Heaven to take Notice of! But it will not be long before you and they come at length to be together in the Heavenly City.[12]

Mather employs various epithets to establish a sense of connection between the masters and their slaves; the latter are called "your servants" and "your vassals," which intended to convey a relationship of domination and subjectivity between the two entities. In the same rhetorical pattern, he uses different felicitous terms for the Christian slave masters including "happy masters," "pious masters," and "our masters." These titles aimed at conveying the dignity of the New England Christian community that was engaged actively in the selling of human (Black) flesh for profit—with the blessing of the colonial American church. He assures Christian masters that the enslaved Africans will render better service if they are indoctrinated in the Christian religion: "Be assured, Syrs ; Your Servants will be the Better Servants, for being made Christian Servants."[13] According to Mather's judgement, the enslaved African should not be granted access to earthly advantages or privileges nor should he or she be allowed access to social mobility unless the master deems it necessary and appropriate. The welfare and happiness of the slave is determined decisively by the sovereign will of the master. While Mather proposes that the enslaved population could be denied of earthly goods, but slave masters should not withhold from them the blessings of the spiritual world.

Evidently, Mather exploited Christianity to make the slaves docile and obedient to their masters and that they could remain in their

11. Ibid., 12.

12. Ibid.

13. Ibid.

God-assigned role as slaves in colonial America. His version of Christianity did not provide any corrective and moral teachings that could radically transform the darkened soul of the Christian masters who had put their brothers and sisters in Christ in chain. The moral failure of colonial Christianity in New England lies in its inability to transform a (Christian) slaveowner to an (Christian) abolitionist. Writing from a Calvinistic-theological viewpoint, Mather reminded Christian that "God has brought a Servant unto thee, and said, Keep that Soul, Teach it, and Help it, that it may not be lost."[14] Accordingly, Christian masters should never lose sight of this divine providence and kindness toward them; yet, Mather reassured them that the stupidity of the enslaved Africans was a 'discouragement,' and that the purpose of the individual Christian master was "to teach, as to wash" the African.[15] Teaching and washing in reference to the master's duty to his slave implies both the full integration of the enslaved population to the Christian faith and complete assimilation into the white-European culture and worldview—which may infer the suppression or eradication of the imported cultural values and religious practices of African slaves in the colony.

Moreover, in 1701, the colonial New England Christian merchant, politician, and judge John Saffin published *A Brief and Candid Answer to a late Printed Sheet Entitled the Selling of Joseph* in response to the Boston lawyer Samuel Sewall's *The Selling of Joseph*, the first anti-slavery track published in New England in 1700. Sewall's central thesis is that slavery was immoral and unlawful; it was unbiblical (for Christians) to own, buy, and sell slaves. Because of this (abolitionist)conviction, Sewall called upon the representative governing officials and authority to emancipate the enslaved population. In his counter-response, Staffin has eloquently argued that slavery as a system was "the constant practice of our own and other Christian Nations in the World,"[16] and that the institution of slavery should not be "condemned as irreligious . . . which is diametrically contrary to the rules and precepts which God hath given the diversity of men to observe in their respective Stations, Callings, and Conditions of Life, as hath been established."[17]

14. Ibid, 11.

15. Ibid., 15–16; also see, Kendi's careful analysis of the contradiction between early American Christianity and the slave system which it supported in colonial America, *Stamped from the Beginning*, 47–76.

16. Staffin, "A Brief and Candid Answer," 823.

17. Ibid.

Moreover, he also added, "God hath set different orders and degrees of men in the world, both in Church and Common weal,"[18] and that it was not an "evil to bring [Africans] out of their own heathenish country"[19] and to convert them to the Christian religion. Like Mather, Staffin interprets the enslavement of the Africans theologically and construes this aberration as an essential facet of God's providence in human history, especially in the history of white rule and hegemony in human civilization. About the outcome of the slavery debate, historian Ibram X. Kendi concludes "Samuel won the battle—Adam was freed in 1703 after a long and bitter trial—but he lost the war. America did not rid itself of slavery or of Black people."[20] He also points out the bewildering correlation between white supremacy, slavery, and American Christianity, for example, in the legal system in the colonial state of Virginia.

> The Virginia legislature also denied Blacks the ability to hold office. Evoking reportedly the term "Christian white servant" and defining their rights, Virginia lawmakers fully married Whiteness and Christianity, uniting rich White enslavers and the non-slaveholding White poor.[21]

Hence, the godliest and gracious duty Christian masters could render to their slaves is not emancipation from the bondage of slavery, but spiritual emancipation from the bondage of sin through dispensing effective religious instruction to their slaves. For Staffin and pro-slavery Christian theologians and (Puritan) ministers, slavery "was a positive good, for it enabled Africans to accept Christian truth."[22] Historian Sydney Ahlstrom's observation is quite insightful about this great American paradox, the dialectic of American slavery and American Christianity:

> That the United States—the first new nation, the elect nation, the _____ ____ with the soul of a church, the great model of modern _____ he nineteenth century with one of the _____ systems in its midst with full consti- _____ one of the world's greatest ironies.[23]

[handwritten annotations overlaid:] the way America has treated black lives - robbing them of their humanity - directly appeals to their ideals. white supremacy loves christianity for these ideals: their belief in god's determined servitude. Africans were enslaved by the Church and abused by the rampent white supremacy within the christian faith.

_____ Beginning, 67.

_____ , 495.

23. _____ ..story of the American People, 635.

It is in the same historical perspective that the editors of *Religion and the Antebellum Debate Over Slavery* could come to a similar conclusion:

> The reformist impulse inherent in evangelical religion did not lead inexorably to an opposition of slavery. Rather, the tenets of evangelicalism, in a different social and cultural context, could be channeled into a slaveholding ethic for maters . . . In denominations in which evangelicalism's impact was weak, there was usually a conservative element that declared slavery a secular matter toward which religious bodies should remain neutral . . . Both popular revivalists and local ministers complained that preaching against slavery would interfere with their missionary and other purely religious work.[24]

In short, slavery challenged black dignity and reduced the self-worth of black folk to non-being while White theologians and clergy correspondingly declared unapologetically and theologically the equal self-worth of every person, or as they say it in Haitian Creole "*tout moun se moun*" ("Every Person is a Person"). The idea that "every person has the same worth as every other is a revolutionary principle" in both (James Cone's) Black liberation theology and Third World Liberation theologies.[25] African American ethicist Peter J. Paris asserts that white American Christianity experienced no conflict between its theological thought, white Christian action, and the mistreatment of black people in America—including black Christians who share with them a common spiritual heritage; certainly, white American Christianity is less concerned about the practice of true biblical ethics or the biblical notion of justice for the advancement of the black population in society. Paris explains further, "Rather, in that respect, the white churches actually experienced no alienation between their thought and practice. This is evidence by the fact that any ʔʼ *american Christ-* ʼality in the pulpits of white churches has ʼ *ianity does not* of hostility against their prevailing eth *Care for genuine* theology and ethics, thought and actic *ethics, happily leading* nporary American Evangelicalism. *to slavery — american Christianity offered no forms of justice for the black population in society.*

24. McKivijan and Snay, *Relig.*

25. Bigo, *The Church and Third Wo.*

26. Paris, *The Social Teaching of the Blac.*

The Dignity and Struggles of Black Folk

It is within the cultural memory of racial slavery coupled with America's systemic racism and oppression towards its black and brown population that James Cone could introduce the theory of "Black Power" in the 1960s as a warning sign and theological account to the problem of whiteness and white hegemony in the American society. Black Power offers an alternative discourse to reason theologically, intellectually, and morally about the omnipresent perils associated with white privileges and the plight of black people in America. Cone explains that Black Power as a humanizing force because it is the black man's attempt to affirm his being, and his attempt to be recognized as "Thou," in spite of the "other, the white power which dehumanizes him."[27] Further, influencing by Fanon's positive anthropology as the quest for (black) recognition and (black) agency, Cone elaborates on the ontological meaning of blackness and the predicament of black people in this overwhelmingly-white world in America:

> To be human is to find something worthy for. When the black man rebels at the risk of death, he forces white society to look at him, to recognize him, to take his being into account, to admit that he *is*. And in a structure that regulates behavior, recognition by the other is indispensable to one's being . . . Black Power, in short, is an *attitude,* an inward affirmation of the essential worth of blackness . . . and the power of the black man to say Yes to his own "black being," and to make the other accept him or to be prepared for a struggle.[28]

The South African political-theologian Allan A. Boesa brilliantly explains the problem of of black existence, space, and white supremacy.

> The right to live in God's world as a human being is not the sole right of whites that eventually, through the kindness of whites, can extended to "deserving" (obsequious?) Blacks as a "special privilege." Human dignity for all is a fundamental biblical right. Nevertheless, many whites seem to think that Blacks live by the grace of whites.[29]

As it were in South African apartheid and American Jim Crow, it took extreme courage to be black and to exist in white spaces in the white

---

27. Cone, *Black Theology and Black Power*, 7.

28. Ibid., 8.

29. Boesak, *Black and Reformed*, 6.

world. It took more resilience to proclaim unapologetically that Black was/is beautiful, and the color of our skin was/is not a curse from God. Race both as a theological problem and a form of social dysfunction in the American cultural fabric is arguably a central theme in Cone's theology of culture and race; as he keenly observes,

> If whites are honest in their analysis of the moral state of this society, they know that all are responsible. Racism is possible because whites are indifferent to suffering and patient with cruelty . . . White America's attempt to free itself of responsibility for the black man's inhuman condition is nothing but a protective device to ease her guilt.

Not only there exists an intellectual irregularity and epistemology crisis regarding white interpretation of the black life in the American society, Cone points out among white theologians and American Christians there's an intentional ignorance or the refusal to know about the black experience, as that false memory may serve in the suppression of the white conscience and guilt. As it were the case when Cone penned the powerful words of indictment in *Black Theology, Black Power* in 1969, the attitude of whites regarding Police brutality toward the blacks, and the violence and pain inflicting upon them in the twenty-first century American society is still a matter of moral and ethical issue. This was especially true in the emergence of the Black Power Movement in the 1960s and the emergence of Black Lives Movement in 2013; both freedom movements campaigned to make sense of the countless of black deaths in the streets of America and to seek racial justice against the cruelty of America's Police forces, white terrorist groups, anti-black public policies, as well as lawmakers and politicians who supported the racist ideologies and actions of white supremacists. As Cone reminds us:

> White Americans do not dare to know that blacks are beaten at will by policemen as a means of protecting the latter's ego superiority as well as that of the larger white middle class. For to know is to be responsible. To know is to understand why blacks loot and riot at what seems slight provocation. Therefore, they must have reports to explain the disenchantment of blacks with white democracy, so they can be surprised. They must believe that blacks are in poverty because they are lazy or because they are inferior. Yes, they must believe that everything is basically all right.[30]

30. Ibid., 25.

Cone is correct to state that "What is at stake is the credibility and promise of the Christian gospel and the hope that we may heal the wounds of racial violence that continue to divide our churches and society." [31] The tragic history of racial violence against blacks and the lynching of the black man, woman, and children, and periodically an entire black family was lynched compels Cone to write prophetically and relationally, "Until we can see the cross and the lynching tree together, until we can identity Christ with a 'recrucified' black body hanging from a lynching tree, there can be no genuine understanding of Christian identity in America, and no deliverance from the brutal legacy of slavery and white supremacy." [32] Yet faith in God the Liberator does not simply contemplate the world, it changes it and radically alters the human condition and social structure;, this is the idea of Christian conversion, a *metanoia*; that Christian faith is revolutionary because it orients us to action. [33] The gruesome history of American lynching has informed Cone's theology of the cross, and his Christology is deeply influenced by a creative reinterpretation of the history of black suffering through the American lynching project. The Southern lynching tree was inevitably the cross in the United States.

Accordingly, the American society and American Christianity must reckon with the trauma of race, and the crushing narrative of whites terrorizing blacks for seemingly white preservation and the fear of the negroes. Lynching as a form of white terror, as Cone puts it, is "an unspeakable crime and a memory that most White Americans would prefer to forget." [34] The famed American theologian and ethicist Reinhold Niebuhr has voiced his own criticism about the dilemma of whiteness in America: "The white race in America will not admit the Negro to equal rights if it is not forced to do so." [35] In his seminal work *Moral Man & Immoral Society*, Niebuhr explains sociologically the complex nature of group interest grounded on racial solidarity of (whiteness) and (white) middle class unity.

> The limitations of the human mind and imagination, the inability of human beings to transcend their own interests sufﬁciently to envisage the interests of their fellow-men as clearly

31. Cone, *The Cross and the Lynching Tree*, xiii–xiv.

32. Ibid., xv.

33. Bigo, *The Church and Third World Revolution*, 9.

34. Cone, *The Cross and the Lynching Tree*, xiv.

35. Quoted in Burrow, *Extremist for Love*, 120.

as they do their own makes force an inevitability part of the process of social cohesion. But the same force which guarantees peace also makes for injustice . . . The individual or the group which organizes any society, however social its intentions or pretensions, arrogates an inordinate portion of social privilege to itself . . . The moral attitudes of dominant and privileges groups are characterized by universal self-deception and hypocrisy. The unconscious and conscious identification of their special interest with general interests and universal values, is equally obvious in the attitude of classes.[36]

The attitude to white people toward black progress in the history of race relations and the problem of racial privileges and economic unfairness in the American society between white and black Americans are moral and theological problems of paramount weight. As Niebuhr reasons fairly:

Southern whites in America usually justify their opposition to equal suffrage for the Negro on the ground of his illiteracy. Yet no Southern States gives equal facility for Negro and white education; and the educated, self-reliant Negro is hated more than the docile, uneducated one . . . Sometimes a dominant group feels itself strong enough to deny the fitness of a subject group to share in its privileges without offering any evidence of a lack of qualification.[37]

Niebuhr was also convinced that "it has always been the habit the privileges groups to deny the oppressed classes every opportunity for the cultivation of innate capacities and then to accuse them of lacking what they have been denied the right to acquire."[38] Niebuhr, who had had an enormous intellectual impact on Cone's theological ethics and anthropology, offers an indictment on the white Christian practice and thought in the American society.

The Bankruptcy of American White Theology

For Cone, the pivotal question concerning the relationship between American white theology and black oppression in the American society

36. Niebuhr, *Moral Man*, 6–7, 117.
37. Ibid., 119.
38. Ibid., 118.

is this: "how to reconcile the gospel message of liberation with the reality of black oppression."[39] In the American experience, it is unfortunate that "the public meaning of Christianity was [is] *white*."[40] American white theology is bankrupt in many ways as it maintains its silence on matters of life and death in the contemporary culture, especially life threatening-issues that confront the welfare and happiness of people of color in the United States. As Cone has remarked, "Consequently there has been no sharp confrontation of the gospel with white racism."[41] African Theologian John Mbiti affirms that Black theology is "a judgment on American Christianity," especially white Christianity.[42]

Notably, Cone describes the bankrupt nature of American theology in this striking and powerful paragraph:

> Throughout the history of this country, from the Puritans to the death-of-God theologians, the theological problems treated in white churches and theological schools are defined in such a manner that they are unrelated to the problem of being black in a white, racist society. By defining the problems of Christianity in isolation from the black condition, white theology becomes a theology of white oppressors, serving as a divine sanction from criminal acts committed against blacks.[43]

Also, he establishes a pivotal rapport between God's exercising his righteousness in society and vindicating the cause of the helpless against their enemies and oppressors, and the morally-wicked:

> Theologians and churchmen have been of little help in this matter because much of their intellectualizing has gone into analyzing the idea of God's righteousness in a fashion far removed from the daily experiences of men. They failed to give proper emphasis to another equally if not more important concern, namely, the biblical idea of God's righteousness as the divine decision to vindicate the poor, the needy, and the helpless in society.[44]

Besides, Cone outlines specifically seven characteristics of white theology corelating with the social fabric of America and the chronology

---

39. Cone, *The Cross and the Lynching Tree*, xiv–xvi.

40. Ibid., xvii.

41. Cone, *Black Theology and Black Power*, 31.

42. Mbiti, "An African Views American Black Theology," 379.

43. Cone, *A Black Theology of Liberation*, 9.

44. Cone, *Black Theology and Black Power*, 43.

of American history and Christianity. First, white theologians are silent about black pain and suffering, and do not confront the moral evil of anti-black racism in America. Second, white theologians seem to hold a neutral position on social, economic, and political issues concerning the oppressed and the poor; when white theologians fail to be in solidarity with those who are victimized by the dominant class, they're directly or indirectly siding with the individuals in position of power and influence in society. Third, the language of white theology does not challenge the oppressive structures of society and systems of power that dehumanize the poor and the vulnerable. Fourth, American white theology and American white Christianity have been overwhelmingly patriotic and in solidarity with the racist government instead of siding with the poor and God to radically transform systems of inequality and injustice to structures of equity and justice, callous hearts to sympathetic hearts.

Moreover, fifth, American white theology is unable to define human nature in the light of the Gospel for the poor and the experience of the weak in society. Rather, the human nature or human identity is defined within the structures of whiteness and white values. As Cone puts it, "The human person in American theology is George Washington, Thomas Jefferson, and Abraham Lincoln."[45] Sixth, white theologians are reluctant to address or confront directly the pressing issues of this age: human poverty and greed, physical deprivation and destitution, economic dispossession and income inequality, oppression and injustice, child and sex slavery, suffering and hunger, white supremacy and racial discrimination, imperialism and capitalism.[46] Finally, American white theology has also been unsuccessfully to champion better race relations, economic uplift programs for the poor and the lower-class, to support protest activism for racial and social justice politics, and to sustain Gospel-centered peace and reconciliation conversations. As Cone thunders in this insightful and provocative paragraph:

> The sin of Americ... without passion . . . When i... it has been so cool and calr... t implicitly disclosed who... rican theology has sim... on of the victims of th... ological silence dur... munity

[Handwritten annotation overlaying the blockquote:] Black power is neccessary to make sure POC know they are beautiful and that their deaths matter— BP forces white people to allow for equal rights. whites often remain silent when people of color face life-threatening situations, historically, white theologians are silent on Black pain, Black oppression, racism, poverty, injustice, and bad race relations.

45. Cone, A Blac...

46. Johnson, Sharing .

in this nation? How else can we explain the inability of white religionists to deal relevantly with the new phenomenon of black consciousness? And how else can we explain the problem white seminaries are having as they seek to respond to radical black demands? There is really only one answer: American theology is racist; it identifies theology as dispassionate analysis of "the tradition," unrelated to the sufferings of the oppressed.[47]

Elsewhere, Cone questions the exclusive content and particularity of white theological and curriculum suggesting that white religious education is not adequate and universal for all people, contrary to the traditional belief. In so doing, seminaries in America

> emphasize the need for appropriate tools in doing theology, which always means white tools, i.e., knowledge of the language and thought of white people. They fail to recognize that other people also have thought about God and have something significant to say about Jesus' presence in the world . . . My point is that one's social and historical context decides not only the questions we address to God but also the mode or form of the answers given to the questions.[48]

The overwhelming emphasis on a white theological education and white representation in the Faculty-staff body in America's theological schools demeans the significance of theological contextualization in the classroom and the necessity for more inclusive and multicultural religious training to serve non-Anglo churches and faith communities. To strengthen his claim, Cone's remarks on the racial identity and deficiency of white theological expression is worth noting further:

> Theology is always identified with a particular community. It is either identified with those who inflict oppression or with those who are its victims. A theology of the latter is authentic Christian theology, and a theology of the former is a theology of the Antichrist . . . American white theology is a theology of the Antichrist insofar as it arises from an identification with the white community, thereby placing God's approval on white oppression of black existence.[49]

---

47. Cone, *A Black Theology of Liberation*, 18.

48. Cone, *God of the Oppressed*, 14.

49. Cone, *A Black Theology of Liberation*, 6.

The lack of ethnic and racial diversity in America's seminaries and divinity schools give the false impression that one size fits all. As Cone has asserted, "In a racist society, God is never color-blind. To say God is color-blind is analogous to saying that God is blind to justice and injustice, to right and wrong, to good and evil."[50]

Cone goes further to denounce the irrelevance of theological guilds and (American) theologians who are indifferent to the existential crises of the community named above, "It seems that much of this abstract theological disputation and speculation—the favorite pastime for many theological societies—serves as a substitute for relevant involvement in a world where men die for lack of political justice."[51] By contrast, the attentive theologian must see it as a Christian responsibility to address "what the gospel has to say to a man who is jobless and cannot get work to support his family because the society is unjust;"[52]

Similarly, it is a moral duty for the Christian thinker to discuss openly the relevance of the Gospel to the woman who has been abused, beaten, raped, and oppressed in the hands of evil men. What does the Gospel have to say to the innumerable black and brown boys and girls who have no economic standing in society and who are orphans because of the repressive structural systems and societal-political arrangements against them that do not recognize their humanity and dignity simply because of the color of their skin and that they do not belong to the dominant white culture? What is the meaning of Christian theology for the undocumented immigrants and illegal refugees from the Caribbean and Latin American countries currently incarcerated in American prison cells just because they are here to seek a better life in America? Does the Christian Gospel have any relevance to the thousands of refugee children American Border Polices have illegally snatched away from their parents' hands at the U.S.-Mexican borders? What does Christian theology have to say to the oppressed communities in earnest search for economic mobility, political rights, and social equality in their own land? How should Christian theologians help the oppressed community cope with and overcome Police brutality and the burden of racial injustices, hunger, and poverty in the "Land of Freedom" and the "Land of the Braves"? Cone interrogates the problematic nature of American theology, and it is a

---

50. Ibid.
51. Cone, *Black Theology and Black Power*, 43.
52. Ibid.

legitimate and relevant concern Christian theologians and clergy should contemplate in their contemporary times:

> Unless there is a word from Christ to the helpless, then why should they respond to him? How do we relate the gospel of Christ to people whose daily existence is one of hunger or even worse, despair? Or do we simply refer to them to the next world?[53]

To move forward in our analysis, in his seminal text, *The Cross and the Lynching Tree*, Cones attempts to recapitulate the American narrative of terror and viciousness toward the country's black citizens and the inadequacy of white theologians to address constructively with the wisdom of the Christian gospel and the terrific message of the cross the crisis of black death and black dehumanization motivated by white (aggressive) rage and (intense) hatred. Writing with deep personal anguish and discontent, he reflects profoundly on the historical trajectories of his life:

> I found my voice in the social, political, religious, and cultural context of the civil rights and black power movements in the 1960s. The Newark and Detroit riots in July 1967 and the assassination of Martin Luther King Jr. in April 1968 were the events that shook me out of my theological complacency, forcing me to realize that bankruptcy of any theology in America that did not engage the religious meaning of the African American struggle for justice . . . Silence on both white supremacy and the black struggle against racial segregation made me angry with a fiery rage that had to find expression. How could any theologian explain the meaning of Christian identity in America and fail to engage white supremacy, its primary negation?"[54]

For Cone, the three great historical heresies and antitheses to the Gospel in America are anti-black racism, the silence of white churches about social justice issues and the plot of the poor, and the silence of white theologians on black death and alienation in the American society. Cone suggests, however it was "self interest and power corrupted their understanding of the teachings and motivated many white theologians and m *univer sal — especially* Christian faith to support the social evil *for the children of* slavery and a century of racial segreg *color who were* ectories and

white religious teachings are not universal — especially for the children of color who were orphaned by the system. → white theologians are then inadequate as they never address how poo are killed and constantly alienated.

53. Ibid., 43–44.

54. Cone, *The Cross*

55. Ibid.

particularly the history of black suffering Cone could write reactionally, "If theology had nothing to say about black suffering and resistance, I could not be a theologian."[56] To substantiate Cone's above thesis, we shall provide various forms and articulations of America's cultural and theological predicament.

The Crisis of White Theological Discourse

The prominent Swiss-born American church historian Philip Schaff (1819–1893), a proponent of white supremacy and pro-slavery theologian, articulated an ambivalent view on race relations. He defended the institution of slavery through his publications. Schaff energetically contended that slavery would one day be recognized in the American society as "no doubt an immense blessing to the whole race of Ham";[57] he was also convinced that "The negro question, lies far deeper than the slavery question."[58] Unquestionably, Schaff strongly believed that "The Anglo-Saxon and Anglo-American, of all modern races, possess the strongest national character and the one best fitted for universal domination."[59]

Similarly, the eminent nineteenth-century Reformed theologian and Professor of Theology at Princeton Theological Seminary Charles Hodge (1797–1878) was a slave owner and therefore did not view slaveholding as a sin or America as a slaveholding Christian nation as contrary to biblical ethic.[60] In the "Slavery" article, which he penned in 1836, he claimed nowhere in the New Testament are Christian slave masters commanded to emancipate their slaves: "If we are right in insisting that slaveholding is one of the greatest of all sins; that it should be immediately and universally abandoned as a condition of church communion, or admission into heaven, how comes it that Christ and his apostles did not pursue the same course?"[61] Notably, antebellum Proslavery theologians established their theological conviction and hermeneutical interpretation on slavery and the subjugation of black Africans on the seemingly proslavery Biblical passages, found in both Old and New Testaments.

56. Cone, *A Black Theology of Liberation*, xii.

57. Quoted in Noll, *The Civil War*, 51.

58. Ibid.

59. Quoted in Cone, *The Cross and The Lynching Tree*, 6.

60. Torbett, *Theology and Slavery*, 79.

61. Quoted in Gutjahr, *Charles Hodge*, 172.

1. Genesis 9:25–27, for the sin of Ham, who exposed his father Noah's nakedness, Ham's descendants through his Son Canaan were to be owned as slaves by descendants of Noah's other sons.

2. Genesis 17:2, God sanctioned and regulated the slaveholding of the patriarch Abraham, father of all believers.

3. Deuteronomy 20:10–11, God sanctioned the enslavement of Israel's enemies.

4. 1 Corinthians 7–21, while a Christian slave may welcome emancipation, that slave should not chafe if emancipation is not given.

5. Romans 13:1, 7, the Apostle Paul urged Christian believers to conform to the Roman imperial system, which practiced a harsh form of slaveholding.

6. Colossians 3:22, 4:1, The Apostle regulated the master-slave relationship, but did not question it.

7. 1 Timothy 6:1–2, the apostle explicitly taught that the conversion of slaves did not provide cause for even Christian masters to emancipate those Christian slaves.[62]

White theology coupled with the question of race in the antebellum America indicates that the slaveholding America was morally bankrupt, and that the nation must undergo a radical evaluation of ideals and values. It also signals that, in principle, slaveholding contributed to the moral failure of Christian America and American Christianity, equally. The French philosopher Diderot, in his anti-slave trade article and argument against the institution of slavery, correspondingly, which he co-published with Alembert in the first modern encyclopedia (*Encyclopedie*, 1751–77), denounces, "If a trade of this sort can be justified by some principle of morals, there is no crime, however atrocious, that one could not legitimate."[63] When a particular theological expression articulates such a conviction or a theological system promotes such as a (human) practice, it invites us to assess the seriousness of its message and its relevance to human flourishing. Cone, however, reminds us that "The black church in America was founded on the belief that God condemned slavery and that Christian freedom meant political emancipation."[64] How can

---

62. Noll, *The Civil War*, 34–35.

63. Quoted in Appiah, *The Honor Code*, 109.

64. Cone, *A Black Theology of Liberation*, 35.

a society flourish when one group progresses, and the other group suffers oppression and exploitation and is deprived of its goods?

Incontestably, human suffering is too urgent in our contemporary times and the omnipresence of evil in our city and the modern world threatens every area of human existence for theologians to focus exclusively on theological jargons of Christian theology and to be disengaged with the realities of the moment. The fragility of human life, the uncertainty of the present, and the vacillation of future possibilities should be sufficient reasons for theology to be the most relevant guide to our existential troubles and challenges. It is critical for Christian religious thinkers to use their craft aptly to foster hope and healing. About this pivotal matter, cone could write convincingly, "With clever theological sophistication, white theologians defined the discipline of theology in the light of the problem of the unbelievers (i.e., the question of the relationship of faith and reason) and thus unrelated to the problem of slavery and racism."[65] White theologians do not question the system that produces the subjugation and abuse of the poor and people of color, and the culture of despair that engenders hostility in society. Human domination is taken for granted in American theological inquiry, resulting in a theology that is incapable to respond adequately to the needs of the people and the demise of American civilization.

The issue at stake is that American white theologians have turned off the economic, political, or social concern at will in most human contexts, as if it were not part of the their lifeblood.[66] The pressing matter is that human suffering should be interpreted as a profound theological problem, and theologians must provide hope to the abused, the exploited, and the damned; theologians must speak of God's liberating presence to the common people in society. Likewise, they must confront the moral matters of their culture and this age. Christian theology must provide an adequate answer to individuals trapped in the socio-economic difficulties and political uncertainties in society.

Finally, Cone makes a resounding case for moral and ethical reform within American Christianity and the practices of American churches. He declares, "If white Protestant churches failed to be a beacon of leadership in America's racial crisis, part of the responsibility for the failure was due to the way its leading religious spokespersons ignored race

65. Ibid., xiii.

66. Assmann, *Theology for a Nomad Church*, 9.

in their interpretation of the Christian faith."[67] To put is simply, weak churches may have devastating effects on the life of the people in society. Evangelical historian Mark Noll, who traces the causes associated with Christianity in the mid- nineteenth century American culture, writes observably, "One momentous-by-product of religious expansion was the fact that the institutional life of the major Protestant churches worked an echoing effect on the body politic.[68]

In his acclaimed text, *Theology in America*, historian E. Brooks Holifield highlights some of the major shortcomings associated with White American theology including the inability of white theologians to mobilize the American people toward better race relations (i.e. unity and reconciliation) and to transcend the cultural pitfalls and political differences between white and black Christians. These concerns are thus followed: (1) "the theological impasse meant that theology could no longer articulate the moral vision that held that culture together;"[69] (2) for others, theology is unable "to unite Americans or to help them transcend the pull of economic and political interests,"[70] and finally, (3) "The cultural language that supposedly united Americans proved itself able to contribute even more forcefully to their division."[71] What should then be the task of theology in the life of the church and in culture in twenty-first century?

The Task of Christian Theology

One of the major theological questions in Western theological tradition has been the concerns for proper theological method and structure. Many theologians trained in the Western theological canon have focused their theological analysis on the abstract ideas when attempting to elaborate on the major Christian doctrines of divine revelation, God (theology proper), the Word of God, humanity (anthropology), sin (hamartiology), Jesus Christ (Christology), the church (ecclesiology), the Holy Spirit (pneumatology), and the doctrine of the last days (eschatology). Theologians have not arrived at a consensus on the underlying role of Christian theology.

67. Cone, *The Cross and the Lynching Tree*, 57.

68. Noll, *The Civil War*, 27.

69. Holifield, *Theology in America*, 503.

70. Ibid., 504.

71. Ibid.

Equally, various propositions about the task of Christian theology in the church and society that have been suggested often conflict each another. For example, Reinhold Niebuhr construes the chief role of theology as "an effort to construct a rational and systematic view of life out of the various and sometimes contradictory myths which are associated with a single religious tradition."[72] In the introductory page of his well praised *Systematic Theology (Volume One)*, Paul Tillich establishes a strong rapport between theology and the life of the church; he interprets theology as a function of the Christian church, that is, theological conversations must emerge from the practices and experiences of the people of God, and that the basic task of theology is to respond satisfactorily to the needs of the church.[73] Hence, theology is simply "the statement of the truth of the Christian message and the interpretation of this truth for every new generation."[74]

The content, shape, and method of theological discourse is created within the ideological worldview of the given culture, as well as in the socio-political, and the historico-cultural trajectories of the associated generation. Karl Barth in *Church Dogmatics* articulates a similar perspective that Christian theology is an impossible enterprise without the active participation and experience of humanity, and that divine revelation enlists men and women into service. The idea of theology as service in Barth is central in Cone's theological development; the notion denotes that God has chosen the church in society to be a community that fosters healing, care, comfort, and hospitality, and that "the work of theology is thus wholly related to the task of the Church which is that of every Christian."[75] Therefore, divine revelation has called followers of Christ to work collaboratively to restore the broken humanity and to integrate men and women into the beloved community of Christ Jesus toward a better humanity, as God himself continues to effect renovation in society through the cooperation and submission of his ambassadors (the church as people of God) in the world.

Moreover, in *Towards Christian Political Ethics*, Liberation theologian Jose Miguez Bonino advises that the engaged theologian should carefully examine the dialectic of praxis and theory in theological

---

72. Niebuhr, *An Interpretation of Christian Ethics*, 9.

73. Tillich, *Systematic Theology*, 1:3.

74. Ibid.

75. Barth, *Church Dogmatics*, 81–82.

analysis, and the end of such endeavor is not to produce a perfect harmonization between these two poles; "on the contrary, instead of a balanced harmony we must think in terms of two poles that challenge each other, making change and movement possible."[76] For Bonino, human action should challenge the theory that has informed it, and human thought should drive action to new explorations; to put it another way, the reality individuals create should transform human (their) action, and action is oriented toward and by that reality.[77]

From this vantage point, the conscious theologian should be mindful that every human act has both a social and political content, and that "a theology of the historico-political development of man is only possible in so far as it relates to an ethic of change, and in so far it accepts political action as a means of transforming society."[78] In the words of Clodovis Boff, Black and Liberation theologies (i.e. Womanist, Feminist, Third World, Postcolonial, indigenous) call for "a positive, contextual, and concrete knowledge of society . . . the theology of liberation pleads for a reading of scripture in continual mindfulness of and orientation to concrete challenges and problems . . . it appears as a demand of the praxis of faith, to the extent that this faith seeks to be incarnate."[79]

In addition, James Cone and the religious thinkers who labor from liberationist and constructive theological angles find some serious shortcomings within the contours and workings of the Western theological canon; in the words of Cone:

> There is no "abstract" revelation, independent of human experience, to which theologians can appeal for evidence of what they say about the gospel. God meets us in the human situation, not as an idea or concept that is self-evidently true. God encounters us in the human condition as the liberator of the poor and the weak, empowering them to fight for freedom because they were made for it. Revelation as the word of God, witnessed in scripture and defined by the creed and dogmas of Western Christianity, is too limiting to serve as an adequate way of doing theology today.[80]

76. Bonino, *Toward a Christian Political Ethics*, 39.

77. Ibid.

78. Assmann, *Theology for a Nomad Church*, 33.

79. Boff, *Theology and Praxis*, xxi.

80. Cone, *A Black Theology of Liberation*, xiv.

Cone has advanced that the goal of Christian theology, whether confessional or public theology, is "the liberation of man"[81] and woman. By providing a succinct definition of the discipline, he asserts clearly that "Theology is not only rational discourse about ultimate reality; it is also a prophetic word about the righteousness of God that must be spoken in clear, strong, and uncompromising language."[82] Cone questions the validity and relevance of Western theological tradition that often seeks to supply "the rational justification of religious belief in a scientific and technological world that has no use for God"[83] while ignoring the problems of this age and the urgent care for the poor in society. With personal conviction, he declares unapologetically, "When I thought about the long history of black suffering and the long silence of white theologians in its regard, I could not always control my pen or my tongue. I did not feel that I should in any way be accountable to white theologians or their cultural etiquette."[84] Understandably, Cone's theology is a political theology that is concerned primarily with the personhood and dignity of black people. Critics often find shortcomings in Cone's Negritudinist theology and the absence of theo-political analysis on the economic disfranchisement of the poor and blacks.

Cone's political theology has two dimensions: the human aspect and the political consciousness coupled with social action. He construes the role of liberation theology as a revolutionary force in society that should not accept the "established order;" it must disturb it, alter its content, and deracinate its unjust structures. To put it simply, "such a political theology has to desacralize not only nature, but all the institutions of the status quo. It also has to put the new institutions brought about change in a human perspective. It must ever accept the ethics of the 'establishment.'"[85] The great impetus of Cone's theological corpus is human flourishing and wholistic shalom in society, and the welfare and freedom of the poor and the sweeping renovation of societal powers and forces in which they live.

81. Cone, *Black Theology and Black Power*, 39.

82. Cone, *A Black Theology of Liberation*, xii.

83. Ibid., xiv.

84. Ibid., xv.

85. Assmann, *Theology for a Nomad Church*, 33.

Theology and the Quest for Human Flourishing

Theology must always be an on-going exercise as time changes and society evolves for good or bad. This is a common theme found in Caribbean decolonial and postcolonial theological discourses. The theological task as that which it is emerged from "the covenant community with the sole purpose of making the gospel meaningful to the times in which men live."[86] The essence of the Gospel message is unchanged, and it remains the same regardless of the crisis of the time; nonetheless, as Cone proposes, "every generation is confronted with new problems, and the gospel must be brought to bear on them. Thus, the task of theology is to show what the changeless gospel means in each new situation."[87] However, since theology is always contextual and the message of the Gospel is transcultural and transracial, Christian theology, shaped by the redemptive news of Christ, must respond directly to the black condition in American and the living and economic situations of the vulnerable in their respective country—especially individuals in the developing world living under the constant threat and ruse of American-European imperialism, and the neo-colonial and economic global capitalism. Theologians should not ignore the real nature of society—the rapport between infrastructure and superstructure, the socioeconomic determinations, cultural and political ideologies, the nature of the state—and the ways that social dynamics have shaped theological language and exposition, as well as theological praxis.[88]

Toward the quest for human flourishing, Christian theologians must participate enthusiastically in public advocacy and render satisfactory civic service toward the common good. Because the Gospel is about human liberation, salvation, and optimism, when the oppressed of the world "begin to hear Jesus' message as contemporaneous with their life situation, they will quickly recognize that the "political hermeneutics of the gospel." [89] For example, Caribbean theologians discuss the role of the Caribbean church to serve the embattled community and to help alleviate the pain and suffering, as well as contribute to ameliorate infrastructures in the Region. Davis in his Caribbean theology of emancipation seeks "emancipation connections" among the people in Africa and the Black

---

86. Cone, *Black Theology and Black Power*, 31.

87. Ibid.

88. Bonino, *Toward a Christian Political Ethics*, 37.

89. Cone, *Black Theology and Black Power*, 36.

diaspora and declares that "For wherever there are the linkages of bondage, there are also the emancipatory linkages are indicated.[90]

Hence, Christianity becomes for the marginalized and the poor "a religion of protest against the suffering and affliction of man,"[91] which Jesus (through the agency of the Church) came to eradicate. This Jesus now dwells in the community of the world's poor, the afflicted, and the outcast who lodge in the ghetto of human despair and labyrinth of death; correspondingly, Jesus the Liberator lives among the postcolonial exploited individuals and families which American military forces and European interventionist powers have pushed in the margins of society. Cone teaches us that the relevance of Jesus' liberating message is not only good for the black and brown people in America; the person and work of Jesus is a life-changing experience to the orphan in the streets of Cape Town, South Africa; the widow in the shanty towns in Haiti and Jamaica; the mine worker in Ghana and Kenya; the sugar cane workers in the sugar industry in Dominican Republic and Cuba; the undocumented African immigrants in the ghetto of Paris and Tel Avis ; and the single mother in the war zone in Afghanistan and Pakistan. As the Caribbean liberation theologian Idris Hamid remarks, "From the Exodus to the Resurrection, God leads man from all sorts of bondage, external and internal, even from the bondage of death."[92] Cone complements this conviction by declaring:

> If we can believe the New Testament witness which proclaims Jesus as resurrected and thus active even now, then he must be alive in those very men who are struggling in the midst of misery and humiliation. If the gospel is a gospel of liberation for the oppressed, then Jesus is where the oppressed are and continues his work of liberation there. Jesus is not safely confined in the first century. He is our contemporary, proclaiming release to the captives and rebelling against all who silently accept the structures of injustice. If he is not in the ghetto, if he is not where men are living at the brink of existence, but is, rather, in the easy life of the suburbs, then the gospel is a life.[93]

On a personal level, Cone, reflecting on the tragic collective experience of Black Christians in the segregated Bearden, Arkansas in the 1950s and 1960s who came face to face with white terror and white supremacy,

90. Davis, *Emancipation Still Comin'*, 127.

91. Cone, *Black Theology and Black Power*, 36.

92. Hamid, "Theology and Caribbean Development," 126.

93. Cone, *Black Theology and Black Power*, 38.

writes optimistically and courageously about the meaning of Jesus in their everyday life; Jesus was a

> trusted friend who understood their trials and tribulations in this unfriendly world . . . Jesus was always there, as the anchor of life, giving it meaning and purpose and bestowing hope and faith in the ultimate justice of things. Jesus was that reality who empowered black people to know that they were not the worthless human beings that white people said they were.[94]

Consequently, contemporary theological reasoning must promote a Christology that empowers the weak toward self-liberation and collective agency, as well as a doctrine of Christ that boasts about the enduring presence of Jesus the Deliverer among the economically-disfranchised poor, and the disadvantaged races and ethnic groups in the world. In Cone's Christology, the oppressed is always the protagonist and actor by the virtue of Jesus' intentional closeness and solidarity with them. The Christian theologian should commit to the struggle and deliverance of the underrepresented individuals and families in society; he or she must attempt to create a new theological language that prioritizes the plot of the underserved population and the historical fight of the poor for justice, equity, and rights.

In addition, In *A Black Theology of Liberation*, Cone introduces the threefold tasks of Christian theology:

1. The task of theology is to explicate the meaning of God's liberating activity so that those who labor under enslaving powers will see that the forces of liberation are the very activity of the being of God. Rat̴͜   ` study of God's liberating activity in the ͙͙   ͙͙al   'n behalf of the oppressed.[95]

2. T̴ the   ͙   nalyze the meaning of
   ͙   ͙   essed community of
   a   ͙   edom, a freedom
   n   ͙   The language of
   t̴   ͙   e it is insepa-
   r̴

3. T   ͙   , the nature of the
   g(͙   e experience of the)

[handwritten, overlaid: "always the gospel is contextual because the gospel is about politics of those is about oppression or Jesus the government community under dwells in the outcasts. dwells to help the"]

94. Cone, "Lou..   /.
95. Cone, *Black Theology an̴* ͙   ͙.
96. Ibid., 4.

oppressed (blacks) so they will see the gospel as inseparable from their humiliated condition, and as bestowing on them the necessary power to break the chains of oppression.[97]

In *God of the Oppressed*, Cone articulates three complementary tasks and roles of the Christian theologian as an exegete, a teacher, and a preacher, and each function relates to his work in the church and responsibility in society:

1. The task of the theologian, as a member of the people of God, is to clarify what the Church believes and does in relation to its participation in God's liberating work in the world. in doing this work, the theologian acts in the roles of exegete, prophet, teacher, preacher, and philosopher. [98]

2. The task of the theologian is to probe the depths of Scripture exegetically for the purpose of relating that message to human existence . . . this task involves, as Abraham Heschel said, the "exegesis of existence from a divine perspective," disclosing that God is not indifferent to suffering and not patient with cruelty and falsehood.[99]

3. The task of theology is to show the significance of the oppressed's struggle against inhuman powers, relating the people's struggle to God's intention to set them free. Theologians must make the gospel clear in a particular social context so that God's people will know that their struggle for freedom is God's struggle too.[100]

On the other hand, he interprets the discipline of theology as a cross-cultural dialogue and intellectual activity in which the theologian engages energetically the lived-worlds and lived-experiences of the people living in the periphery of postcolonial nation-states; as he notes below:

I am convinced that no one should claim to be doing Christian theology today without making the liberation of the Third World from the exploitation of the First World and the Second World a central aspect of its purpose. There is an interconnectedness of

97. Ibid., 5.
98. Cone, *God of the Oppressed*, 8.
99. Ibid.
100. Ibid., 90–91.

all humanity that makes the freedom of one people dependent upon the liberation of all.[101]

Liberation theology as a subset of Biblical theology allows the Christian thinker or theologian to always be in connection with the subject and object of his or her inquiry. Biblical theology as the theology that liberates and connects with the poor calls for genuine relationship with the community of faith. One cannot work toward the integral liberation of the poor and the dispirited while separating oneself from their real presence or social reality. Liberation theology is a theology of proximity, interconnectedness, and relationship. It is plausible for Cone to assume that "Theology is always done for particular times and places and addressed to a specific audience. This is true whether theologians acknowledge it or not. Although God is the intended subject of theology, God does not do theology, *human beings do theology*."[102] Elsewhere, he clarifies that "if theology is to be relevant to the human condition which created it, it must relate itself to the questions which arise out of the community responsible for its reason for being."[103] Because human liberation is the telos of Christian theology, Cone could define the discipline of theology as

> *a rational study of the being of God in the world in light of the existential situation of an oppressed community, relating the forces of liberation to the essence of the gospel, which is Jesus Christ.* This means that its sole reason for existence is to put into ordered speech the meaning of God's activity in the world, so that the community of the oppressed will recognize that its inner thrust for liberation is not only *consistent with* the gospel but is the gospel of Jesus Christ. There can be no Christian theology that is not identified unreservedly with those who are humiliated and abused. In fact, theology ceases to be a theology of the gospel when it fails to arise out of the community of the oppressed.[104]

101. Cone, *A Black Theology of Liberation*, xvii.

102. Ibi., xix.

103. Ibid., 36.

104. Ibid., 1.

Theology and Social Activism

In the most fundamental Barthian dialectics, Cone's theology begins with God's revelation to the needs of humanity and maintains that theological inquiry should not start from human needs to God. Therefore, the ethos of the incarnation is that God has intervened in the human situation as to deliver humanity from the predicament of sin and human oppression.[105] The God of the Bible, he contends, "stands against the culture of the oppressors"[106] and social injustice and inequality that often delay human flourishing and the common good. To borrow a central principle from the Latin American Theology of Liberation, "Protestant theology needs to recover not the one history, but the one just God as the radical counterforce of all unjust history,"[107] including the history of women oppression and abuse in the church and in society. Further, Cone also suggests that theology should address contemporary problems of sexism in the church, classism in society, the downsides of capitalism and globalization, and the exploitation of the developing nations by the developed nations. Correspondingly, the task of Christian theology today is to denounce the quandary of poverty, world hunger, colonialism, human rights, and the monopoly capitalism of the United States and the (Western) European nations in Latin America, Africa, the Caribbean, and Asia.[108] (Africana critical theological discourse not only interrogates the politics of the empire and its destructive weapons; it evaluates the logic that sustains the capitalist order, the current market value, and the inhumane economic structure in Western societies. African critical theology also rejects the politics of Western globalization that disfranchises the darker people and exploits the developing nations in the world.)

Concerning the question of sexism in Christian churches, Cone believes that "sexism dehumanizes and kills, and it must be fought on every front . . . Anyone who claims to be fighting against the problem of oppression and does not analyze the exploitive role of capitalism is either naïve or an agent of the enemies of freedom."[109] Therefore, the critical theologian must not analyze the race question apart from the effects of capitalism on race, class, and gender; racism, classism, sexism,

---

105. Cone, *God of the Oppressed*, 90.

106. Ibid., 89.

107. Assmann, *Theology for a Nomad Church*, 7.

108. Cone, *A Black Theology of Liberation*, xvi-xx.

109. Ibid., xvi-xvii.

and capitalism are the worst antagonists of human deliverance and self-determination. Sexism postpones women's freedom and agency and undermines Christian women's use of their gifts in the church to empower the community of faith.

Particularly, as much as racism is America's original sin that has affected millions of American poor and specifically the black and brown (oppressed) population, Cone reckons that American theologians should examine the human condition and not simply the issue of American racism. It is from this viewpoint he could make this declaration: "We must the not allow racial solidarity to distort the truth. Without class analysis, a global understanding of oppression will be distorted and its domestic manifestations seriously misrepresented."[110] While racial solidary can be effective at certain moments of struggle, human unity is the transcendent value that outdoes the problem of race, sexism, and classism in the church and society.

Cone's stated claim above is justified that it is necessary for the Christian theologian to be both a nationally and internationally-minded, and culturally and transculturally-concerned thinker as the issues he or she analyzes engulf the human condition in the world.

> [Theologians] must be concerned with the quality of human life not only in the ghettos of American cities but also in Africa, Asia and Latin America. Since humanity is one, one cannot be isolated into racial and national groups, there will be no freedom for anyone until there is freedom for all. This means we must enlarge our envision by connecting it with that of other oppressed so that together all the victims of the world might take charge of their history for the creation of a new humanity . . . Liberation knows no color bar; the very nature of the gospel is universalism, i.e., a liberation that embraces the whole of humanity.[111]

The clarion call for contemporary Christian theology is to be a theology for the people and from the people. Theology from below should never be the articulation of theoretical ideas that can't reach the ear of the poor and the uneducated and are inaccessible to their understanding. The theology of tomorrow must remain true to its never-ending search for comprehensive justice and steadfast commitment to the good of the poor, the

110. Ibid., xviii.

111. Cone, "Black Theology and the Black Church," in Cone and Wilmore, *Black Theology: A Documentary History*, 271–4.

orphan, the widow, the abused, the victim, and the exploited. The global perspective in theology would enable the engaged Christian thinker to take seriously the struggles of the troubled population in his or her own country and be proactive about the cries for justice from the lips of mistreated racial and ethnic groups in other parts of the world. Within this line of reasoning, Cone offers some words of wisdom and exhortation:

> The Christian theologian, therefore, is one whose hermeneutical consciousness for an interpretation of the gospel defined by the oppressed people's struggle of freedom, seeking to adhere to the delicate balance of social existence and divine revelation. In this situation, the theologian must accept the burden and the risk laid upon him or her by both social existence and divine revelation, realizing that they must be approached dialectically, and thus their exact relationship cannot be solved once and for all time.[112]

Evidently, Christian theology is a commentary on the life and experience of the church in relation to God and society; it is a conscious analysis on the daily interaction of the community of faith. Theology done for the sake of the church must empower the church as the people of God to identity with the whole of people's misery and suffering, not what they suffered yesterday and may know tomorrow, but the suffering that they are experiencing at the moment; as Bigo warns us, "A Christian begins at that point and always comes back to it for two reasons: misery goes on propagating itself without end and it reappears in forms every new."[113] Therefore, the work of the Church in doing acts of compassion and service and in demonstrating the love of God in Christ through hospitality (that is welcoming the stranger, the unknown, and the immigrant), feeding the hungry, clothing the naked, visiting the prisoner, and caring for the orphan and widow does not have an end. The Church's duty in improving the human condition in society and transforming people's lives for better through serving, loving, and connecting people in its community is the greatest manifestation of divine hospitality, love, and justice in public.

---

112. Cone, *God of the Oppressed*, 89.

113. Bigo, *The Church and Third World Revolution*, 10.

The Vocation of the Church Today

Cone's ecclesiology is an important category in his theological corpus, which he connects with the theme of human liberation and human flourishing. He insists that the vocation of the Christian church is unique as to serve and liberate people, and to help create a new social order of human freedom and future possibilities. He interprets the church as having a prophetic role in society. (The phrase "prophets of social consciousness" associating with the Christian church play a similar role in Mays's politico-theological vision of the church in society.) Hence, we must begin with Cone's concept of the church before we undertake the task of exploring the vocation of the church in contemporary society. Cone advances the proposition that the church consists of

> a new people which the New Testament calls the *ekklesia* (church). Like the people of Old Israel, they are called into being by God himself—to be his agent in this world until Christ's second coming. Unlike Old Israel, their membership is not limited by ethnic or political boundaries but includes all who respond in faith to the redemptive act of God in Christ with a willingness to share in God's creative activity in the world. . . . Its sole purpose for being is to be a visible manifestation of God's work in the affairs of men. The Church, then, consists of people who have been seized by the Holy Spirit and who have the determination to live as if all depends on God. It has no will of its own, only God's will; it has no duty of its own, only God's duty. Its existence is grounded in God.[114]

His proposal about the vocation of the church in the world is linked to God's initial purpose in Christ Jesus to call out an inclusive community into existence to forge a new human race empowered by the Spirit of God. For Cone, the church as God's redeemed people exists in society to carry out God's sovereign desires and objectives—which may include the trinitarian ministry of reconciliation, unity, fellowship, and peace. Cone provides further analysis about the vocation of the church by accentuating its philosophy of inclusion, democratic values, non-discriminatory character, and its ecumenical nature:

> The Church of Christ is not bounded by standards of race, class, or occupation. It not a building or an institution. It is not

114. Cone, "The White Church and Black Power," in Cone and Wilmore, *Black Theology: A Documentary History*, 68.

determined by bishops, priests, or ministers as these terms are used in their contemporary sense. Rather, the Church is God's suffering people. It is that grouping of men who take seriously the words of Jesus: "Blessed are you when men revile you and persecute you and utter all kinds of evil against you falsely on my account" (Matt. 5:31). The call of God constitutes the Church, and it is a call to suffering.[115]

The inclusive content of Cone's ecclesiology intends to be a counter response to white American ecclesiology that is racially selective and whose foundation is built on the exclusion of non-white Christian members of other races and ethnic groups. White churches in America are bound both by race and class, cultural ideologies and political consciousness. In his important work, *King and Malcolm and America*, Cone substantiates his thesis that Marin Luther King and Malcolm X, "two masters critics of American Christianity," believed that racism is a fundamental characteristic of American Christianity and society.[116] King once said, "Sunday morning is the most segregated hour in Christian America," and that the church fails to be a true witness of the message of the Gospel in the public sphere. King challenged White American Christians to embody the Gospel in their quotidian dealings with black people because of his conviction that God is not a color-blind deity; the universal message of the Gospel is transracial and transcultural, but contextual, ethnically sensitive. He proclaimed that God created all people in his image to be one human family; before God, we are brothers and sisters to one another, and we are one race. For King, the tragic failure of the White church in America is its intentional ignorance and practice of racism, and equally its implicit support of the power-structure of the oppressive state. King sustained the notion although racism was the fundamental moral dilemma in the American society, black and white American Christians should not ignore it and concurrently maintain their Christian identity and announce the message of reconciliation, unity, and the Gospel of peace.[117] In addition for Malcom, as Cone has argued:

> The public meaning of Christianity remained almost exclusively identified with the cultural values of white American and Europeans . . . Malcom's race critique of Christianity is as important for genuine Christian living in the world as Marx's class critique.

115. Ibid.

116. Cone, *Martin and Malcom and America*, 295.

117. Ibid.

> In clear and forceful language, Malcolm's life and thought tell us about the great difference between Christianity as preached and taught, on the one hand, and about the practice of white and black Christians in their communities, on the other.[118]

Accordingly, what contemporary American churches and Christians should learn from both King and Malcolm about public Christianity include their fierce activism to challenge America's inequality and injustice system and their robust campaigns against the racist structure of American Christianity. Both Malcom and King "supposedly" believed that Christians should be the guiding conscience of this nation. Disappointedly, that was not true and always the case in their America. The white church has also failed King and Malcom's moral expectations.

In his harsh criticisms of the "White Church" in America, Cone has consistently demonstrated that the White church is intrinsically a racialized-and-power-hungry institution that has fallen from grace and short of the New Testament vision of the *ekklesia* of God.

> If the real Church is the people of God, whose primary task is that of being Christ to the world by proclaiming the message of the gospel (*kerygma*), by rendering services of liberation (*diakonia*) and by being itself a manifestation of the nature of the new society (*koinonia*), then the empirical institutionalized white church has failed on all counts. It certainly has not rendered services of reconciliation to the poor. Rather, it illustrates the values of a sick society which oppresses the poor.[119]

Furthermore, he laments with great sorrow and grief that

> The white church has not merely failed to render services to the poor, but has failed miserably in being a visible manifestation to the word of God's intention for humanity and in proclaiming the gospel to the world. it seems that the white church is not God's redemptive agent but, rather, an agent of the old society. It fails to create an atmosphere of radical obedience to Christ . . . The society is falling apart for want of moral leadership and moral example, but the white church passes innocuously pious resolutions and waits to be congratulated.[120]

---

118. Ibid., 296.

119. Cone, "The White Church and Black Power," 72–73.

120. Ibid.

While we have highlighted in previous analysis Cone's criticisms toward the White church in America, this same Cone is calling upon the Black Church to be an active force and revolutionary church in society that will do in practice what it is theologically confessed or preached. The Black Church, according to Cone's assessment, does not mobilize its people for social justice and to care for the black poor and the economically-disadvantaged Americans:

> Our church is an impostor, because we no longer believe the gospel we proclaim. There is a credibility gap between what we say and what we do. While we may preach sermons that affirm the church's interests in the poor and the downtrodden, what we actually do shows that we are committed to the "American way of life," in which the rich are given privileged positions power in shaping the life and activity of the church and the poor are virtually ignored. As a rule, the church's behavior toward the poor is very similar to the society at large: The poor are charity cases.[121]

At this juncture, Cone condemns both the white and black churches/christianities in their negligence to engage in transformative projects of social justice and integral liberation, to make a *preferential option for the poor and the disadvantaged*, and to alter their present situation toward one that is more humane, optimistic, and sustaining. This could be well due to the absence of a strong theological conviction, what we may call "an aggressive justice theology system;" the latter pertains to the lack of robust commitment of these American churches to actualize in the practical sense what the people of God have traditionally professed theologically and ethically.

The Role of Theology in the Church

Christian theology must not only commit to peace and justice in society. Theology in the church should propose practical and concrete ways for doing effective pastoral ministry and fulfilling the public role of the church toward a fuller humanization of life. On a parallel note, theology in the life of the church should help mature the laity by stressing the importance of incarnating the professed faith in the reality of social and political conflict.[122] On the other hand, theologian Leonardo Boff laments

121. Cone, *Risks of Faith*, 111.
122. Boff, *Church*, 31.

that "there are practices that limit basic human rights, justified by their corresponding theological theories."[123] Theological education and praxis in the life of the church thus must promote, sustain, and guarantee human flourishing, deliverance, mutuality, reciprocity, interdependence, fraternity, and service; "these are the imperatives that foster our hope and lead us to shape practices that strive toward those ideals."[124]

Cone places great emphasis on the experience of *the community of the oppressed* as the source of Christian theology and ecclesiology because "God is the God *of* and *for* those who labor and are over laden."[125] Cone goes on to bring greater clarity on the role of theology in the life of the church, and its interface with Scripture:

> What is certain is that the theologian brings to the scripture the perspective of a community. Ideally, the concern of that community is consistent with the concern of the community that gave us the scriptures. It is the task of theology to keep these two communities (biblical and contemporary) in constant tension in order that we may be able to speak meaningfully about God.[126]

His reasoning is that the biblical communities that produced the Scriptures should shape contemporary churches' practices and values; reciprocally, the experiences and realities of today's churches impact scriptural interpretation and the relevance of the Bible in those congregations. The South African Liberation theologian Itumeleng J. Mosala advises that we should cultivate a healthy attitude toward the biblical texts and construes them as "ideological products of social systems and of the configurations of social relations internal to these systems."[127] Cone underscores that "the real Church of Christ is that grouping which identifies with the suffering of the poor by becoming one with them."[128] Caribbean Liberation Idris Hamid proposes that the the church should make new commitment to the people as "to work with the people instead of for them, listen to them instead of speaking at them, standing with them in suffering and shame instead of scolding and judging."[129] Hamid's

123. Ibid., 43.
124. Ibid., 43–44.
125. Cone, *A Black Theology of Liberation*, 1.
126. Ibid., 36.
127. Mosala, *Biblical Hermeneutics*, 45.
128. Cone, "The White Church and Black Power," 78.
129. Hamid, "Theology and Caribbean Development," 127.

call for ecclesiastical solidarity echoes Cone's theology of racial solidarity with black Christians and in the context of the Black church. How does then Cone conceive the function of theology in the life of the church? In what ways should theology inform the activities and doings of the church? According to Cone, theology is a corrective mechanism to prevent the church from committing grave sins—moral, cultural, economic, political, etc.; as theology itself "functions within the Church. Its task is to make sure that the 'church is the church."[130]

In other words, theology is a (symbolic) purifier for the church, and its role is to fortify the redemptive mission of the church by declaring and acting out "the gospel it has received."[131] Christian theology has a central responsibility to continually examine and reexamine "the proclamation of the Church of Jesus Christ."[132] Because the church is in the world and must engage it perpetually, the role of theology, then, "is to serve the need of the Church"[133] as the church should become "worldly church theology." By this concept, Cone insists that the thrust of Christian theology, in relations to its ecclesiastical practices and traditions, is to

> make sure that the Church is in the world and its word and deed are harmonious with Jesus Church. It must make sure that the Church's language about God is relevant to every new generation and its problem. It is for this reason that the definitive theological treatise can never be written. Every generation has its own problems, as does every nation. Theology is not, then, an intellectual exercise but a worldly risk.[134]

The shortcoming of American theology is and has been its failure to guide adequately the church in accomplishing its divinely-appointed mission in society, that is by truly being the catalyst of change and the defender of the poor and the oppressed. Cone laments that churches in America have not produced a theology of risk to confront this culture at risk associated with the actuality of the poor.

> American theology has failed to take that worldly risk. It has ignored its domestic problems on race. it has not called the Church to be involved in confronting this society with the

130. Ibid., 80.

131. Ibid.

132. Ibid.

133. Ibid.

134. Cone, "The White Church and Black Power," 80–81.

meaning of the Kingdom in the light of Christ . . . The lack of a relevant, risky theological statement suggests that theologians, like others, are unable to free themselves from the structures of this society.[135]

Within the same logic, he believes that theological education in America has also been tragically influenced by this said theological tradition above. He calls upon theologians to develop a theology of risk as a possible hope to engage the world of uncertainty and despair. In this respect, theological schools and seminaries in the United States have not only failed the church, they also failed the church's poor and the disfranchised Christians. Cone is more specific that the white curriculum of religious education or theological schools in the United States has ignored the black experience in history and the contributions of black religious scholars and theologians in the discipline of theology and biblical studies.

> The seminaries in America are probably the most obvious sign of the irrelevance of theology to life. Their initiative in responding to the crisis of black people in America is virtually unnoticeable. Their curriculum generally is designed for young white men and women who are preparing to serve all-white churches . . . Most seminaries still have no courses in black church history and their faculties and administrators are largely white. This alone gives support of the racist assumption that blacks are unimportant.[136]

Therefore, ineffective churches could be construed as a by-product-of a deficient theological education that is selective, exclusive, and racially-biased. As Cone has remarked, "For the sickness of the Church in America is intimately involved with the bankruptcy of American theology."[137] Cone justifies this claim by providing three examples. First, "When the Church fails to live up to its appointed mission, it means that theology is partly responsible. Therefore, it is impossible to criticize the Church and its lack of relevancy without criticizing theology for its failure to perform its function."[138] Second, when the Church fails in its appointed task to glorify God and empower the weak, it would accomplish its own selfish agenda and becomes subservient to other cultural forces that counter the Gospel of liberation.

135. Ibid., 81.
136. Ibid.
137. Ibid., 78.
138. Ibid., 80.

Third, in the intriguing text entitled *The Good Society,* the authors suggest that contemporary churches in America have lost their moral vision and sense of social mission due to observable theological symptoms; in particular, they maintain, "Mainline Protestant theology fails to map a course for socially concerned Christians, to move them to follow it, and to guide them along it because it fails to ring true to their actual experience of social life."[139] Perhaps, one of the contributing factors to this bankrupt nature of contemporary churches is that current theological discourses do not emerge from the experience of the people of God, and thus, the conveyed message of theologians do not connect with the (ordinary) people in the church.

Contemporary theological discourses should empower the people in the church to serve and care for one another, practice hospitality to strangers, and care for the poor and the socially-disadvantaged and the economically-disfranchised. In the same line of thought, contemporary theological thought should help churches to cast new vision for overcoming poverty, hunger, and infant mortality in contemporary society. Orlando E. Costas employs the phrase the "missionary-liberation issue" of theology to designate especially the all-encompassing activities of the church.[140] Toward this goal, the practices of contemporary churches would be grounded on the ethic of Jesus, which is the realization and telos of prophetic religion and the kingdom of God on earth. Complementarily, Vuyani Vellem calls for the articulation of a vigorous Prophetic Theology in which the Christian theologian can make use of "other modes of moral discourse so as to include rational, apologetic modes of argumentation between prophets and policy makers in public life."[141]

Envisioning the Church of Tomorrow

The goal of the church in Cone's understanding is to create a new community of freedom and new humanism in which the poor could experience their full potential in life. Cone construes the true role of the church as a faithful witness to God's kindness and emancipating movement in society; as he declares firmly, "If the church is to remain faithful to its Lord, it must make a decisive break with the structure of this society

---

139. Bellah et al., *The Good Society,* 192–93.
140. Costas, *The Church and Its Mission,* 221.
141. Vellem, "Interlocution."

by launching a vehement attack on the evils of racism in all forms. It must become prophetic, demanding a radical change in the interlocking structures of this society."[142] For example, in the context of the American racism, Cone boldly declares that

> The White structure of this American society, personified in every racist, must be at least part of the New Testament meant by the demonic forces. . . . these powers can get hold of a man's total being and control his life to such a degree that he is incapable of distinguishing himself from the alien power. This seems to be what has happened to white racism in America. It is a part of the spirit of the age, the ethos of the culture, so embedded in the social, economic, and political structure that white society is incapable of knowing its destructive nature.[143]

The proper response to the various cultural and political expressions of "the demonic forces of white racism," according to Cone, is to resist them and fight their allies in society. Cone interprets the church as a new community that actively participates in Christ's liberating work in history; as a result, the church should never endorse public policies and 'law and order that causes suffering or the exploitation of individuals.[144] Rather, the Christian church should be the voice of reason in society. Assmann proposes that followers of Christ need to see the Church not just a place for spiritual healing and reformation, but "as an institution of social criticism, and institution of the critical freedom of faith."[145]

Moreover, Cone highlights three major functions of the Church, as observed in the New Testament: preaching (*kerygma*), service (*diakonia*), and fellowship (*koinonia*):[146]

1. First, it proclaims the reality of divine liberation. This is what the New Testament calls preaching the gospel. The gospel is the proclamation of God's liberation as revealed in the event of Jesus *and* the outpouring of the Holy Spirit. It is not possible to receive the good news of freedom and keep it to ourselves; it must be told to the whole world.

---

142. Cone, *Black Theology and Black Power*, 2.

143. Ibid., 41.

144. Cone, *A Black Theology of Liberation*, 130.

145. Assmann, *Theology for a Nomad Church*, 31.

146. Cone, "The White Church and Black Power," 69.

2. Secondly, the church not only proclaim the good news of freedom, it actively shares in the liberation struggle. Though the battle against evil has been won, old rulers pretend that they are still in power . . . The function of the church is to remind them that they are no longer in power . . . The church is the community that lives on the basis of the radical demands of the gospel by making the gospel message a social, economic, and political reality. It has the courage to take the risk, knowing that, at this early state, it lives in a society that refuses to believe the gospel message. It thus goes against the grain of societal existence because its sole aim is to share with Jesus Christ in his liberating activity.

3. Thirdly, the church as a fellowship is a visible manifestation that the gospel is a reality. If the church is not free, if it is a distorted representation of the irruption of God's kingdom, if it lives according to the old order (as it usually has), then no one will believe its message.[147]

Cone advances his claim forward by placing accent on the international dimension of the work of the church as the people of God partake in the mission of God in all cultures; the God-church joint-partnership places "the church squarely in the context of the world. Its existence is inseparable from worldly involvement."[148] As the Head of the Church, the mission of Christ in the world is to liberate those in chain, restore the brokenhearted, reinstate the outcast into the beloved community, and deliver hope to the hopeless. Ultimately, the great hope of Christianity is that Jesus Christ will eradicate death and evil in the world.

> Because the church knows that the world is where human beings are dehumanized, it can neither retreat from the world nor embrace it. Retreating is tantamount to a denial of its calling to share in divine liberation. It is a complete misunderstanding of the Christ-event, which demands radical, worldly involvement in behalf of the oppressed.[149]

Arguably, the church in action must continue maintaining a constant presence among the weak, the vulnerable, and the disfranchised in society. As Cone interprets:

147. Cone, *A Black Theology of Liberation*, 130–32.

148. Ibid., 132.

149. Ibid., 132–33.

> If the white and black churches do not represent Christ's re-
> demptive work in the world, where then is Christ's church to be
> found? As always, his church is where wounds are being healed
> and chains are being struck off. It does not matter in the least
> whether the community of liberators designate their work as
> Christ's own work. What is important is that the oppressed are
> being liberated.[150]

The Christian church in America looks too much like the American culture and is entrapped in American political games. It needs to
exit from this cultural predicament, the political Babylon of this age.
Yet, the Christian church should be an engaged and dynamic church by
responding creatively and constructively to the human condition and
in particularly to "the problems which are unique to this country."[151]
The American Church should be a servant to the culture by relating the
transforming impact of the Gospel to life situations of individuals and
families and by addressing the cultural, economic, political, and social
factors that affect their daily.

If the central message of the church is the proclamation of the good
news of God's reign, peace, and liberation through Jesus Christ and by
the empowering presence of the Holy Spirit, this same message should
be the center of the church's missionary project in the world. The goal
of humanization should be an integral part of the church's missionary
endeavor, which should advance the cause for "social reform, health,
education, welfare, relief, technology, and development"[152]—especially in
the underserved and developing nations.

Comparatively, Caribbean theologian Idris Hamid in *Search of New
Perspectives* interprets development as a fundamental mission of the
church, and that ecclesiastical project may include developing or supporting a balanced economic model that is related to the human commitment of the society and its growth and transformation; ameliorating the
public education system to reach the poor and underperformed students;
"church's mission must inform the goal and direction of our development plans."[153] Hamid's philosophy of human development as it relates
to economics and education is critical here; it is anti-capitalist and stands
against the exploitation of the poor and the economically-disadvantaged,

150. Ibid., 134–35.

151. Cone, "The White Church and Black Power," 81.

152. Costas, *The Church and Its Mission*, 175.

153. Hamid, *In Search of New Perspectives*, 14–16.

and its basic goal consists in improving the living and economic conditions of the marginalized and the poor:

> The economics of a human oriented society will serve, not the interest of efficiency or the profit motive, but man's humanity and community. If the economic models do not help to humanize our condition, then, it must be modified or rejected. All systems must serve man and is community, not man serving the systems. This is why we cannot accept a capitalist oriented economy with apologetic patches of planning. Our whole history has been darkened by this evil system which catered to the greed and base passion of men . . . We may have also to forge a new business ethic predicated on the human-community, oriented society . . . .Now, since the education programme in any society has always been geared to the goals of that society, it follows that if the goals of our envisioned society are going to be different, then the education programme will be different . . . A society which seeks to inculcate respect for the person, emphasize the human, and promote community-mindedness would have to have an educational programme suited to its goals.[154]

Because the message the church announces is about God's Kingdom in the world, and human liberation, it is important for the church to help create communities of freedom and places of healing in society by challenging structures of human oppression and systems of human degradation. Toward this end, the church will be true to its vocation in fostering human flourishing and enhancing human freedom.[155] The duty of the church of today and tomorrow entails the clarion call for various Christian communities and churches to join hands together to emancipate

our community from its own internal destructiveness, will be free to fight against oppression in the larger society. Accordingly, the test of the authenticity of our commitment is found not only in what we say about freedom generally what we do about the liberation of victims within our community.[156]

154. Ibid., 16–17.

155. Cone, *Risks of Faith*, 118.

156. Ibid.

The Prophetic and Postcolonial Church

Africana critical theology makes a case for former colonized people to create solid postcolonial and decolonial congregations that reflect the indigenous way of serving God and their religious habitus. In the context of global Christianity in the developing world and postcolonial nations, new postcolonial congregations must be formed to reflect the indigenous culture and the religious habitus of the people, not to be a replica of American and Western church practices. Non-Anglo Christian theologians and parishioners have a vital role to play in the urgent project of decolonizing Christian churches in their land; likewise, they must create new expressions of Christian piety that is relevant to their postcolonial condition and a decolonized faith that sustains the values and identity and the cultural heritage of their people. They also have a tremendous charge to decolonize the imported ecclesiastical rituals of Western Christianity in their respective culture and correspondingly to deracinate the irrelevant Western values embedded in Christian tradition in their own postcolonial context. Toward this aim, non-Anglo Christian thinkers and clergy could would be able to produce a veritable decolonial faith of indigenous agency and determination that is true to their cultural identity in Christ, as well as to their religious worldview compatible with the Christian religion.

The vocation of the (postcolonial) church in the twentieth-first century should also include a robust campaign toward better social justice theology, equitable forms of economic fairness, and the alleviation of poverty and hunger in society. Correspondingly, the church should commit its resources and power to constructive social actions contributing to healthy and productive individuals and families society; this could be done in the church's relentless support of government-sponsored programs and uplift projects to ameliorate the condition of the unfortunate and the economically-challenged people.[157] As previously noted, the church as a teacher of the nation's moral conscience of right and wrong, and the protector of the poor should encourage individual men and women to keep their promises to each other and stay close to a spouse in moments of sickness and health; to raise morally-responsible children and compassionate future citizens; to reach out to the hungry; to respect the rights of others; and to offer hospitality to strangers and

---

157. Bellah et al., *The Good Society*, 188–89.

immigrants.[158] These propositions represent some of the prophetic roles of the church in the twentieth-first century global culture. A prophetic church is a church in emancipative action and a revitalizing Christian community in which its members assume their leadership role in transforming the culture of oppression and despair into a culture of optimism, as well as contributing to the wholistic transformation of the unfortunate condition of the wretched and poor of the world. In summary, the characteristics in the paragraph below may also be inclusive to the vision and role of a prophetic church of tomorrow:

> church friends could provide emotional and economic support in times of unemployment, sickness, and death . . . Faithful Christians not only care for the poor and call them to forsake sinful choices and destructive behavior, Christians also why people are poor—and advocate change. A faithful church will issue a ringing summons to the middle class and rich to transcend their self-centered materialism and change what is unjust. A faithful church knows that great imbalances of power foster injustice and, therefore, acts to strengthen honest unions and encourage grassroots community organizing. A revitalizing Christian church—truly understanding that God measures societies by how they treat the poor and that the Bible demands economic justice for all—could provide the critical leadership necessary to dramatically reduce poverty.[159]

Boff comforts the church, whose hope is in Christ and his wealth, not to be subservient to the power and authority of the state or be dependent upon the riches and resources of the dominant class that subjugates the poor and economically exploits underclass workers.

> There is also another, of the Gospel, upon which the Church stands, that constantly criticizes and denounces every abuse of power and calls for respect and service. Jesus' message does not favor the domination of some over others or the curtailment of their rights; the same holds true for the Church that exists because of the message and that incarnates him in the world[160].

158. Sider, *Just Generosity*, 100.

159. Ibid., 101–2.

160. Boff, *Church*, 43.

Conclusion

Contemporary churches must reckon with the idea that everything in society has a political dimension and that there's a political dimension of faith that should compel followers of Christ not to remain indifferent to the suffering of the poor and the disinherited.[161] Sharing possessions and gifts with the needy is a tremendous shortcoming in contemporary churches because of the absence of a genuine theology of possession and giving in today's churches. New Testament scholar Luke Timothy Johnson writes compellingly about the performative role of theology in character formation of the Church and the individual Christian toward the cultivation and embodiment of moral virtues of sharing, distribution, (alms-) giving, and hospitality:

> Theology can discover and contemplate this: the sharing of pos-
> sessions is an essential articulation of our faith in God and of
> our love for our fellow humans. But how and in what fashion
> that sharing is to take place is not the task of theology but of
> the obedience of faith . . . One of the reasons the Jewish ideal
> of almsgiving (doing justice) recommends itself to our medita-
> tion and implementation is, beyond the fact that it is communal
> without being communistic, beyond the fact that it deals with
> humans in concrete rather than ideal terms, is the simple fact
> that is rooted in God's commanding Word and has been subject
> to the most critical and searching reflection for thousands of
> years. Christians need only pay attention.[162]

As previously observed in Cone's theology and ecclesiology, the marriage between theological imagination and ecclesiastical practices cannot be divorced. Theology, informed by the life of the church, must give serious consideration about the predicament and welfare of the poor and the vulnerable in society, such as the liberating message we encounter in James Cone's theology of the vocation of the church and the task of Christian theology in the twenty-first century.

Finally, Cone interprets the sacred duty of the Christian church is to set the oppressor free from his or her own sin of oppressing the oppressed: "The Good News of freedom is proclaimed also to the oppressor, but since he mistakes his enslaving power for life and heath he does not easily recognize his own mortal illness or hear the healing

161. Assmann, *Theology for a Nomad Church*, 31.

162. Johnson, *Sharing Possessions*, 116, 139.

world."[163] Moreover, he heightens the importance of clarity and precision in church's communication to the world in its outreach programs:

> The Church should speak in a style which avoids abstractions. Its language must be backed up with relevant involvement in the affairs of people who suffer. It must be a grouping whose community life and personal involvement are coherent with its language about the gospel.[164]

Finally, Cone reminds us of the essential task of Christian theology and the church in fostering intentional relationship with the culture which gives them a public stage and shapes the content of their message. For the Gospel proclaims that God is with us now, actively fighting the forces which would make man captive. And it is the task of theology and the Church to know where God is at work so that we can join him in this fight against evil.[165] The church as the divine ambassador in the world must follow God's footsteps where he is already present and active in the culture to recreate the world, reestablish the poor and the downtrodden, and ultimately to make all things right to his glory. Christian theology, based on the message of the Gospel, must emerge from the experience of the church, that is the people of God.

163. Cone, "The White Church and Black Power," 69.

164. Ibid., 78.

165. Cone, Black Theology and Black Power, 39.

5

Black Theodicy and Liberation

Caribbean Theology and the Problem of God, Suffering, and Violence

WHILE IN THE PREVIOUS two chapters on James Cone, I explored the problem of black theodicy in the Black American experience and Cone's constructive theological anthropology grounded on a Christology of suffering and atonement, this present chapter studies the issue of black theodicy associating with imperial intervention, famine, hunger, and the historic enslavement of the African people (as seen in Cone) within the trajectories of the Caribbean experience. Africana theological ethics and anthropology is a lament and protest theological discourse that reflects critically on the history of suffering and dehumanization of the African people and their descendants in the African Diaspora. This politico-theological narrative contemplates on the practice of racial segregation in public spaces and Christian meetings (Mays), Caribbean slavery and American imperialism (Price-Mars, Hamid, Aristide, Erskine), American slavery and lynching (Cone), the colonial legacy and European hegemony in continental in Africa (Mbiti, Idowu, Megasa), and each of these transforming-life events radically shaped Africana intellectual discourse and theological musings.

Within this intellectual framework and historical consciousness, in this chapter, I examine the contributions of four Caribbean theologians to the disciplines of theology and anthropology, and human rights conversations. These Caribbean thinkers write informatively, contextually, and intelligently from the *Sitz im leben* of the Caribbean experience. Jean-Bertrand Aristide (Haiti), Idris Hamid (Trinidad), Noel Leo Erskine (Jamaica), and D.H. Kortright Davis (Antigua and Barbuda) articulate a common vision of a Caribbean theology of emancipation and decolonization. Arguably, their political theological discourse is an attempt to engage the Caribbean experience within the framework of the postcolonial life and the anti-imperial reason. There exists substantial convergences and confluences, as well as ideological parallels and connections in the political theology and contextual theology of freedom and hope in the work of these four thinkers who emerged from four different geographical corners in the Caribbean.

Caribbean theology of emancipation, decolonization, and hope is emerged out of the labyrinth of European slavery and colonialism, American imperialism, white supremacy, and globalization. It could shed tremendous light on American Christian theology, and American Christians and churches have a lot to learn from the Caribbean people, especially their everyday experience with suffering, violence, hunger, famine, and political interruption and corruption.

The Caribbean Setting as the Context of Caribbean Theology

Caribbean theology is a postcolonial and decolonial discourse in which Caribbean theological thinkers and scholars are chiefly concerned with a new theological paradigm grounded in the Caribbean landscape toward the radical transformation and liberation of Caribbean societies and the betterment of the Caribbean people. What is then Caribbean Theology in which to situate geographically and regionally the theology of these four Caribbean thinkers? At this juncture, it will be important to explore what constitutes precisely Caribbean theology from the writings of selected Caribbean theologians and thinkers.

First of all, there is not a unified Caribbean theology as the Caribbean landscape is religiously, ethnically, linguistically, and culturally diverse. The Caribbean society is not homogeneous, so its theology. Although the

Caribbean people share a common history of slavery, colonialism, imperialism, poverty, and alienation, there are sharp distinctions between the corresponding societies. For example, in Haiti, Cuba, Martinique, and Dominican Republic, Roman Catholicism is a major religious tradition; whereas, in Jamaica and Antigua, Protestant Christianity plays an important place in the everyday experience of the people. Vodou is practiced in Haiti; Obeah in Jamaica; Santeria in Cuba; the Orisha religion in Trinidad. Nonetheless, the common thread of all of these Afro-Caribbean societies and Afro-Caribbean religious traditions is the African element and impact. Therefore, we should speak of Caribbean theologies, not Caribbean theology as it is a monolithic or homogeneous narrative. Caribbean theology should give thoughtful attention to the way in which Caribbean peoples organize their lives and construct their spiritual worldview; equally, Caribbean theology should not be an antagonist to Afro-Caribbean cultures, but should work to maintain its integrity.[1]

Martinican Literary theorist and philosopher Edouard Glissant[2] construes the Caribbean life as a poetics of relations. As he has observed, "We are not prompted solely by the defining of our identities but by their relation to everything possible as well—the mutual mutations generated by this interplay of relations."[3] Dominican scholar Silvio Torres-Saillant contends that the people of the Caribbean have suffered a long history of exclusion from Western historiography and from the human meta-narratives the winners of history (the West) produced.[4] Torres-Saillant refers to the Caribbean as the "historical center of colonialism"[5] because its plantation economic system was the most prosperous and successful industry in Western society—from the middle of the seventeenth through the end of the eighteenth century. He proceeds to describe both the historical quandary of Caribbean societies and the contemporary plight of the people in the Region:

> Split into several distinct colonial domains—with the same territory at times changing colonial hands more than once—the region has housed all the races, religions, cultures, and desires of the globe. The colonial transaction broke this part of

1. Davis, *Roots and Blossoms*, xviii.
2. Glissant, *Caribbean Discourse* (1989), and *Poetics of Relations* (1997).
3. Glissant, *Caribbean Discourse*, 89.
4. Torres-Saillant, *An Intellectual History* (2006).
5. Ibid., 17.

the world into imperial blocs and caused the various societies there to look in the direction of different metropolises abroad. Linguistically and politically the Caribbean comes from a history of fragmentation. Most societies in the region today exist as independent nations, but some territories remain colonially attached to foreign policies.[6]

Haitian-born novelist Myriam Chancy states that the human condition in the Caribbean, particularly that of Haitian women, implies an awareness of the cultural modes of production in which the Caribbean people understand themselves within the cultural and epistemological framework that define their identity, societal function, and future destiny in the Caribbean.[7] Chancy suggests a feminized reading of Caribbean history as a valid approach to acquire better understanding of the people; it gives the impetus to or accentuates the voice of Caribbean women who have contributed enormously to Caribbean societies and changed Caribbean intellectual landscape. Chancy proceeds to elaborate that the life and self-definition of women in the Caribbean, women of color in the United States, as well as women in the Developing World "reveal that the creation of identity in the face of imperialist and colonial oppression begins with the transmutation of the personal into the creative, into modes of self-empowerment that in and of themselves create a theory of self-definition."[8] She insists that the Caribbean experience is pinched profoundly by a sets of historical memory and cross-cultural connections; in the case of Haitian women, she notes, "it is a complex history of sexist oppression at the hands of white and black, at the hands of French, Haitian, and American men whose identities cross racial lines."[9]

From this angle, paradoxically, Caribbean memory also "serves as the paradigm survival transhistorically; it is not a claim to an evasion of history, but rather a challenge to remember that cultures are shaped by what survives from one generation to the next."[10] Chancy maintains that the history and experience of Caribbean Women can provide us with a penetrating insight into Caribbean societies and of the intersections of history, memory, sexuality, and gender. To complement Chancy, Haitian-born novelist and short story writer Edwidge Danticat has characterized

6. Ibid., 19.

7. Chancy, *Frame Silence*, 5–7.

8. Ibid., 5.

9. Ibid., 19.

10. Ibid., 11.

Haitian history as a narrative that is obsessed with memory (of the past).[11] In the Haitian psyche, historical memory never goes away; it functions as an invisible scar on the Haitian soul. Memory as a marker of the human experience in Haiti bears both tragic remembrances and historical events that stimulate Haitian resistance and Haitian proud in time of despair, exile, and alienation. According to Danticat,

> We have, it seems, a collective agreement to remember our triumphs and gloss over our failures. Thus, we speak to remember our triumphs and gloss over our failures. Thus, we speak of the Haitian revolution as though it happened just yesterday but we rarely speak of the slavery that prompted it. Our paintings show glorious Edenlike African jungles but never the Middle Passage.[12]

In addition, Danticat explains further the uneasiness of the Haitian people to confront their historical past—a past that was shattered by slavery, colonialism, forced labor, American military occupation, dictatorship, etc.; as a result, she pronounces that "our shattered collective psyche from a long history of setbacks and disillusionment."[13] As other people in the Caribbean, Haitians find different mechanisms to create alternative meanings and cope with their painful history. As she puts forth, "we cultivate communal and historical amnesia, continually repeating cycles that we never see coming until we are reliving similar horrors."[14] Haitian society like other societies in the Caribbean is fragmented, disorientated, and in the words of the Cuban novelist Antonio Benitez-Rojo, the Caribbean space is

> the union of the diverse . . . and that the Antilles are an island bridge connecting, in 'another way,' North and South America . . . Since within the sociocultural fluidity that the Caribbean archipelago presents, within its historiographic turbulence and its ethnological and linguistic clamor, within its generalized turbulence and its ethnological and linguistic clamor, within its generalized instability of vertigo and hurricane, one can sense the features of nan island that "repeats itself, unfolding and bifurcating until reaches all the seas and lands of the earth,

---

11. Danticat, *Create Dangerously* (2010).

12. Ibid., 64.

13. Ibid.

14. Ibid.

while at the same time it inspires multidisciplinary maps of un-expected designs.[15]

In addition, Guadeloupean novelist Maryse Condé in an interview conducted in December 2, 1992, affirms both

> the diversity of the islands as well as their common problems
> ... We saw the differences between the various linguistic zones
> we've mentioned. We reached the conclusion that within their
> diversity, unity existed among the Caribbean islands, the affir-
> mation of a personality that was neither African, nor American,
> nor European ... This personality was based on a common his-
> tory and rather similar social and political evolution, and evolu-
> tion that was more social than political.[16]

Hence, Caribbean theology must integrate the memorial experience of the Caribbean people and highlight the agency of Caribbean women, as the Caribbean experience is particularized through a range of relations and identity politics: gender, class status, memory, racial difference, po-larized religious beliefs, etc. Secondly, there is a great divorce between Anglophone Caribbean, Francophone Caribbean, and Hispagnophone Caribbean, as the matter pertains to theological articulations and theo-logical reflections on the Caribbean life. The theological narrative of each Caribbean Region is contextualized and nationalized.

Interestingly, theologians and biblical scholars from Anglophone Caribbean—especially from the country of Jamaica—have gained prominence in this particular are of study and contributed enormously to a theological identity of the Caribbean world that is both regional and trans-regional, particular and universal. Because of linguistic difference (i.e. Creole, Spanish, French, English, Dutch, and Portuese) and ideo-logical conflict between Caribbean thinkers, theologians from the Carib-bean shores do not interact with each other's work and often overlook the contributions of their West Indian/Caribbean interlocutors. Conse-quently, the promise of theological ecumenism in the Caribbean which Laënnec Hurbon,[17] Edmund Davis,[18] Idris Hamid,[19] Noel Leo Erskine,[20]

---

15. Benitez-Rojo, The Repeating Islands, 2–3.

16. Pfaff, Conversations with Maryse Conde, 109.

17. Hurbon, Dieu dans le Vaudou haïtien (1972).

18. Davis, Roots and Blossoms (1977).

19. Hamid, In Search of New Perspectives (1979).

20. Erskine, Decolonizing Theology (1981).

Kortright Davis,[21] Howard Gregory,[22] Fritz Fontus,[23] Jean Fils-Aime,[24] Jules Casseus,[25] and many others championed never came to fruition in Caribbean theological program or interreligious diaologue.

Idris Hamid, who is dubbed one of the founding fathers of Caribbean Theology, was probably correct to refer to "Caribbean perspectives in theology" rather than "Caribbean theology;" he articulated a fourfold vision of Caribbean theological tradition (s):

> The ways in which Caribbean people have experienced God over the years should be analyzed, structured, and clarified, so that "the power of intellect [will] make that experience persuasive to the rest of the community, and keep it alive. (2) The deeply rooted understanding of freedom and dignity in Caribbean people must be fully expressed. (3) The experience of the consolation of God among Caribbean people, because of their suffering and pain, also must be expressed. (4) The cumulative effect of these experiences on our people should be carefully and clearly analyzed and expressed.[26]

Haitian Theologian Jules Casseus enunciates a Caribbean perspective of theology from the Haitian experience in which he makes a clarion call to Haitian theologians and thinkers to reimagine a contextual theology that embodies the Haitian way of life.[27] In order to develop an authentic theology that communicates Haitian values, Haitian Christians must reinterpret the Biblical text creatively and contextually "without being the hostage of a North American or European Orthodoxy."[28] He summons Haitian churches and ecclesiastical leaders to reassess the imported Christianity which they received uncritically from Western missionaries, as well as to reconsider the relevance of "foreign hermeneutics and exegesis" which demonizes Haitian cultural practices, philosophy of life, and defies Haitian Christian experience. Toward a contextual Haitian theology, the content of an acceptable Haitian theological discourse will incorporate the following elements:

21. Davis, *Emancipation Still Comin'* (1990).

22. Gregory, *Caribbean Theology* (1995).

23. Fontus, *Effective Communication of the Gospel in Haiti* (2001).

24. Fils-Aime, *Vodou, je me souviens* (2007).

25. Casseus, *Toward a Contextual Haitian Theology* (2013).

26. Quoted in Davis, *Emancipation Still Comin'*, 95.

27. Casseus, *Toward a Contextual Haitian Theology*.

28. Ibid., 25.

The gospel we are preaching in Haiti should be clothed with Haitian values. Our understanding of God, our interpretation of his word, our ecclesiology, and our practical Christian lives should reveal the positive aspects of Haitian culture . . . The Haitian theology will embrace all the provinces of the Haitian Christian life. It will help us take off our western masks so that we can present ourselves in the presence of God-the Great Master (*le Grand Maître*), with our emotions, our feelings as true Haitians and as true Haitians at the same time. This Haitian theology will be contextual, dynamic, liberating, transforming, and truly Haitian.[29]

Another Haitian theologian Fritz Fontus has also proposed that Caribbean theology from the Haitian worldview must not replicate the American-European theological hermeneutics. In other words, the experience of the Haitian people with God should not be "a carbon copy of the ones held in American and European churches."[30] He writes convincingly that

When one remembers the great difference which exists between Western culture and Haitian culture—in spite of some similarities—one can understand the interest the tension between the two has created among missionaries, national pastors and Christian leaders. They realized that the cultural conflict, we have just described, has consequences for the life of the individual Christian, the vitality of the churches, and the existence of the national culture. There is no doubt that such a conflict can disorganize the latter so much that it leads to what a Haitian cultural anthropologist has called a process of *deculturation*.[31]

Both Cassesus and Fontus imagined a Caribbean theology that continues to interrogate the grammar and logic of colonial theology and simultaneously, they advance a theological project that is postcolonial, decolonial, and pro-Caribbean values and cosmology. On the other hand, both Cassesus and Fontus envisioned a Haitian theology that is contextual, dynamic, pedagogical, and relational, and concurrently, a theological project that could radically transform the economic and political conditions of the Haitian people. In the same line of thought, Noel Leo Erskine, who writes theologically from a Jamaican point of view, proposes a Caribbean theology of freedom and hope that integrates the theological reflection,

29. Ibid., 25–26.

30. Fontus, *Effective Communication*, 3.

31. Ibid., 3–4.

the postcolonial experience, and the socio-economic aspect of the Caribbean people. He theories a Caribbean theology that gives prominence to the relevance of the Afro-Caribbean community systems and promotes the significance and values of the family in the Caribbean life.

Correspondingly, the Jamaican theologian Edmund Davis asserts that the notion of "Caribbean theology" is a discourse that seeks to vindicate the Caribbean people, and it establishes "the attempt to find points of similarity and of peculiarity between the nature and the experience of 'the Caribbean man' [the Caribbean woman] and that of the European culture from which the expatriate ministry sprang."[32] Davis explores the definitional element of Caribbean theology as "an emotive phrase and because of this it is easy to forget the significant questions hover about its use."[33] He points out three components of Caribbean theology: theological motivation, theological methodology, and its relevance to Caribbean society. The theological motivation of Caribbean theology is an effort to merge or bring in conversation the constituents of Christianity with the "socio-cultural and psychological heritage of the Caribbean."[34] The underlying purpose of Caribbean theology is corrective and vindicative, in view of the colonial history of the Region and the colonial theology that degrades Afro-Caribbean religion and culture.

The methodology of Caribbean theology is an alternative to Western Christian theology's focus on the doctrine of God. According to Davis, Caribbean theological method

> is a product of the open predicament? Moreover, a theological audience is also a product of such a predicament. If theologians and their clientele both self-consciously exist in the stream of world history, how can a theology which focuses exclusively or even predominantly on traditional world be considered either fully Caribbean or fully adapted?[35]

Consequently, Caribbean theology, as an expression of the world and traditional habits of the Caribbean people, must critically confront the Caribbean predicament in a meaningful and responsible way. The charge of the Caribbean theologian is to interpret the Christian faith from the world of the Caribbean people and concurrently to reflect

32. Davis, *Roots and Blossoms*, 115.
33. Ibid.
34. Ibid.
35. Ibid.

upon the social and intellectual history and the development of Caribbean societies to the postcolonial moment.[36] On one hand, Casseus,
Fontus, Erskine, and Davis endeavored to particularize and contextualize the Christian experience of the Caribbean people and summoned
Caribbean theologians and religious leaders to be masters in their own
households and to speak the language of their people; on the other
hand, Emund Davis recommends that Caribbean thinkers need to go
beyond the open predicament of the Caribbean. By this notion, he seeks
to convey that Caribbean theology

> cannot be limited to a dialogue with the intellectual and social
> history of the Caribbean alone. To do such a thing would place
> the theological task in the Caribbean in too narrow a context.
> The universal as well as the particular must be maintained in the
> development of theological education.[37]

Furthermore, in 1973, the Caribbean Conference of Churches held
a historic conference in Jamaica, resulting in the publication of a collection of seminal essays entitled *Troubling of the Waters*, edited by Idris
Hamid. According to Erskine's evaluation,

> This is perhaps the most significant theological work to have
> appeared in the Caribbean in the last decade . . . The book's main
> task is to indicate the common search for identity among Carib-
> bean people. *Troubling of the Water* is not a search for roots, but
> an attempt to indicate areas in which further research is needed
> in Caribbean history and spirituality.[38]

In the paragraph below, Hamid succinctly summarizes the various
perspectives of Caribbean theology expressed by the assembled Caribbean theologians and church leaders in that writing:

> The view as expressed that Caribbean theology has to be in-
> tuitive and symbolic, and while saw the need for an emerging
> architectonic framework within which to do our theologizing,
> it was felt that insight is what is more important. Many thought
> that we should move along tentatively in our search rather than
> await some new philosophical framework.[39]

36. Ibid., 116.
37. Ibid.
38. Hamid, *Troubling of the Waters*, 11–12.
39. Ibid., 9.

In a complementary note, Antiguan theologian Kortright Davis insists on a Caribbean theology that focuses on the emancipation of the Caribbean people.[40] The components of a Caribbean theology of emancipation include theological self-reliance, theological praxis, theological ecumenism, interreligious dialogue with the Afro-Caribbean religions in the Region, and the liberating function of the Caribbean churches as a vanguard of change and human flourishing. For Gregory, Caribbean theology must first begin with the human experience (method: theology as a "first act") of the Caribbean people, and then one can formulate a theological discourse (as a "second act" of theology) about the collective world of the individuals in the Region. It is in this manner that the human experience and God's revelation come in proximity in theological dialogue.[41]

According to Gregory, Caribbean theology should not only signify the articulation of the new; its purpose is to serve, to confirm, to correct, to echo earlier experiences of the Caribbean people, and ultimately to allude to the contemporary life of the Caribbean people.[42] Gregory interprets the role of Caribbean theology as the promotion of constructive and relevant theological education toward the long-term and holistic development of the Caribbean.[43] He construes theological education in the Caribbean as a vehicle leading to the economic progress, and sociopolitical transformation of Caribbean societies; equally, he argues that Caribbean theology should redefine ministerial formation "beyond the narrow 'spiritual' categories."[44] For Gregory, "A Caribbean theology must involve emancipation from the impact of [these] oppressive forces in the life and experience of Caribbean peoples."[45] Finally, he avers that Caribbean theology must be able to respond to the challenges of globalization in the Caribbean societies and should appropriate its advantages to benefit and liberate the Caribbean people.

Similarly and finally, like Caribbean theology, a liberation theological hermeneutics seeks to pursue a "'tri-focal critique (1) of the oppressive powers of state, economy, and culture; (2) of how the church has absorbed, justified, and benefited from these powers; and (3) also of the ways the

40. Davis, *Emancipation Still Comin'*, 88–104.

41. Gregory, "Ministry Formation for the Caribbean," 80.

42. Ibid., 81.

43. Ibid., 79–100.

44. Gregory, "Introduction," xi.

45. Ibid., xvii.

people, the poor, the oppressed (often but do not always considered as Christians) have themselves internalized oppressive patterns, requiring hence a process of conscientization, a 'pedagogy of the oppressed.'"[46] Our interest is ultimately to promote an ethics of life, and for life. In the same manner as Dussel and other Black theorists of liberation (i.e. Fanon, Cabral, Senghor, Cesaire, Du Bois), Caribbean theologians do not divorce theology, politics, ethics from anthropology and ethics of communal reciprocity and coexistence. As Dussell has intelligently remarked:

> The abolition of the political is the negation of human life, not just as naked existence but as collective, communitarian, dialogical, communicative freedom. Without others, without the other, there is neither ethics nor politics. Without others, without the other, there is no politics as the horizon of the possible—the possibility of continued existence. It is this continued existence as coexistence, as surviving and flourishing with others, that is the source of the political.[47]

Moreover, theological anthropology as imagined in the postcolonial and decolonial theological framework within the Caribbean logic "imagines subjectivities that resist the homogenizing and divisive tendencies of racial and ethnic labels, normative appearances, or religious and national tendencies.[48] This point is very important in Caribbean theological anthropology. Comparatively, "Theology can rethink its understanding of the *imago dei* with the help of theories of the split subject-as the embodiment and internalization of colonizing ideals, but also as the site of *spirited* resistance."[49]

The Imperative of Decolonization and Emancipation in Caribbean Theological Discourse

To establish points of contact and linkages between Hamid, Davis, Erskine, and Aristide in theological conversations does not mean points of difference and variation do not exist. These thinkers are predominantly concerned on how to use theology as a method of analysis to address the pressing needs of the Caribbean people. Below, we shall consider these

46. Keller et al., *Postcolonial Theologies*, 3; Freire, *Pedagogy of the Oppressed*.

47. Dussel, *Twenty Theses on Politics*, viii.

48. Keller et al., *Postcolonial Theologies*, 19.

49. Ibid., 17.

convergences and confluences in their political works, and in particular, the call to decolonize the Caribbean life and the imperative to emancipate the Caribbean people from the yoke of neocolonialism, globalization, imperialism, starvation, and political totalitarianism.

Kortright Davis

Kortright Davis suggests that Caribbean theology must articulate new methods that are grounded "within the context of local communities, to respond to current pressures: the need for more formal training of women, the growing inability to sustain appropriate standards of living (economically) among their clergy, the revolution of ethical perspectives and rising expectations in the Caribbean, and the inevitable imperatives of ecumenism."[50]

He proposes "theological self-reliance" as a mode of thinking theologically and doing theology within the context of the Caribbean experience. He makes an appeal to Caribbean theologians to reject the theological dependence from the metropolitan North from which they imitate theological forms and methods.[51] Davis calls into question North American and European theological methodologies into question because they "appear to offer a ready-made set of solutions to complex theological problems, so that the temptations to import them is strong than the will to seek new and indigenous ones."[52] Davis articulates a radically and innovative theological methodology that is rooted in the Caribbean spirit and that which embodies the experiences, the needs, religious beliefs, and plight of the Caribbean people. From Davis' groundbreaking text, *Emancipation Still Comin,'* (1990) we have identified six distinctive traits on how to do theology within the context of the Caribbean people.

Foremost, Davis offers the suggestion that Caribbean theologians and thinkers should provide "a radical assessment of the needs of the Caribbean constituency which is attempting to interpret the meaning of the Gospel of emancipation in the Caribbean context."[53] Second, he interrogates the traditional way of doing systematic theology or moral theology in the Caribbean, which focuses on the writings and ideas of

---

50. Davis, *Emancipation Still Comin'*, 88.

51. Ibid., 89.

52. Ibid.

53. Ibid.

Western white theologians—whose cultural experiences and economic-political context differ than those of Caribbean theologians. He contends within the milieu of the Caribbean life, Western moral theology and systematic theology "need not continue to be the basis for contemporary theological and moral insights."[54] Third, he places a clarion call upon Caribbean theologians to return to their own sources and to construct theological paradigms and categories by using "Caribbean folk wisdom and cultural history."[55] Fourth, he suggests Christian theologians in the Region to establish dynamic rapport with the Afro-Caribbean religious traditions and indigenous rituals that "had long been a source of spiritual and cultural power for the underclasses of Caribbean societies."[56] Fifthly, Davis emphasizes the urgency of theological praxis (Practical theology) in order for Caribbean theology to respond responsibly and empathetically to the pressing needs of the Caribbean people.

The new Caribbean theological vision should give serious attention to the economic life, political distresses, and the socio-historical circumstances of Caribbean societies. In other words, practical theology and theological formation executed within the life-experiences and lived-worlds of the Caribbean people "must take place in the midst of congregational life social and political witness and the actual hands-on-situations of ordinary people who struggle on the margins of poverty and frustration."[57] In particular, Davis makes a burning request to Caribbean male theologians and churches to allow greater participation of Caribbean women in the life of Caribbean churches, theological dialogue, and theological education.

> Women are by far the more dominant sector, numerically, in the life of the church in the Caribbean just as they are in other areas of the Christian world. The lifeblood of the church would be seriously malnourished if women were to withdraw their full participation and support. Yet church leaders in the Caribbean continue to be ambivalent and hesitant about the significance of such participation and about the value of women in the leadership structures of the Christian movement.[58]

54. Ibid.
55. Ibid., 90.
56. Ibid.
57. Ibid.
58. Ibid., 90–91.

The Haitian saying, "*Fanm se poto mitan*" (Women are pillars of society), affirms the centrality of women in Haitian society and religious life. The final distinctive mark of the new Caribbean theological discourse is the importance of ecumenism. The new theological method should strategically and intentionally promote "ecumenical sharing and ecumenical engagement."[59]

> Realistic and serious dialogue between groupings of different persuasions is required, as Well as formal opportunities for fellowship and mutual learning between Christian and non-Christian bodies. Caribbean theological formations must seek Christian unity at all levels of the church, as well as Caribbean unity at other levels. The unity of the Christian church and the unity of the human family in the Caribbean cannot be maintained in separate compartments. The emancipation we seek cannot afford to be at the expense of human division and religious bigotry.[60]

Furthermore, Erskine argues that Caribbean theology cannot ignore the world of the Caribbean people in which they struggle to create meaning and to reclaim their humanity. Caribbean theology must consider the sociological context and historical trajectories that shape the Caribbean experience. "As the church in the Caribbean decolonizes theology, it must be willing to put aside a timeless, universal, metaphysical theology and become existential as it seeks to relate to the living history of blackness."[61]

The Call to Reject Foreign Theology

Likewise, in an important chapter book entitled "Method in Caribbean Theology," Jamaican theologian Theresa Lowe-Ching articulates some relevant propositions pertaining to the method, meaning, and message of Caribbean theology. She begins her critical analysis by asserting that American and European imperialist intervention in the Caribbean is fatal and hinders the human spirit in the Caribbean in the search for wholeness and freedom. She denounces colonial powers and missionary Christianity in the Caribbean for equating Christianity with civilization. She advances that the Caribbean people must reject the theology

---

59. Ibid., 92.

60. Ibid.

61. Erskine, *Decolonizing Theology*, 45.

of imposition that was forced upon them by Christian colonialists. Western imperial forces supported by colonial Christianity have denigrated the conquered population and destroyed their collective identity and self-esteem.[62] Lowe-Ching projects that the Caribbean people must not only discard the "European sources" that shaped their theology, social and intellectual life, and Christian practices, they must reclaim the main sources of Caribbean theology, which she lists: "the Bible; the history of Caribbean people; the writing of certain Caribbean sociologists and economists and the history of the Church in the Caribbean and statements of conciliar and ecumenical bodies in the Caribbean."[63] She also lists non-religious but influential Caribbean women, intellectuals, poets, cultural critics, and public intellectuals—e.g., V.S. Naipaul, Bob Marley, Marcus Garvey, Derek Walcott, Walter Rodney—as possible sources for Caribbean theology.

In the Francophone Caribbean, we should also consider Toussaint Louverture, Joseph Antenor Firmin, Jean Price-Mars, Jacques Stephen Alexis, Jacques Roumain, Rene Depestre, Aime Cesaire, Jane Nardal, Paulette Nardal, Frantz Fanon, Edouard Glissant, Maryse Conde, Marie Chauvet, Cleante Desgrave, Annie Desroy, Nadine Magloire, etc., as potential sources for constructing an innovative and meaningful contextual Caribbean theology. These individuals symbolize Caribbean experiences in various ways.[64] Lowe-Ching, however, has failed to consider the African heritage which has substantially defined the Caribbean religious life and cosmology.

Furthermore, Lowe-Ching affirms that Caribbean theology, like its Latin American counterpart, gives preference to orthopraxis; prioritizes preferential option for the poor and the cause of the oppressed and marginalized; aims at uprooting oppressive structures and systems that hold the poor captive; maintains that the Black experience as the hermeneutical base of Caribbean theological conversations and reflections.[65] She advises that Caribbean theologians should rigorously and dynamically engage with other disciplines in the Humanities and concurrently enter in constructive dialogues with social scientists and professionals in other academic fields of knowledge; the advantage of cross-disciplinary

62. Lowe-Ching, "Method in Caribbean Theology," 24–25.

63. Ibid., 25.

64. Ibid., 110.

65. Ibid., 24–25.

engagement is that it will strengthen Caribbean theology and assist Caribbean theologians to creatively reread the Bible and Christian symbols scientifically and from different angles.[66]

Lowe-Ching reiterates a common practice among Caribbean thinkers and Developing World theologians: "The dual challenge confronts Caribbean theologians to not only express their understanding of option for the poor and oppressed in theological categories, but also to engage more seriously in a spirituality of liberation involving actual participation in the struggles of the poor and oppressed."[67] Finally, she infers that a major deficiency of Caribbean theology is the woman question that is Caribbean male theologians have failed to incorporate "the feminist agenda in Caribbean theological reflections."[68]

The matters outlined above are critical in the articulation of black theological anthropology and black theological ethics from the Caribbean context and the global Black Diaspora. We should now explore the ideas of Idris Hamid in the project of reconstructing black personhood and humanity toward a Caribbean theology of emancipation, hope, and decolonization.

Idris Hamid: Toward a More Promising Caribbean Future

First of all, Jesus's solidarity with the poor and the economically-oppressed individuals is Hamid's point of departure for theological inquiry and reflections. Secondly, the Caribbean milieu is critical for his theological development. According to Hamid, in the incarnation, through the person and work of the historical Jesus, God became identified with humanity and took sides by establishing friendship and fellowshipping with the poor, the sick, the disadvantaged, and the underclass.[69] According to Jesus, for anyone to enter the Kingdom of God, he/she "must identity with and the minister to the imprisoned, the naked, the sick, the hungry, (Matt. 25:31–46)—and we may add, the unemployed, the brutalized, the dehumanized . . . To follow Jesus means therefore to identity with the liberating forces and to imitate such forces."[70] Hamid does not believe

66. Ibid., 27.

67. Ibid., 28.

68. Ibid.

69. Hamid, *In Search of New Perspectives*, 3.

70. Ibid.

that Christian salvation is possible unless one deliberately partakes in the life of the poor and the sufferings of the oppressed. If anyone desires to be saved and become Jesus' disciple, he/she must actively involve in the lived-experiences and lived-worlds of disfranchised individuals in society, and intentionally walk in solidarity with them resulting in caring and serving them, and sharing in their sufferings.

For Hamid, the hope of Caribbean theology is decolonization. In other words, decolonization is the departing point to think through black personhood and humanity intellectually and theologically. Decolonization as a project may lead to decolonial praxis and contribute to a life of anti-colonial and anti-imperial practices. Hamid construes the decolonization process of Caribbean societies from the yoke of economic dependence and cultural imperialism of the U.S. A. and European countries as full emancipation. This emancipation encompasses the sphere of the religious experience of the Caribbean people. Hamid suggests that the Caribbean people must search for a new theological orientation and political vision that is based on the historical experiences of the Region and "the future to which God calls us."[71] The Caribbean past has been an exploited past, and the people have been dehumanized and denigrated by various colonial and imperial forces. Slave masters and colonialists have thoroughly robbed Caribbean people of their labor, production, and resources. Western colonialists have undermined African retentions in the Region and denigrated Afro-Caribbean identity and cultural practices. Like the colonialists, Western missionaries have devalued the African-derived religions and spirituality of the Caribbean people. According to Hamid, Western missionaries introduced a God who was "foreign" to the Caribbean religious experience, and that in the religious imagination of the Caribbean people, God is construed as "a benign white foreigner—'an expatriate.'"[72]

This white God has not walked in solidarity with the Caribbean people, has not involved in their history, and has not empathized with them nor shared in their sufferings. European missionaries catechized the Caribbean people to worship God through somebody else's lived-experiences and lived-worlds that is those of the European Christians. To achieve theological emancipation, the Caribbean people must reject the foreign and white God and embrace God who can sympathize with them in their sufferings and shame. A healthy doctrine of God will lead

71. Ibid., 7.
72. Ibid., 8.

to a healthy theological anthropology. The transformation and future of Caribbean societies should be understood in God's love for and promise to the Caribbean people. Hamid seems to imply that God has been silent in the historical plight and sufferings of the enslaved Africans in the Caribbean; as a result, he challenges the Caribbean people to ask God honest, what he has termed "unholy questions" including the following: Where hast Thou been in our history? What meaning can there be to all this—genocide, slavery, indentured labor, poverty, colonialism? Why, Why, Why?"[73] At this point, Hamid puts God on trial to answer the most pressing issue in modernity; the problem of black theodicy in the Caribbean and in the world.

Idris Hamid interprets the interplays between God and the Caribbean people as divine abandonment and black theodicy. According to Hamid, Because God has intentionally distanced himself from the Caribbean experience and the Caribbean people, the Caribbean past

> has been a deculturized past. Hopelessness reigned. We were the ploy of other people's future. We had to peg our future on a beyond for we could find no future here. Ours was an existentialised transcendent future, not a historically imminent one. Our lives and communities were ordered to benefit and stabilize the future of others. While they gained a future, we lost ours . . . In our religious training one is hard put to find any attempt to see God operating in our former cultures and in our Caribbean history.[74]

For Hamid, the question of black theodicy is more than a theological issue. It is an anthropological, a moral issue, eve an existential crisis—considering God's seemingly hiddenness from the Caribbean people in the triumphal era of slavery and colonization. Where was God? Hamid supposes that it is inconceivable to theorize an operative and healthy black theological anthropology and ethics if God is/has been absent in black lives. The clarion call is for God's drastic reintervention in the Caribbean experience leading to renewed hope and radical divine closeness.

The question of Caribbean future is a central characteristic in Hamid's Caribbean theology of emancipation and decolonization. He links Caribbean theology to Caribbean identity in which the Caribbean people is recommended to search for alternative modes of thought, new expressions, new ways to exhibit their self-agency, collective will, and collective

73. Ibid.

74. Ibid., 7.

determination. In Hamid's vantage point, Caribbean perspectives in theology should enrich Christianity in Caribbean societies as a result of critical retrospective on Caribbean anthropology and the Region's historical past. Caribbean theology of emancipation should also contribute to more dynamic Caribbean cultures and human relationships and improve infrastructures and the human condition in Caribbean societies; correspondingly, Caribbean theology should contribute to projects of development in the light of God's promises for the Caribbean people.[75]

In the search for a new theological orientation in the Caribbean landscape, Caribbean theologians should seek to ameliorate the future of humanity in the Region. In order to create an inventive Caribbean theological discourse and orchestrate a more promising Caribbean humanism, the Caribbean people must deconstruct the theology that was imported and integrated in their cultural matrix. In order to be fully emancipated, Hamid puts forth the idea that the Caribbean people must decolonize the "foreign way of life" and the irrelevant theological categories that do not reflect their cultural fabric and native experiences.[76] The emancipation of Caribbean societies will involve a series of radical interventions and progressive actions in the realm of politics, culture, economics, health, ethics, human and social interactions, and the religious life:

> We must break loose and seek one which will not threaten our future creativity. This acceptance of responsibility for our future is far reaching. It goes far beyond responsibility for our political life and the search for new cultural forms. It involves the value system of a new society, the life-styles of our people. It involves rejecting the cultural imperialism and life-styles and values which are now inflicted on us through the printed word and the mass media.[77]

Hamid is persuaded that the role of the Caribbean church in Caribbean societies should be "essentially creative and militant."[78] The next three issues that pertain to the church's civic engagement in Caribbean societies are as follows: development, unemployment, and education. Hamid understands development as the collective work of the Caribbean church and Caribbean government. Development in the context of Caribbean

---

75. Hamid, *Troubling of the Waters*, 4.

76. Ibid., 8.

77. Ibid.

78. Ibid.

societies implies the radical transformation of systems, power relations, human dynamics, and structures that have hindered development and societal reformation, as well as those that have blocked human flourishing. If development entails total change, it must also encompass serious changes in Caribbean churches, Caribbean theology, and the social and political societies in the Region.[79] Effective development in the postcolonial Caribbean societies must engage the field of education with a decolonial outlook. The ultimate goal of education—both secular and theological—in Caribbean societies is to enrich the lives of the Caribbean people, strengthen Caribbean societies, and to contribute to holistic change.

Hamid laments that the (neo-) colonial education in the Caribbean remains most alienating to Caribbean students; he points out two central shortcomings of the education program in the Caribbean.

> First, from the very first day in school the child is confronted with "A for Apple". His Education begins and continues with reference to a point from outside. This education system has been extended to cater for more people, but not transformed to any effective extent to produce suitable people . . . Secondly, it alienates people. One of the ironies of the system is that it purports to train people to be of service, but in acquiring that education it alienates from the people to be served. It is elitist in character.[80]

The education system must be decolonized to reflect the values, attitudes, culture, worldview, and thought-process of the Caribbean people. A decolonized education should give primacy to the native tongues (Creole, Jamaican English) of the Caribbean people as the language of instruction. Caribbean students should cultivate a sense of respect for their primary language as it is often the case for the langue of the colonizer: English, French, Spanish, and Dutch. The Caribbean people must reimagine an alternative source of educational epistemology and pedagogy that is both liberative and sensitive to Caribbean needs. A decolonized education program would consider the achievements of Caribbean men and women in Western civilization and universal civilizations. In the educational curriculum, Caribbean students need to be acquainted with the works or writings of Caribbean heroes and heroines, poets, painters, musicians, thinkers, politicians, inventors, engineers, educators, historians, philosophers, religious figures, etc. Education in the Caribbean must always elevate the

79. Ibid., 18.
80. Ibid., 17.

collective and not the individual; it should also aim at national progress and the common good in Caribbean societies. A decolonized education program in the Caribbean would focus on the nurturing of the Caribbean mind and the nurturing of the Caribbean soul toward both individual progress and collective success; it should promote national consciousness and be community-oriented.

In the case of Caribbean churches, Hamid insists that "The Christian education programme of the churches which emphasizes hard work for individual success as a reward for personal holiness will have to be altered so that "success" is viewed in terms of community service and human development."[81] In other words, Caribbean Christianity must commit itself to the permanent and holistic development of Caribbean societies, and that Christian intervention in the Region is "necessary for development, for social justice and the liberation of our people, even more necessary is the deep thought and theological reflection which enable the Caribbean man [woman] to find his true itself."[82] The decolonial education project in the Caribbean has also a spiritual dimension if it is going to be authentic and comprehensive development.

In the same line of thought, Caribbean societies must reject the capitalist economic model that are characteristic in Western societies and detrimental to the Caribbean life. The new economic model in the Caribbean should seriously consider both the nature of Caribbean societies and the destiny of the Caribbean people. Caribbean economy must give primacy to human relationships and the improvement of people's lives and communities in the Region. According to Hamid,[83] transformative economic activity in the Caribbean must accentuate human commitment to the success of the society; it should incorporate the role of religion in promoting and contributing to a human-centered economic model. Ultimately, the core goal of a successful and effective economic model is to stimulate the good life and better social and human relationships. An economic model that does not use humans as commodity would not also treat work as a commodity to be shared by all people in the Caribbean.

Caribbean economic model must not emulate the free trade model of Western societies that exploits the resources and productions of the working class and the disadvantaged. Similarly, job should not be the

---

81. Hamid, *In Search of New Perspectives*, 17.

82. Hamid, *Troubling of the Waters*, 5.

83. Hamid, *In Search of New Perspectives*, 15.

end of life and relationship; the improvement of human relationship and social interactions should be a directive force for employment. A fair distributive economic system bears considerable implications for equal employment, distributive work, and wealth distribution. Work must be shared among the Caribbean people. In the paragraph below, Hamid provides a practical example on this matter:

> If there is limited work, then it must be shared. This would mean that instead of having three men work full time and one totally unemployed, that work be so distributed that all four men work nine months of the year, with the salaries so adjusted that it would be the same during the "off" period shared by all, to be sued for leisure, rest, hobbies, studies, creative and cultural activities, etc., and catered for bye special services of government.[84]

Finally, education as holistic development and decolonization project lies in a new Caribbean self-understanding, a reexamination, and reinterpretation of Caribbean history and experience in the postcolonial context and era of globalization and neoliberalism.[85] Hamid's political theology forestalls a dynamic and resourceful black theological anthropological and ethics. Hamid sees Caribbean churches as protagonists and agents of these democratic promises.

Kortright Davis: Interrogating Cultural Alienation and Overcoming Cultural Suicide

Similarly, Kortright Davis suggests that the Caribbean Church must become the catalyst and "the social conscience" for Caribbean societies by mobilizing the Caribbean people to organize themselves toward self-determination and self-agency; the role of Christian churches in the Caribbean is to become fully engaged in the Caribbean drama and regional developmental efforts, and to reclaim political sovereignty, cultural renewal, economic dependence, and the unification of Caribbean societies.[86] Davis is convinced that the program of Caribbean emancipation must also "be realized in all its dimensions and structures, not merely as a political or economic objective of history but also as a

84. Ibid., 16.

85. Hamid, *Troubling of the Waters*, 6.

86. Davis, *Emancipation Still Comin'*, 47.

concrete manifestation of the work of a Divine Emancipator. Change and renewal, liberation and maturity."[87]

Davis presents God as the one who has willed the economic success of Caribbean societies; the divine presence in the Caribbean ensures the human partnership and an optimistic future: "The focus on economic growth through imaginative creativity and resourcefulness finds it religious motivation in the fact that God, and in the meaning of God's assured and favored presence in the Caribbean condition."[88] He gives prominence to human self-efficacy and resilience in the Caribbean, and presumes that the Caribbean people will persevere through challenges which will increase the likelihood of development and sustainability. Through the ethic of self-reliance and determination, and through communal collaboration, the Caribbean people will achieve economic dependence and political sovereignty

> Caribbean people need only to match the making of their own 'bread' with their understanding of the making of children as instance of divine-human collaboration; and the theological implications and imperatives for economic growth and creativity, productivity and self-determination will cry out for articulation. The ethical imperative here is clearly the need for moral persistence . . . The emancipatory ethic of persistence is therefore enjoined at this point.[89]

Economic freedom and national sovereignty require moral consistence and resistance to both disruptive internal and external forces. The ethic of moral consistence includes "consistency with local values, realities, and priorities; with long-term goals and objectives; and with the highest ideals of national prestige and human self-esteem. The popular will must insist on such moral consistency instead of the political norms of expediency and the principle of the zigzag."[90] Davis bases his premise about Caribbean future and economic success on the analogy of the consistency of Christ's faithfulness to God; similarly, Christ will be faithful to the Caribbean people. He encourages the Caribbean people to model their self-determination after this Christological motivation.[91] The role

87. Ibid.
88. Ibid., 80.
89. Ibid., 81.
90. Ibid., 82.
91. Ibid.

of Caribbean Christianity and political government is to warn the Caribbean people and ensure that they "are no longer for sale and that their
dues have already been paid, not only by their ancestors in slavery but
also by their brother Jesus-Christ."[92]

Not only economic freedom will enhance black lives in the Caribbean and the Black diaspora, belonging to a community will also
increase the individual's life toward sustainability, sociability, and interdependence. In the previous analysis, we have pointed out that Davis
identified alienation in Caribbean societies as a devastating effect of
colonialism. Davis proposes the African concept of community as a
mechanism to cure the problem of individual and collective alienation.
Observably, the colonial life not only orchestrated cultural alienation, it
also engendered human alienation. Caribbean people came to embrace
Western individualism which challenges the community life, which has
sustained them during the time of slavery. The conundrum of cultural
alienation according to Davis is that it

> encouraged Caribbean people to become mutually contemptuous
> and to accept patterns of self-contempt, sometimes as a means of
> social progress or acceptance by others. That which was foreign
> was good; that which was local was not good. So people were
> alienated from each other inducement. They were also alienated
> from their natural cultural endowment (race, color, language, be-
> lief systems, relationships, entertainment and leisure, work sched-
> ules, family mores, personal aspirations) and from their rightful
> corridors of power, influence, and social classes.[93]

In the same line of thought, Jean Price-Mars in his innovative book,
Ainsi parla l'Oncle (1928), made a similar remark about the Haitian society that it has suffered from "collective bovarisme," a form of cultural
alienation and psychological anomaly that forces the Haitian people to
question the relevance of African cultural values and practices in the
Haitian soil. Haitian cultural alienation as a powerful phenomenon in
the Haitian society makes the Haitian people depreciate their maternal
tongue (Creole) and undermine the African culture of Haitian peasants.
As Davis has remarked, "The imposed forms of alienation have tended to

92. Ibid.
93. Ibid., 83.

decimate the people's communitarian sprit, by pitting neighbor against neighbor and class against class."[94]

To remedy the enigma of cultural alienation in Caribbean societies, it is sufficed for Caribbean people to return to the African system of communal living. Through the community, the Caribbean people would be able to collaboratively create social institutions and communities that are strong and effective, which would respond adequately to the needs of the individual and the community. The community encourages collective solidary and communal life; it also helps maintain an orderly life that promotes full personhood in Caribbean societies. Life in community will enable the Caribbean people to find a common solution to a shared problem and allows them to "participate together in the sociopolitical and cultural processes of the region."[95] Finally, Davis highlights additional benefits of the community that could fortify black personhood and black humanity:

> The virtue of community involves not merely collectivity but, more particularly, the rights and obligations of communicating and sharing; the responsibility to resist fragmentation in all its forms, as a continuing regional crisis; and the need to contribute to the creation of a more wholesome generation of self-affirming, self-accepting, de-alienated young people, whose pride in their heritage would render the return to alienation an impossible dream.[96]

In a similar note, Noel Erskine interprets the African concept of community as the place that enables the individual to become more fully human. Erskine interprets the African concept of community as the place that enables the individual to become more fully human. Nonetheless, in slavery, the African people in the Caribbean were forced "to live outside the indigenous community,"[97] which was detrimental to their collective growth or communal progress.

94. Ibid.
95. Ibid.
96. Ibid.
97. Erskine, *Decolonizing Theology*, 36.

Noel Erskine: The Call to Wholeness and a Harmonious Life in the Caribbean

Erskine conceives the freedom of the individual only within the (collective) experience of and harmony with the community. He asserts that "with this understanding of being-in-community, one ceased to experience a brother or a sister as the limit of one's freedom but, rather, as the possibility through which the search for identity and meaning was [is] more fully realized. Existence-in-relation sums up the pattern of the African way of life."[98]

Consequently, it is through the community the individual develops his agency and it is the community that makes life meaningfully or worth living. Life outside the community is not productive or effective. In the African tradition, to live independently from the community is to defer the success and happiness of the individual. Within the community, suffering and joy are shared collectively, and that men and women become social beings. This idea of African corporate personality insists that

> the individual discovers herself or himself in terms of duties, privileges, and responsibilities to self and peers . . . An important feature of this corporate relationship is the demand on the individual to engage in a lifestyle that will enhance the well-being of the community. One way to achieve this is for the individual to fulfill his or her destiny in the context of the community.[99]

In this way, African anthropology is framed within a theological framework. The life in the community is not only preconditioned by social sanctions; it is also directed by God. It is both God and individual members of the community that mutually shape individual's life in the community. The success and freedom of the individual and the community is determined by both entities. While Erskine deduces black theological anthropological from the African experience as a life of freedom and sustainability in the community, he reads black theology from the Caribbean context as the pursuit of freedom and hope, and social transformation.

Like Hamid, Erskine sustains the idea that while the task of Caribbean theology should include the promotion of social change, optimism, and freedom in Caribbean societies, it "must guard against imports . . .

98. Ibid.
99. Ibid.

[because] an imported theology would not be able to address this need with specificity and clarity."[100] Hence, Caribbean theology reflects both the historical experience and existential struggle of the Caribbean people towards radical change, emancipation, decolonization, self-agency, and disalienation.

A major characteristic of Caribbean theology Erskine suggests is hope. Caribbean theology projects the idea of redemptive hope but denounces all sources of human oppression. In Erskine, Caribbean theology seeks to establish the dynamics between hope and freedom. When one hopes in God the Liberator, freedom becomes the vision of this liberating trust because God himself is the ground of human hope and freedom; he will not disappoint the oppressed and poor who take refuge in him. The freedom of God is a radical critique of the society and a confrontation of people who have the power and influence to create systems and structures of oppression and subjugation. Hope firmly rooted in the freedom of God provides satisfying optimism in the most hopeless human situation. Jesus has shown himself to be the Protagonist of hope and the paramount Agent of human freedom; his testimony to John the Baptist substantiates this claim: "The blind receive their sight and the lame walk, lepers are cleansed and the deaf hear, and the dead are raised up, and the poor have good news preached to them" (Matthew 11:5).

Erskine, who pronounces a Caribbean theology of hope and freedom, claims that hope is not only one of the most prized aspects of Christian theology; Christian optimism reveals an intrinsic divine attribute.

> This question is central to Christian theology because, if hope does not mean struggle for freedom in history, then it is the opium of the oppressed. For Christian theology to talk about hope without relating it to the struggle of the oppressed for freedom in history is for it tacitly to sanction the structures oppressions, which deprive the oppressed of their dignity. To hope, then, is not merely to plan the future. Hope is more than anticipation of freedom. It gives both form and content to human freedom.[101]

Hope is situational and contextual. By nature, it is a reactionary human emotion to certain forces or phenomena—both internal and external. Suggestively, we should understand Caribbean theology of hope as a reactionary and corrective theology to the insufficiency of colonial

100. Ibid., 118.
101. Ibid., 118–19.

theology that failed to portray God as the Emancipator of African slaves. Another equally valid problem is that missionary Christianity in the Caribbean has also failed to denounce the bondage of slavery and to establish the rapport between divine freedom and human hope in slavery. Rather, colonial Christianity approved of the institution of slavery and the colonial order, and their cruel structures and systems of domination in the Caribbean landscape.

In addition, Erskine has posited that the contemporary Caribbean church, entangled with neocolonial mentality and practices, often neglects its role as a liberating force in Caribbean societies and belittles its own responsibility "to slums and shanty towns, which destroy black family deny children their future. The inaction and unconcern of the church is due to its failure to discern God's liberating work in the word of human bondage."[102] In contemporary Caribbean societies, Caribbean churches can no longer disregard its social setting, the unfavorable human condition of the Caribbean poor and disfranchised families, as well as the Caribbean experience which continues to shape its content, message, and rhetoric.

Furthermore, Erskine sees continuity between his Caribbean theology of hope and freedom with the rhetorical language and theological vision of the historic meeting of the Second General Assembly of the Caribbean Conference of Churches, held in Guyana in 1977, in which Caribbean ecclesiastical leaders and theologians declared that "God is the basis of human rights and freedom for black people;"[103] together, they affirmed their conviction about the significance of upholding Human rights in the Caribbean:

> In our journey of struggle for rights through self-reliance, we resolve that our rights nature have their foundation in our God and in his faithfulness. And while this might be a difficult principle to uphold in a characteristically cynical, scientific age, with not many dramatic examples of "the God who went before his people, winning their battles and demanding justice for them," there is a latent and indefatigable confidence that he sees "our condition" and "struggles" with us in our determination to change the present order.[104]

102. Ibid., 119.
103. Ibid., 120.
104. Ibid.

Because the Caribbean people are also created in the *imago dei,* they are eligible to live freely and have conclusive human rights. God's decisive execution to endow sustaining breath and life upon the people in the Caribbean is linked to his "commitment to the ordering of a new society" in the Caribbean.[105] Caribbean theology is premised on the possibility of an alternative future and emancipative society in the Caribbean because it is the will of God. Caribbean theology is an enterprise that involves the collaborative partnership between God and the Caribbean people as artisans of new historical trajectories and agents of transformation and emancipative future in the Region. Toward the goal in engineering this new Caribbean community and Caribbean humanism, Erskine accentuates the responsibility and contributions of Caribbean Christians and churches to challenge and reject the current social order characterized by unequal distribution of wealth, abject poverty, hunger, political conflict, economic dependence, imperial domination, and the conflict between social classes. However, he ascertains that God's dedication to social equality and justice, and humanization in the Caribbean is deliberate, transformative, and intentional.

> God's freedom ensures the determination to realize his justice in
> the world. With divine freedom as the basis of human freedom,
> Caribbean Christians affirm the Kingdom of God as the kingdom
> of free humanity. The understanding that the Kingdom of God
> has everything to do with the social and political responsibility
> of Christians in the world is upheld by Caribbean Christians.[106]

From Erskine's perspective, a Caribbean theology of freedom and hope must incorporate the hope of decolonization and the logic of decoloniality. Like Hamid, he deduces that a shortcoming of colonial theology is that a link was not forged between saving black souls and redeeming black bodies; colonial theology deliberately divorced the economic productions by enslaved Africans and their material or physical needs to be economically self-sustained. Colonial theology upheld a false consciousness between the spiritual need and the bodily need, the heavenly realm and the earthly realm; such pseudo theological discourse maintained the idea that "While the soul belonged to God, the body belonged to the master."[107] In other words, the African slave planted, the master reaped;

105. Ibid.
106. Ibid.
107. Ibid.

the slave produced, the master consumed the production. Consequently, Erskine could assign two central characteristics of the decolonization (theological) project: spiritual and political, an important feature in Aristide's political theology.

> The decolonization of theology would require "a form of spiritual rebirth and not merely an external political process. It connotes change in the relationship between peoples resulting from a transformation." For the dominated people, that would mean a consciousness of their own status as human beings, their strength to bring an end to their domination and subjugation; their ability to decide on the quality and direction of their future." The call, then, is to affirm that to be Christian is to be free and that to be free for the Kingdom of God is to be Christian. To be Christian is to be human, because the locus of freedom is the Kingdom of God.[108]

From the viewpoint of Caribbean political theology and Caribbean theology of decolonization, the purpose of the kingdom of God relates to the project of radical humanization of the oppressed and outcast, and the incontestable proclamation of their emancipation, which necessitates the freedom of the mind, socio-economic freedom, and political freedom. The program of a theology of decolonization converged with a Caribbean theology of hope and freedom anticipates the social and political activism of followers of Christ as a way to effectuate (or share) the values and benefits of the Kingdom of God in Caribbean societies. Human agency is paramount in this decolonial project as it aims at deracinating zones and sources of domination and subjugation. In a nutshell, Caribbean theology is a discourse that champions the democratic life and the ethics of human interconnectedness, two central features of Jean-Bertrand Aristide's political theology.

Aristide: A Theology of Democracy and Cultural Renewal

It is in this framework that Aristide in his new book *Haiti-Haitii? Philosophical Reflections for Mental Decolonization* and his doctoral dissertation—"Umoya Wamagama (The Spirit of the Word)" (2016)—completed at the University of South Africa, made a clarion call for the mental and ideological decolonization of the Haitian psyche, as well as for the

108. Ibid.

de-Westernization of Haitian culture and worldview. The history of the Haitian and Caribbean people has been marked by colonial domination and subjugation, imperial hegemony, and alienation and humiliation.

Aristide's theology can be characterized as Caribbean, postcolonial, liberative, and indigenous. Like Erskine, he has called to link Haitian cultural practices and traditions to their African roots, making his work in close conversation with African theology that affirms African cultural identity and the relevance of indigenous way of life for doing contextual African theology and creative postcolonial practice, within the African worldview and context. Drawing on indigenous culture's focus on solidarity and reciprocity, Aristide called for an ethic of solidarity that can inspire popular economics and social development and transformation. Like Davis, in his theo-political discourse, he champions the causes of the poor and the idea that the poor and oppressed of the world should achieve a life of emancipation and shalom. He is also aware of the imperial and neocolonial exploitation of the Caribbean region, and the common history of suffering and slavery the people of Haiti and the Caribbean share.

> Sisters and brothers of Jamaica, Barbardos, Trinidad, Cuba, the Dominican Republic, Guadeloupe, Martinique: our past struggle colonialism has led us inevitably toward the establishment of deeper ties in the course of our long march toward the democratic table. A new social contract at the Caribbean, Latin American and international level is clearly necessary for us to join together one day, all of us, around the democratic table.[109]

On one hand, Aristide's urgent demand for regional solidarity against future unwarranted political and economic interventions of American and European forces in the Caribbean demonstrates his collaborate spirit to create a new alternative future for the people in the Caribbean. On the other hand, he articulates the necessity to foster new forms of international solidarity and alliance in the process to resist the lure of American and Western economic capitalism and neoliberalism. As Noel Erskine reiterates:

> The Caribbean falls within the ambit of Third World countries and as such shares a common history with these countries—a common history in which the European search for expansion of empire and religious freedom brought Third World countries under political, economic, cultural, and religious

109. Aristide, *Aristide*, 202.

domination by European people. The European zeal to "Christianize" and "civilize" the world often provided a rationale for Third World Oppression.[110]

Aristide's democratic vision, framed within the discourse of political theology, is a direct repudiation of absolutism, totalitarianism, and imperialism. It is within these wide-ranging and transnational contexts one must also investigate the development of Aristide's political theology. Theology is always born out of a particular social reality and cultural context. Aristide's theological discourse and framework is primarily located within the *Sitz im Leben* of his native land. Aristide's theology must also be discussed in relation to wider Caribbean theological discourse. Yet, his politico-theological articulation must be seen within the tradition of liberation theologies and freedom movements, as well as the struggles of oppressed nations, peoples, and "minority races" and "ethnic groups" to resist Western epistemic and cultural hegemony, colonial imperialism, White supremacy, and the politics of globalization and theory of economic dependence.

In an important passage, Argentinian philosopher of Enrique Dussel (2013) in his groundbreaking and interdisciplinary work *Ethics of Liberation in the Age of Globalization and Exclusion* describes in specific term how Western domination and Eurocentrism works closely:

> In the context of modernity, the European variant of ethnocentrism was the first 'global' ethnocentrism (Eurocentrism has been the only global ethnocentrism thus far known in history: with it, universality and European identity became fused into one; philosophy must be liberated from this reductionist fallacy). Under such circumstances, when the philosopher belongs to a hegemonic system (be it Greek, Byzantine, Islamic, or medieval Christian, and particularly in the modern period), his or her world or ethical system has the claim of presenting itself as if it were equivalent to or identical with the epitome of the human 'world'; while the world of the Others is that of barbarity, marginality, and nonbeing.[111]

On the other hand, Western civilization has made remarkable contributions to the histories of cultures and civilizations of the modern world. Mignolo cautions that "But, it by no means should be taken as the point of

110. Erskine, *Decolonizing Theology*, 2.

111. Dussel, *Ethics of Liberation*, 41.

arrival of human existence on the planet . . . The fact that Western civilization was the most recent civilization in human history doesn't mean that it was the best, that the rest of the world should follow suit."[112] Black Lives in the Caribbean equally matter, as those in other worlds. As pointed out in the above analysis, the humanity and dignity of black people in the theological works examined symbolize a point of commonality and consensus between the four designated interlocutors.

The connections between Aristide and the works of the Caribbean theologians and thinkers named above are numerous. For example, like Hamid, Erskine, and Davis, Aristide's political theology is orthopraxis that calls for cultural renewal, sustainability, better education system and economic progress in the Caribbean region. It is a public theology that seeks to resist cultural alienation and simultaneously is concerned with the welfare and emancipation of the Haitian people and those living in the margins of society. Emancipation is anticipated from economic independence and political dictatorship. Aristide seeks to foster a decolonization of the mind in the Haitian society by rejecting the vestiges of colonialism in the Haitian society. Caribbean theology argues for a fair and equal distribution of wealth and job access in the Region.

Aristide's theology is simultaneously, anti-colonial, anti-imperial, postcolonial, and decolonial. Aristide's political theology addresses the pressing needs of the Haitian society such as free access to public education, the eradication of poverty and hunger, and free healthcare for all Haitians. As Aristide points out Haiti is a country where "85 percent of the population, crushed under the weight of economic violence, is still illiterate: illiterates who are not animals."[113] Aristide, however, is very optimistic that together we can help

> these victims to read . . . You who are our friends, do not be observers. Be actors, inasmuch as you are citizens of the world. Together, let us participate in a campaign for literacy. . . . All cooperation at this level testifies to a willingness to struggle against economic violence through active nonviolence."[114]

In the language above, Aristide demonstrates both the necessity of regional and international solidarity and alliance to find a common solution for Haiti's economic woes and educational crisis. Another common issue

112. Mignolo, *Darker Side*, xiv.
113. Aristide, *Aristide*, 198.
114. Ibid., 198–99.

that threatens the human condition in the Caribbean is cultural alienation and imitation, which Hamid, Davis, and Kortright brought to surface. Aristide's ninth commandment of democracy, which insists on "fidelity to our culture," should be understood as a campaign against the tragedy of cultural alienation and imitation of foreign habits in Caribbean societies. He pleads that the people of Haiti and the Caribbean must resistance cultural alienation which will guarantee "the psychological health of the democratic issue. In fact, every kind of cultural suicide results in deviance in the social body and inevitably threatens the democratic cells."[115] For Aristide, in order for the people to create the democratic life, they must reject cultural alienation. He insists that the democratic life demands for the people to preserve their own cultural traditions and practices because "To live, and to live fully, also means nourishing oneself at the sources of one's culture; it means plunging the roots of being into those sources . . . No truly deep change can be accomplished democratically without an articulation of the indigenous values that are closely linked with any genuine socio-cultural fabric."[116]

Comparatively, like Davis, Aristide emphasizes the role of the Haitian church as harbinger of hope and freedom in the Haitian society to work collaboratively with the Haitian government and the private sector to increase employment opportunities and improve Haiti's infrastructures problems. His democratic vision coincides with the politico-theological program and the pressing needs the above theologians carefully discussed in our previous analysis.

In a speech delivered at the General Assembly of the United States in New York in September 25, 1991, Aristide articulated ten propositions which he christened "the ten commandments of democracy," which transcend territorial and geo-political locations and zones and the politics of the nation-states.

1. The first commandment of democracy: liberty or death.

2. The second commandment of democracy: democracy or death.

3. The third commandment of democracy: fidelity to human rights.

4. The fourth commandment of democracy: the right to eat and to work.

115. Ibid., 200.
116. Ibid., 200–201.

5. The fifth commandment of democracy: the right to demand what rightfully belongs to us.

6. The sixth commandment of democracy: legitimate defense of the diaspora, or tenth department.

7. Seventh commandment of democracy: No to violence, yes to Lavalas.

8. The eight commandment of democracy: fidelity to the human being, the highest form of wealth.

9. The ninth commandment of democracy: fidelity to our culture.

10. The tenth commandment of democracy everyone around the same table.[117]

Aristide's democratic vision consists of an amalgam of various traditions: the Haitian Revolution (commandments one, two, and three), Judeo-Christian Tradition (commandments three, four, and eight), universal Catholic Social Teaching (commandments three, four, eight, and nine), African communism (commandments five, nine, and ten), and Western Democratic Tradition (commandments three, five, and ten). Aristide informs the international audience that his democratic program emerged from the democratic praxis of his administration. The first two commandments of democracy are grounded on the radical rhetoric and activism of the Haitian Revolution in which Haitian revolutionaries and the maroon communities at Saint-Domingue Haiti made a decisive commitment to each other to live free, independent, and as abolitionists.

The collective pledge of the African slaves at Saint-Domingue-Haiti to live free then to live under the hell and horrors of slavery began in Africa when African anti-slavery revolutionaries fought valiantly against European slave merchants to stop the slave trade. This commitment was renewed with Makandal, a radical religious leader and freedom fighter, who in collaboration with other slaves, in 1757, poisoned 6,000 white oppressors in the colony. As a charismatic leader, Makandal inculcated a sense of communal solidarity among the slaves in their struggle to fight colonial oppression. He also developed an extensive cross-plantation network of resistance and mobilized the enslaved population toward cathartic violence, decolonization, independence, and abolitionism.[118] In this manner, the

117. Ibid., 189–205.

118. For further analysis on this topic, see Joseph, "Prophetic Religion, Violence,

Haitian Revolution is historically and should be understood as a Makandalian revolution that predates the French Revolution of 1789.

Thirty-four years after Macandal's violent death by colonial oppressors, Dutty Boukman, his successor would continue the same vision and talk about freedom in a comparable manner.

The religion of the slaves and Makandal's preaching independence as a theological conviction strategically helped to unite Saint-Dominguan slave population against slave masters and the institution of slavery.[119] As his project of black liberation and decolonial imagination through cathartic violence will be carried out by another influential religious leader, Dutty Boukman, Makandal's rhetoric of reversal of slavery and the colonial system in Saint-Domingue-Haiti would foster a spirit of liberation and a spirit of resistance in the new generation of black revolutionaries who had sworn to declare their humanity and reclaim their human rights.[120] Boukman's clarion call for "liberty or death" was brazenly announced in the night of August 22, 1791 in which he summoned the mobilized enslaved population to

> throw away the symbol of the god of the whites
> who has so often caused us to weep,
> and listen to the voice of liberty,
> which speaks in the hearts of us all.[121]

Furthermore, the motto for "liberty or death" was expressed through various means of collective resistance against the unholy trinity of slavery, colonial imperialism, and white supremacy in the French colony of Saint-Domingue. For many enslaved Africans in the colony, the process of marronage was parallel with the very idea of freedom, in which they became the author of their own freedom, a practical liberty "from below." The desire for freedom was central to slaves' daily experience and marronage provides that catalyst. Freedom in the sense of independence and the eradication of the institution of slavery has always been the expression of the enslaved in the colony. Slaves at Saint-Domingue manifested the aspiration for freedom in various forms of resistance to slavery including marronage, infanticide, consistent slave

---

and Black Freedom."

119. See, for example, Joseph, "The Rhetoric of Prayer."

120. Joseph, "Prophetic Religion, Violence, and Black Freedom," 29–30.

121. See Joseph, "The Rhetoric of Prayer."

insurrections, religious superstition or sorcery, on -going abortions among slave women; slave committing suicide in large numbers, slave nurses poisoning newly-born babies; slaves poisoning their masters and their children, and the decimation of livestock by deliberate sabotage.[122] The Haitian Revolution was the most democratic revolution in the Western world. It is the roots of the declaration of human rights and the basis of universal emancipation in the West.

In the third commandment, Aristide reiterates the promise of the Haitian Revolution in which human rights are projected as the most sacred rights that should be defended and preserved by the community of faith and by laws. The third commandment of democracy is premised on the dignity and equality of every human person, and as Aristide has categorically declared, "Every human being is a person." For Aristide, "fidelity to human rights"[123] simply means not only the protection of those inalienable rights to life, liberty, and the pursuit of happiness, as the Universal Declaration of Human Rights and American Constitution put it; the third commandment of democracy makes a clarion call to legally guarantee those indefeasible rights, so individuals could live in a socially-and, economically-free, and politically- self-governing nation-state. Fidelity to human rights is a tremendous responsibility that involves the sacrifice and collaboration of the individual, the collective, and the nation-state to ensure that human rights are always respected, maintained, and not violated. The premise of the third commandment of democracy categorically affirms that every person has rights and duties towards one another and toward the common good, a better democratic social order, and on-going human flourishing.

The fourth commandment of democracy enunciates Aristide's social justice project and his anti-economic capitalism and globalization philosophy. The fundamental democratic right applicable to every person is the irrevocable right to eat. Developed countries not only regulate the international market, the free trade enterprise, worldwide food distribution, and the (means of) production and resources of international workers from developing nations; their hegemonic control over the free trade economy incorporates access to employment, job distribution, and salaried employees transcends their own geo-political spaces. International workers and the working class become the victims of the politics

122. James, *The Black Jacobins*, 4–20; Joseph, "Prophetic Religion, Violence, and Black Freedom," 7.

123. Aristide, *Aristide*, 192–93.

of economic capitalism and globalization. For example, "In Haiti, the victims have difficulty eating because they themselves are being eaten by the international axes of exploitation."[124] Aristide declares elsewhere that

> We are not against trade, we are not against free trade, but our fear is that the global market intends to annihilate our market. We will be pushed to the cities, to eat food grown on factory farms in distant countries, food whose price depends on the daily number game of the first market . . . We are still moving from misery to poverty with dignity . . . The dilemma is, I believe, the classic dilemma of the poor; a choice between death and death.[125]

In other words, global suffering and global poverty have their roots in unequal distribution of wealth and a lack of (international) social justice. The existential conundrum is never about food or the lack of food for everyone. The underlying thesis of the fourth commandments maintains that "the hunger of one person is the hunger of humanity itself."[126] The increase in food distribution and employment opportunities worldwide will warrant the promise of democratic justice and international collaboration to alleviate poverty, hunger, and human suffering in the word. Thousands of people die daily simply because of hunger and poverty and regulated oppressive systems and structures that hinder free access to eat and work for everyone are "causative demons and woes" to this international crisis.

Finally, Aristide's fourth commandment of democracy alludes to the biblical and theological mandate to care for the poor, the laborer, the stranger and the economically-disadvantaged. This particular commandment and commandments eight and ten have strong biblical and theological antecedents in the Judeo-Christian ethics and anthropology, and social justice project. The author of Proverbs gives a fair warning, "Whoever oppresses a poor man insults his Maker, but he who is generous to the needy honors him" (Proverbs 14:1). To humiliate the poor and exploit the labor and resources of those with dire material needs is to scorn God himself. To act in such an ungodly manner toward the poor and oppressed is to ignore the biblical mandate to treat all people with care, dignity, and respect. When one honors the poor, God is honored;

---

124. Aristide, *Théologie et politique*, 193.

125. Aristide, *Eyes of the Heart*, 10, 13, 16.

126. Aristide, *Aristide*, 194.

when one mistreats the needy, the immigrant, the orphan, and the widow, God is mistreated. This verse in Proverb prioritizes the material needs of the poor, while not undermining their spiritual needs. To give preference to the poor and the needy is to have a God-entranced worldview, and to celebrate the supremacy of God in all things.

In addition, the same author of Proverbs insists, "Whoever has a bountiful eye will be blessed, for he shares his bread with the poor" (Proverbs 22:9). From a biblical perspective, one is counted "blessed" and "happy" because he prioritizes the material needs of the poor and does not withhold his goods from him. Comparatively, the author of Leviticus draws a parallel between the poor and the stranger/immigrant, "When a stranger sojourn with you in your land, you shall not do him wrong" (Lev 19:33). The idea here is to treat both the poor and the immigrant with dignity, because it is simply the will of God. The love for the immigrant and the needy is predicated upon one's love, and affection for God: "You shall treat the stranger who sojourns with you as the native among you, and you shall love him as yourself . . . I am the LORD your God" (Lev 19:34). One's spiritual devotion to God is displayed in one's treatment of the poor, the needy, and the stranger/immigrant among us.

The concept of caring hospitality and generous relationality, and exceptional love toward the immigrant, the needy, and the poor is rooted in God's idea of inclusive justice and God's generous lovingkindness toward all people. It is more pronounced in Deuteronomy. "For the Lord your God is God of gods and Lord of lords, the great, the mighty, and the awesome God, who is not partial and takes no bribe. He executes justice for the fatherless and the widow, and loves the sojourner, giving him food and clothing. Love the sojourner, therefore . . . (Deut 10:18–19). Finally, in chapter 5, we will allude to African communal system and cosmology to establish linkages and parallels with Aristide's ninth commandment of democracy. Correspondingly, in chapter 6, we will make connections between Aristide's theology of Ubuntu and his tenth commandment of democracy.

Conclusion

Evidently, Aristide's ten theses on democracy are connected to Black and Caribbean political theology of development and emancipation. In the work of Benjamin Mays, he associates the notion of development with the work of democracy both in the American society and American

Christianity. The other Caribbean thinkers examined in the chapter interpreted the problem of (under) development in the Caribbean Region primarily as a result of the colonial legacy, the institution of slavery, and American-European economic imperialism and globalization. The fundamental crisis here is how to use theology as a mechanism or tool of analysis to foster hope in the midst of despair, and to give life in the midst of social and existential death, and economic violence. One should always remember that "All thoughts about God and being human reveal the limited autobiography of the thinker and, consequently, invite discussion with other particular reflections on theological anthropology."[127]

The relevance of Caribbean theology of emancipation and decolonization relates to the black condition and experience in the world without undermining the suffering and predicament of the brown people across the globe. These connections have been drawn for many reasons, as outlined below:

> First, the geographical proximity (Cultural proximity in regard to Africa) of the Caribbean and the United States is significant in terms of social development. Second, during slavery black people were often taken from the Caribbean islands to the United States; as they came they brought important elements for black American culture. Finally, and perhaps most importantly, black people in the Caribbean and the United States share a common experience, which may be characterized as the search for freedom in history.[128]

In addition, a pivotal shared historical moment between Caribbean religious experience and the greater Black Diaspora in religion pertains to "the experience of faith as it was fashioned during slavery. This experience was one in which much exchange took place between Caribbean and black American peoples."[129] Black perspectives on theology from the Caribbean, Black America (U.S.A.), and Africa, as well as developing countries have many convergences and confluences; we should also be aware of their differences. Yet, the ultimate goal is to use theology, with other human resources, as a tool of analysis to achieve shalom, decolonization, and emancipation from any form of human

---

127. Hopkins, *Being Human*, 2.

128. Ibid.

129. Ibid.

oppression and subjectivity. Caribbean theology is a theology that promotes human flourishing.

Finally, we should remember that the Cross of Christ is not a symbol of European conquest and hegemonic domination in the world; rather, the cross tells the devastating story of a sacrificial death and gift, and the transformative and redemptive love of God in Christ for the world and on behalf of all people. First, the God of the slave masters and European colonialists is not the true God of the Bible nor the God whose preferential option is for the poor and oppressed. The Biblical God is a God of love, freedom, and justice. God's ultimate desire for every individual is to experience freedom, peace, and love—in relationship with him and in relationship with each other. Second, the Jesus of the slave masters and European colonialists is not the real Christ nor the biblical Jesus. While "Christ" means "the anointed one" or "messiah," the Christ was a historical person the same was Jesus was a historical figure. Interestingly, both early and contemporary Christians believe that "Jesus was/is the Christ/Messiah." Third, colonial Christianity is a false religion and not true or biblical Christianity. Colonial Christianity enslaved people and did not liberate them from oppression and the labyrinth of slavery. Colonial Christianity was an oppressive religion that failed to promote equality, justice, human dignity, reconciliation, and shalom. Fourth, Christianity as a religion was misused to enslave, subjugate, and colonize African slaves and other colonial subjects. One should not equate the use of a religion as a tool or instrument with the essence and teaching of that religion. Any system or institution could use any religion to carry out any desirable goals or intended objectives. This principle also applies to the misapplication of the name of God and the name of Jesus.

Therefore, it is a logical fallacy to state that black people in the African Diaspora, whose African ancestors have been victims of colonial Christianity and Christianity of the slavers, should not become Christians or worship the God of their ancestors' masters. Black Christians do not worship a "dead Messiah," but one who is living and has conquered death on the third day. Correspondingly, Black Christians do not follow a "blind faith," but one that is grounded both in faith and reason, what many thinkers have phrased "reasonable faith." Finally, one should separate the cultural construction of Christianity and biblical Christianity; in the same vein, one should not equate the cultural construction of the person and deeds of Jesus Christ in Western societies and history of thought with the biblical and Palestinian Jewish brown-skinned male named Yeshua.

6

Democracy in Black

Democratizing American Christianity
and Christianizing the People in the Church:
Benjamin E. Mays on Christian Public Witness
and Civic Engagement

Introduction

AS EXAMINED IN THE previous chapters, colonial Christianity and cultural
Christianity in the time of slavery have caused tremendous human pain
and horror in the African and diasporic experience. The historic misuse
of Christianity by slave masters, colonialists, and agents of American and
European imperialism has contributed to the underdevelopment of Africa and the economic regress of black-populated countries like Haiti and
Jamaica or anywhere in the darker nations where Christianity was used
as a vehicle of colonization, neo-colonization, and imperialism. Similarly,
in the American context, white theologians, racists, and Christians who
championed racial segregation in public spaces and ecclesiastical meetings have deployed the Christian faith as a resource to dehumanize black
people and withhold from them the benefits and promises of American

democracy. Consequently, one can infer that the witness of Christianity in the public sphere in the American society has been the antithesis of the liberative message and teachings of Jesus and a dishonor to the biblical theology of the fatherhood of God and the brotherhood of man.

Arguably, one of the cultural trends in contemporary American culture is the puzzling relationship between the message of Christianity and the American society. In other words, the matter pertains to the public witness and civic engagement of Christianity in both America's civil and political societies. Hence, this chapter investigates the relationship between faith and society in the politico-theology and social ethic of Benjamin E Mays. Mays was a fierce critic of American democracy and the practice of racial segregation in public spaces and Christian churches; he was also a fervent critic of the anti-black racism culture and the indisposition of white Christians to use their power and influence to transform the political landscape and cultural dynamics toward the welfare of the African American population.

Through a close reading of the politico-theological and ethical writings of Benjamin E. Mays, this chapter argues that American Christianity must be democratized before it could be deployed as an empowering resource to the triumph of democracy and an unstoppable force of human flourishing in society. As Mays had argued, the second part of this thesis advances the idea that the democratization project is grounded on two central and interrelated propositions: the democratization of the American society and the Christianization of the American culture. The chapter suggests that with the same passion activists in this culture are pushing the government to act democratically in respect to the human rights and dignity of America's racialized and marginalized populations, Mays contended that individuals should use the same energy and enthusiasm to compel the people in the church to become Christian, democratic, and to live out the liberative and redemptive teachings of Jesus Christ.

Benjamin E. Mays was a prominent public Christian theologian, educator, civil rights activist, and the mentor to Dr. Rev. Martin Luther King, Jr. Mays was the first African American to receive a PhD in Theology in 1935, from the University of Chicago. He served as the Dean of the School of Theology at Howard Divinity School, from 1934 to 1940, and President of Morehouse College, from 1940 to 1967. Both his friends and enemies know him as one of the most illustrious critics of anti-black racism, racial segregation, and the denial of constitutional rights to the black population. As a Christian theologian and ordained minister, he used the resources of Christianity to campaign against racial segregation, to demand rights and racial justice on behalf of African Americans, and to promote interracial peace, reconciliation, and unity. It is within this context Mays defined the Christian message as public witness and that Christianity has the most promising resources to lead the American society to strong leadership and triumphant democracy. In many of his writings, Mays associated the ideals and virtues of Christian citizenry with the ideals and virtues of American democracy. For him, the role of Christianity in society is inevitable and integral to the clarion call of Christians to civic engagement and responsibility.

The chapter is divided in three major parts: the problem with American democracy, the problem with American Christianity, and Constructing a democratic America and prophetic Church. The chapter will then proceed to analyze Mays's propositions to construct a democratic order in the United States. Second, it assesses Mays's (politico-theological) regarding the rapport between American Christianity and American democracy in hope that the American churches could genuinely embody a truly missional and democratic faith that is parallel to democratic principles and faithful to the teachings of Jesus Christ. Mays's work is very relevant to the pressing issues confronting contemporary American Christianity in the age of Donald Trump. For example, contemporary American Christians and Evangelicals have sided with the power structure and political hierarchy of this country, which often counters the social vision and emancipative promises of Biblical Christianity toward the betterment of society and the welfare of the downgraded and poor populations, especially the economically-disadvantaged and politically marginalized black and brown people. Mays believed that American Christianity was a major problem to American democracy and human flourishing. Therefore, he summoned the people of the Church to become "Christian" and good American "citizens."

Finally, the chapter will consider Mays's courageous and an unapologetic claim that the Christian Church in America should "Christianize" America and be a "prophetic church," rendering the American society as truly democratic and Christian. Mays did not find the democratic principles embedded in the U.S. Constitution and Bill of Rights sufficient and adequate to respond to pressing contradictions and pressing needs of society. His conviction is very appropriate and relevant for today's American Evangelicalism, Christian Churches as Christianity is progressively declining in the American society, and the American people are leaning more toward the secularist worldview. Mays was convinced that Christianity was the most powerful tool and embodied hope to build an effective democracy in America and to contribute to the common good and human flourishing.

The Problem with American Democracy

In June 8, 1945, Benjamin E. Mays delivered the Commencement Address at Howard University, in which he discussed the crisis of American democracy in relation to the role of Christianity in society. In this address, he made a compelling case for the democratization of America's institutions and Christian practices. This address is very important for us to understand Mays's critique of both American democracy and American Christianity. The central problems in American democracy relate to America's economic structure and America's religious pattern of life.[1] The pivotal problem with American democracy, according to Mays's interpretation, is the idea that the American government has never "deliberately planned to make our democracy function effectively."[2] Mays added that those in seats of political power and influence "have never been excited about a democracy for all the people;"[3] correspondingly, the American democracy has not been extended fully to radically change the living and economic conditions and destiny of African Americans. Mays highlighted seven major areas in the American society wherein democracy was lacking and not fully embedded: the sphere of education, employment opportunities, health care, peacemaking, interracial relations, foreign policy and relations, public housing, social justice issues.

Mays projected the potentiality of the American political system and the democratic ideals embedded in the U.S. Constitution and the Bill of Rights to contribute to a more perfect union, a democratic future, and a more promising life for all people. Mays posited that fascist methods contradict the methods and aims of democracy, as the German and Russian political powers in the first half of the twentieth-century, incorporated fascism, rejected democratic ideals, and denied the rights and will of the Jewish people leading to the death of millions of individuals.[4] Mays

1. Mays, "Democratizing and Christianizing America," 527.
2. Ibid., 528.
3. Ibid.
4. Ibid.

clarified that democratic ideas must embed in the will, the objectives, and the purposes of the American government and public policies. He noted, "If a democratic government really wanted its democracy to function more perfectly, it would find ways and means within the democratic framework to make it function more perfectly."[5] For Mays, the lack of democracy was a structural problem in America's political system. On the other hand, Mays rejected the revolutionary power of violence as a human strategy to bring about the democratic order and process. For example, while he endorsed the freedom struggle of activists of the Black power movement, he rejected violent strategies associated with Black Power and Black Consciousness movements. Being influenced by the Ghandian non-violent philosophy and peacemaking Christian theology, Mays explored alternative options and promising possibilities to introduce radical transformation in social and race relations and religious fellowship between individuals in the American culture.

In Mays's era, racial segregation in public spaces and Christian meetings was legislated. Segregation not only interfered in all of the areas and places named above, segregation altered social relationships, affected the possibility to cultivate interracial friendship, delayed intellectual growth and social progress, and hindered democratic advancement. For example, in the area of public education, Mays inferred that the educational standard of the Southern Region of the United States was below the national average. He correlated the country's economic problem to the educational deficiencies of the Southern states. In his biography on Mays, historian Maurice Jelks discussed the importance of Mays's democratic ethic and philosophy of education:

> For Mays, it was not enough for an educated individual to serve his own needs; education was a privilege requiring that an individual serve others. Being truly educated, he believed, meant that one should practice altruism and self-sacrifice . . . Self-satisfaction was always disastrous. Easy contentment never brought out the best in a person or lead to high achievement . . . He emphasized the goal of education was to instill in a people an appreciation for different philosophical and cultural values as they shaped their own lives [and] and "an appreciation for all values and all knowledge."[6]

5. Ibid., 528–29.
6. Jelks, *Benjamin Elijah Mays*, 145.

For Mays, an essential element of the American democratic experience was to democratize American education and to give all Americans, including black citizens, full equal access to public education, and equality of opportunity to explore their potential and shape their own destiny in this country. In particular, Mays was concerned about the lack of financial support that Historically Black Colleges and Universities (HBCU institutions) such as Howard University and Morehouse College, where he had both taught and served as administrator, received from by both the American government and the wealthy private sector.

> When it comes to support of black institutions, it takes philanthropy a long time to make up its mind, even when the appropriation is relatively meager. Simply put, neither white philanthropy nor state governments have decided what should be done with the black colleges and universities. For good or ill, the white people have in their hands the power of life and the power of death for black colleges, but they do not have the wisdom to determine whether to sustain or to kill.[7]

White Supremacy and the Black Experience

Beyond the American inadequate funding of and support of black education Mays complained about the catastrophic arrangement of America's public housing and the predicament of human suffering in America's slums. He linked America's delinquency in public education with the poor living conditions of the blacks. Not only Mays rooted the problem of America's public housing (i.e. the slums, the ghettos) and structural poverty in the disastrous effects of American capitalism, but also to the Jim Crow segregation that created a wide economic gap and unequal distribution of wealth between black and white Americans. Jim Crow laws had borne devastating effects on Black education and segregated black schools, as compared to the white schools. The Black schools or black students were underperformed because of lack of educational resources and well-trained black teachers and professionals on subject areas. To the Black victims of Jim Crow, as Anthony Pinn has noted, Jim Crow regulations "make equality not only socially unacceptable but also unlawful."[8] The Federal government did not have the will to solve the country's public

7. Mays, *Born to Rebel*, 193.
8. Pinn, *The Black Church in the Post-Civil Rights Era*, 8.

housing problem in the ghettos because it generated economic profits to the rich and kept Black ghetto residents poorer. Contemporary America's ghettos not only indicate inequality of opportunity, they provide a clear window into the country's family disorganization, poverty, delinquency, mental illness, drug addiction, and various social pathologies.[9] In 1971, the Florida State University Political Scientist Thomas R. Dye, in his book *The Politics of Equality*," penned the provocative paragraph, drawing an analogy between America's Black Ghetto and European colonialism:

> The feeling of powerlessness that black ghetto residents posses is reflected in a comparison of ghettos with the "colonies" of an earlier era . . . Ghetto residents feel they have little control over the institutions in their own communities: businesses, schools, welfare agencies, the police, and most other important agencies are all controlled from the outside. Often the agents of these institutions—the store managers, clerks, teachers, welfare workers, and policemen—are whites who live outside of the ghetto. Thus, the important institutions of the ghetto are staffed and controlled almost entirely by outsiders—and hence the analogy with colonialism.[10]

The relevant and practical questions one should be asking is this: What have been the most innovative transformation in Black Ghetto residencies since 1971 to 2020? Have the individual and collective lives of Black ghetto residents improved? Is there a correlation between contemporary segregated communities and low-performing public schools? Arguably, the existence of Black ghetto is indicative of the failure of American democracy and the country's turning its back away from its black citizens. According to Mays's reasoning, the present state of the American democracy could be compared to civilizations of the past that have decayed because of abandonment of a large segment of their citizen population. He provided many reasons underlying the failure of these ancient civilizations (i.e. Rome, Greece) as they restricted the rights and democratic freedom of their citizens, which is akin to contemporary American democracy and the plot of black and brown people. For example, he contended that civilizations just like democratic systems could decay if they are built on human greed and the exploitation of the economically-poor and if they fail to create a constructive welfare systems

9. Dye, *The Politics of Equality*, 92.

10. Ibid., 95.

and uplift programs to address the social ills of the most vulnerable and marginalized members of the population.

According to Mays, the decline of the moral order in society is another pertinent matter that led to the decline of ancient civilizations. Mays attributed all of these contributing causes and deficiencies to the American democracy; he concluded that the conundrum of American democracy pertained to a moral crisis. "The chaos of our time is a moral chaos—located in the will . . . Our problem is not intellectual, it is ethical and moral."[11] The solution to America's democratic problem, according to Mays's inference, is to produce a democratic-minded nation and to make "individuals good as well as intellectual."[12]

Moreover, Mays believed that the bankruptcy of democratic principles in the American society lied in the hegemony of white supremacy in the American society and that white power had had devastating effects on the non-white populations and American history. He noted that white people in the United States have used their power to exploit blacks and keep the country unequally democratized. He associated white power with the cultural, economic, political, and intellectual influence and dominance of white people in America and in the world. For example, he explained the horror of the black experience is the ensuing result of white supremacy:

> The white man has made his way through history on white power. The wonderful things he has done have resulted from his economic, political, and intellectual power. The evil things he has done, as well as the good things, have come from the white man's power and might. White power kept Negroes in slavery for 246 years and freed them without a dime in compensation for their labor. White power kept the black man segregated in the United for one hundred years.[13]

White supremacy is the central hindrance to the spread and applicability of American democracy in all areas of the American life and experience. White supremacy is an enormous block to human flourishing, human rights, and race relations in the American society. Most of all, white supremacy causes much suffering and pain to the black population and the disentangled groups. As a prevention to American democracy, white

11. Mays, "Democratizing and Christianizing America," 532.

12. Ibid.

13. Mays, *Born to Rebel*, 314–15.

supremacy dehumanizes black humanity and defers the destiny and future of a large segment of minoritized and racialized American population. On the pervasive impact of white supremacy on black lives, Mays discussed further its implications on poor black housing, white violence toward blacks, and the subject of inequality of (Black) employment:

> White power robbed the Negro of the ballot, gave inferior schools, lynched him, and saw to it that he has given only menial jobs and deliberately exploited and degraded. White power sees to it that desegregation in public schools moves at a snail's pace. Slums and ghettoes exist because the white man has the power to keep them in operation. In reality, white power determines in large measure the Negro's destiny.[14]

Mays believed that the American democracy was not functioning effectively for a large segment of the American population, chiefly the African American people whose lives were trapped under racial segregation (Jim Crow laws) and a racialist structure. Although, Black people have partially tasted the freedom of democracy, but did not have the full access to the promises and provisions (i.e. employment, voting rights, justice, equal treatment under the law, education opportunity) of the American democracy, he maintained. In his 1971 autobiography, *Born to Rebel: An Autobiography*, he penned terrifying words about how the U.S. government since its birth had robbed the black population of their political and civil rights:

> The United States government and the vast majority of white Americans have never committed themselves to the idea of full-fledged citizenship for the Negro. Black people in America were emancipated 106 years ago, and a century has passed since the enactment of the 13th, 14th, and 15th Amendments to the Constitution. In all these years, the federal government has never been willing to enforce laws to give the black man the rights that are guaranteed to him by the Constitution. Not in needs, hopes, aspirations, fears, sorrows, or dreams do men differ; only in pigmentation! How different history might be had all men the same color![15]

At the time Mays was writing his autobiography in the 1960s, the African American population constituted 10% of the American

14. Ibid.

15. Ibid., 309.

population. Yet the African American population was the most eco-
nomically- disfranchised group in the American society, and one of
the contributing factors was the miseducation of Black people. To this
important wealth inequality:

> It is my considered judgement that not one foundation, not one
> government agency, national or state, has ever thought in terms
> of allocating ten percent of all monies given for education to
> the support of black institutions or for the education of blacks.[16]

The issue of economic disparity between whites and blacks and the
unequal distribution of wealth and public education between these two
groups was arguably a democratic dilemma. Mays cogently challenged
the government's unwillingness to improve the economic gap between the
poor and the rich by stating, "Although the Negro has helped to make the
wealth of the nation, he has not been allowed to help shape the policies of
how that wealth is to be distributed. And this inequity is largely true, too,
in the use of government funds."[17] Mays, who was influenced by Christian Social Democracy and the Social Gospel movement, articulated his
sensibility toward the poor and the disfranchised in this remarkable statement: "My sensitivity for the poor, the diseased and those who have given
their lives for the good of those sick and the poor, the great and the small,
the high and the low."[18] For Mays, the message of the Christian Gospel
is a compelling statement that comes with moral obligations: the sacred
Christian responsibility and civic engagement is to be active agents of social transformation and moral conscience of their society. As Jelks elaborated on Mays's democratic leaning, "What the Social Gospel provided for
Mays was an intellectual and ethical framework for his Christian activism
against Jim crow . . . Mays solidified his belief in the social character of
Christianity and the positive impact that a social faith and sound biblical
interpretation could have on the prevailing social order."[19]

This perspective also helped to explain Barbara Lewinson's interpretation of Mays's social vision of Christianity that it was "a working force
and the church as an institution that should lead rather than follow in

---

16. Ibid., 193.
17. Ibid.
18. Quoted in Burton, "Born to Rebel," 35.
19. Jelks, "Mays's Academic Formation," 118.

developing the rights of Africans."[20] Inevitably, Christian public witness is intrinsic to the ethical and moral responsibility of all Christians.

Mays promulgated his conviction that it was a moral obligation and intellectual responsibility for both the Federal government and white philanthropy to support black education, whether it was channeled through the HBCU's institutions. Mays was equally alarmed about reparations for free black associated with American slavery for he discerned that not only reparation was a moral issue, but also it would be the most democratic project for the American government to invest in.

> I do believe that white churches should invest more heavily in projects designed to help the Negro poor. White philanthropy has an obligation to make amends for its hundred years of neglect of Negro colleges. It is odd that a country feels little or no moral obligation to compensate its own citizens for decades of shameful and savage treatment.[21]

In the 1960s, Mays was correspondingly attentive to the black response to struggle to gain the three major rights: social justice, collective autonomy, and political rights. He understood the black struggle for civil rights and political freedom was structural, collective, and systemic.

> The central questions confronting every black man are what he can do to enlarge his freedom, to create in himself a sense of his inherent worth and dignity, and to develop economic and political security. He must also consider what can be done to help build a society where each person has the opportunity to develop his mind, body, and spirit without the imposition of artificial barriers.[22]

Mays argued that the self-determination and the dignity of the Black population was linked to Black economic power and political right. Black liberation was not an impossibility without a proper reevaluation of Black potentiality and economic power. The work of democracy for blacks in America was and has always been a long journey of black resistance and black optimism toward national recognition and collective dignity. Mays did not divorce the matter of black freedom and right to the significant role of religion in American history. Eddie S. Glaude reminds us that "The task at hand is not about securing the goodness of the American Idea or

20. Lewinson, Mays's Educational Philosophy," 217.

21. Mays, *Born to Rebel*, 193.

22. Ibid., 307–8.

about perfecting the union. It is about according dignity and standing to all Americans no matter the color of their skin."[23]

The Problem with American Christianity

Black and White Churches

In his intellectual campaign for democratic justice or black democracy, Mays raised two major problems in white churches and in the white world: the support of racial segregation in society and the practice of segregation in Christian houses of worship, and the refusal of white Christians to extend Christian fellowship to black Christians. As for the subject of racial exclusivity in black churches, Mays argued that this pattern of practice in black congregations was necessary to ensure that black Christians maintain control of their churches; also, racial segregation occurred black churches because the Black church was an activist space for social activism, leadership autonomy, and political protest in the Black community. Interestingly, Carter G. Woodson suggested the black experience in religion has "become a test of the reality of Christ in American churches" because it demonstrates the hypocrisy of white American Christians who allegedly affirmed the brotherhood and equality of all people, as affirmed in Scriptures, but did not practice these Christian virtues toward black people.[24]

By contrast, it was the Black Church that provided a place of refuge, solace, and fortress for Blacks, especially in the period of American slavery. Woodson summarized the pivotal multi-purposes of the Black Church as (1) a platform for Black forum; (2) a space that served as a clearing house for the Black community; (3) a social welfare agency; (4) a powerful house that empowered and inspired the Black community; and (5) an educational outlet for black collective expression and the training of the black mind for service and civic engagement.[25] It is in the same line of thought, E. Franklin Frasier noted that it was The Negro Church during the time of slavery and to an extent during the era of racial segregation that provided some form of social cohesion to the Black community and fostered racial solidarity among Blacks of various intellectual and ideological leanings and

---

23. Glaude, *Democracy in Black*, 38.
24. Woodson, *The History of The Negro Church*, ix.
25. Ibid., 242–50.

educational background.[26] C. Eric Lincoln and Lawrence H. Mamiay historically documented the development of Black nationalism ideology and Black Power Movement as a counter force to racial segregation in public spaces and white Christian circles; similarly, the emergence of Black Liberation Theology was birthed as a critique to White Christianity and America's anti-blackness practices in the 1960s. [27]

In summary, the creation of the Black Church in the American society during the time of slavery was the result of a profound theological crisis of racial segregation in ecclesiastical meetings and Christian fellowship, and this theological crisis was premised on the pseudo-ideological belief of the inequality of the races; correspondingly, this theological heresy, supported by White theologians and Christian thinkers, claimed that God was a "White God" who favored the white race and endowed it with the intellectual aptitude and hegemonic power to conquer, dominate, and exploit the world and the non-Anglo-Saxon nations and races. This religion of whiteness is idolatrous to biblical religion and wages war against a holy, perfect, and loving God who also fashioned Black people and the multicolored global family for love and relationship and to be the direct ambassadors of the triune God in the world. Jamaican Liberation theologian Noel Erskine reiterates that white churches did not respond positively to the plight of black people during the time of slavery because white Christians "were deeply enmeshed in the system that they were unable to pose a radical alternative to slavery."[28]

Consequently, Mays believed that not only Christian churches in America was divided over theological differences, further division in Christian congregations were grounded on the distinction of race and color. "It is to be regretted this division is too deeply established that even where there is unity in theology, creed, ritual, liturgy and language, we find the body of Christ divided on grounds of race and color."[29] Mays was critical about the witness of Christianity in the public sphere and Christian activism in society to ameliorate the living conditions of the poor and the economically-disfranchised population in the American society. He found faults in both Black Christianity and White Christianity for preaching a Gospel message that was not relevant to the existential needs of the

26. Frazier, *The Negro Church in America*, 13–34.

27. Lincoln, *The Black Church Since Frazier*, 111–68; Lincoln and Mamiya, *The Black Church in the African American Experience*, 164–235.

28. Erskine, *Decolonizing Theology*, 57.

29. Mays, *Born to Rebel*, 256.

American people and a message that was not confronting the social ills of and the plight of the Black population. He observed, "The Gospel in Negro and white churches alike was definitely other-world-oriented and never ever hinted at bringing whites and blacks of the county closer together for the improvement of social and economic conditions."[30]

Moreover, Mays blamed both black and white churches for preaching a message that emphasized the Christian experience in heaven, the eschatological future, while ignoring the existential realities such as the exploitation and mistreatment of the poor and black people "here on earth."[31] In his comparative analysis of the two racialized Christianities, he declared that "The local white church has always been conservative when it comes to taking a stand on social issues, especially so if the issue involves black people. Local black churches have been far more prophetic than the local white churches."[32] On a general note, he found both branches of American Christianity were silenced about the racial and social problems of his contemporary society. American Christianity has been incompetent in responding to the needs of non-religious community and in contributing to the (general) welfare of the American people.[33] Yet he was optimistic about a religion that could be changed for the good of the American people and a faith that could be instrumental to human rights and liberation.

For example, Mays noted that movements and non-religious interactions such as the National Association for the Advancement of Colored People has always had access to black congregations. They served as forces of resistance and an empowering presence for Blacks toward the pursuit of civil rights and political justice. Similarity, The Southern Christian Leadership Conference and the National Conference of Black Churchmen have actively been involved in local black congregations and partnered with black communities in cooperate programs and projects "to bring about social and economic justice for black people."[34]

While racial segregation was evident in both black and white churches in the Northern and Southern Regions of the county, Mays made a distinction between the racial attitude between white and black Christians

30. Ibid., 242.

31. Ibid.

32. Ibid., 243.

33. Mays and Nicholson, *The Negro's Church*, 164.

34. Mays, *Born to Rebel*, 243.

by asserting, "The basic difference between the black and white churches is that the black church has never had a policy of racial exclusiveness. The white church has."[35] In his well-researched book, *The Negro's Church*, which he published with Joseph William Nicholson in 1933, Mays concluded that the idea of a separate church and a divided American Christianity was "satisfactory to white Americans and pleasing to a goodly number of Negroes. The encouragement that Negroes have received from white people to have their own churches has served to increase the number of Negro churches."[36] Mays provided six reasons for the persistent existence of a segregated church in the United States:

1. The whites have stimulated Negroes to build or purchase their own churches by direct acts of discrimination against them;

2. by financially aiding them to purchase or build churches or to start new work;

3. by separating the Negroes under white supervision;

4. by giving church buildings to negroes or encouraging them to remain at old sites when the whites moved or build new churches;

5. by willingly grating the request when Negroes desired their own church;

6. or by friendly counsel and advice.[37]

The noted reasons were not just racial; correspondingly, they related to theological, leadership, and financial matters. Nonetheless, it was the white church that took the lead in those racial and ecclesiastical matters in the American culture. The Black church suffered financial resources, but not it was not lacked in creative imagination and charismatic leadership. Further, Mays highlighted two central reasons black churches were not racially integrated. The first reason pertained to the issue that Black Christians wanted to "to maintain control of their churches;" second, black Christians did not want to be humiliated, hurt, or dehumanized in churches.[38] White Christians fully embraced the dangerous doctrine of white superiority and that whiteness was a mark of their racial identity, heritage, and difference.

35. Ibid., 242.
36. Mays and Nicholson, *The Negro's Church*, 6.
37. Ibid.
38. Mays, *Born to Rebel*, 241.

In addition, the separate church afforded black churches and black Christians with the opportunity for collective self-expression, to assert black agency and autonomy, and to strengthen black Christian leadership and religious freedom in black congregations. In their sociological study of the Black Church, black (church) historians and sociologists W. E. B. Du Bois, Carter G. Woodson, Benjamin E. Mays, E. Franklin Frazier, C. Eric Lincoln, and Joseph William Nicholson all affirmed the historic grassroots mobilization and transformative public function of the Black church in the Black experience in America:

> Nowhere in America is the Negro's opportunity for self-expression and leadership in private and even in public affairs allowed to be equal to that of the white man's except . . . The Negro's political life is still largely found in the Negro Church. . . . Thus, not finding the opportunity that is given to member of other racial groups in civic and political life, in business enterprises and social agencies, the Negro through the years has turned to the church for self-expression, recognition, and leadership.[39]

Traditionally, white churches do not extend leadership opportunities to black Christians attending predominantly white congregations and black Christians belonging even to a multicultural church that is overly white feel that the white leadership does not express genuine concern about the wellbeing about the Black community. The Christian church has not always been the national leader and conscience on moral and ethical issues in this nation. At the time Mays was writing his autobiography in the first half of the twentieth-century, the White Church has historically complied with the racist system and thus contributed to a greater degree to black suffering and pain. The underlying motif for this historic alliance has been an intense desire for white Christians to ascend to political power and cultural influence, as this matter is contemporaneous to the goals and pursuit of contemporary American evangelicalism. The white church has been the cooperative tool of the dominant class to carry out its agendas, which often disfranchise black and brown Christians. Nonetheless, Mays explained that prior to the legal abolition of slavery in the United States, multiple factors—economic, social, cultural, religious, and

---

39. Mays and Nicholson, *The Negro's Church*, 8–9; also see, Du Bois, *The Philadelphia Negro* (1899), and *The Negro Church* (1903); Woodson, *The History of the Negro Church* (1921); Mays and Nicholson, *The Negro's Church* (1933); Frazier, *The Negro Church in America* (1964); Lincoln, *The Black Church Since Frazier* (1974); Lincoln and Mamiya, *The Black Church in the African American Experience* (1990).

psychological—accounted for a divided Christianity in the country, which in turn produced damaging impacts on corporate Christian worship and fellowship. Chiefly, Mays provided five reasons for this interracial separation among black and white American Christians:

> Following emancipation, when the Negro could actually own and aggressively expand his church, the economic factor was added. Therefore, since about 1865 these economic, social, and psychological factors have permeated the structure of the Negro church. Specifically, churches originated from about five causes, namely a growing racial consciousness, the initiative of individuals and groups, splits, migration of Negroes, and mission of other churches.[40]

Moreover, Mays concluded that the non-religious sectors and non-Christian organizations have exceeded Christian churches and institutions in the areas of race relations and social justice issues. One of the profound issues he noted in Christian churches was the matter of cultural accommodation and political appropriation, as well as the failure of the church to be a visible witness of divine justice in America's public sphere:

> The local churches permit secular bodies such as the state and federal courts, the United States, big league baseball, professional boxing, colleges and universities, the public schools, and theaters to initiate social change in the area of race. But even when secular bodies initiate the change, local churches, Negro and white, follow slowly or not at all.[41]

For Mays, the legacy of the Christian church in America was at stake and its future was at risk. Thus, he lamented, "It will be a sad commentary on our life and time if future historians can write that the last bulwark of segregation based on race and color in the United States was God's church."[42] Mays would reason that the existence of a racialized Christianity in the American society justified his basic claim that the American society has never been fully democratized and Christianized. In the same line of thought, the racialized Christianity indicates that the people in the church have never been Christianized, and that people in American churches never made peace with God and their neighbor. He reiterated this thesis elsewhere, "We have been excited about a

40. Mays and Nicholson, *The Negro's Church*, 14.

41. Mays, *Born to Rebel*, 355.

42. Ibid.

Christianity that was to be lived on the earth and that was to function in every area of life."[43]

In the same vein, democracy has never fully graced (or applied in) every area of life in the American society. The economically-disadvantaged and marginalized populations cannot look to the church for hope and protection, the same way the American government has not created a culture of optimism and safety for its brown and black populations. Both the American church and the Federal government have never been the pioneers of equality of opportunity to include black citizens. As the economist Joseph E. Stiglitz advises the nation, "We will never create a system with full equality of opportunity; but we can at least create more equality of opportunity . . . It's not a matter of eliminating inequality or creating full equality of opportunity. It's just a matter of reducing the level of inequality and increasing the extent of equality of opportunity."[44]

The basic problem is an issue of trust and reliability. Mays projected that the end and success of democracy and Christianity in America is bound to the commitment of the Federal government to be democratic and the Church to be Christian.[45] In the paragraph below, Mays articulated the great paradox between democracy and Christianity, and the shortcomings of the American church to become truly "Christian," the latter is a peculiar characterization and distinctive identity that could potentially advance the democratic process and progress in the American society.

> We are what we do and not what we say. We are as democratic as we live and we are as Christian as we act. If we talk brotherhood and segregate human beings, we do not believe in brotherhood. If we talk democracy and deny it to certain groups, we do not believe in democracy. If we preach justice and exploit the weak, we do not believe in justice. If we preach truth and tell lies, we do not believe in truth. We are what we do.[46]

In addition, in his *The Negro's Church*, Benjamin Mays demonstrated how self-interest and greed had prevented certain individuals in society not to be on the side of justice and in solidarity with the poor and the marginalized. Solidarity with the poor and the marginalized is an act of courage that strengthens our democracy and our national belief that

43. Mays, "Higher Education," 108.
44. Stiglitz, *The Price of Inequality*, 287.
45. Mays, "Democratizing and Christianizing America," 531.
46. Ibid.

everyone deserves a second chance toward a transformational society and human flourishing. Also, those in position of power and influence are reluctant to be on God's campaign for justice because of the fear of experiencing social ostracism and alienation from their group as well as losing economic privileges and political leadership. Elsewhere, Mays connected this human behavior to the triumph of white supremacy and structures of class power.

> There is some virtue in being identified with the under-privi-leged. It is usually more likely that the man farthest down will advocate complete justice for all than that the man farthest up will. It is hardly possible for the most privileged to be as sensitive to the injustices, the restrictions and the limitations imposed upon the weak as it is for the weak themselves; or for him to feel these wrongs with the same degree of intensity as they are felt by the under-privileged. They who sit in the seat of the mighty, or those who are racially identified with the ruling class, are more likely to feel that they have too much to lose if they begin to champion too ardently the cause of the man farthest down. It is more difficult for them even to see the wrong. The danger is that they view the evil from lofty heights, if at all. They fear economic insecurity and social ostracism, which may come to them if they identify themselves too openly with the oppressed group."[47]

White Churches and Race Relations

Similarly, Mays assessed the public work of American (White) churches and (White) Christian institutions as inadequate progress toward Biblical-centered race relations and constructive human flourishing. Not only Mays has deemed the nation's Christian institutions bankrupt and fragmented, Christian churches in America were not contributing substantially to the democratization of American Christianity and correspondingly to the Christianization of the American life. This observation is clearly demon-strated in his 1945 Commencement Address at Howard University:

> The United States is obligated by virtue of its Federal Constitu-tion and by virtue of its Christian pronouncements to become Christianized and democratized. If America is to maintain in-tegrity of soul, and if our Government is to escape the label of hypocrisy and deception, it has no choice but to plan deliberately

47. Mays and Nicholson, *The Negro's Church*, 63.

to bring to full fruition the four freedoms—for which we claim we fought on the battlefields of Europe and Africa; and for which we calm we are fighting in the Pacific."[48]

Mays construed "American Christianity" as just another "American institution" that was complicit in the suffering, dehumanization, and disfranchisement of the African American people. He criticized the white church and white Christians for their lack of integrity, moral virtues, and social responsibility to display in public a Christian character that is worth imitating as well as their failure for being an unwavering witness and testimony of change in the American public sphere and civil society.[49] In his writings, it is customary for Mays to complaint about the disposition of white Christians to treat black people with dignity and the practice of racial selectiveness in white congregations. Particularly, he condemned local white churches in the United States. He also condemned white Christians for performing unchristian actions that often contradict Jesus's teaching on brotherly love and Christian fellowship. For example, he remarked that

> The local white church has been society's most conservative and hypocritical institution in the area of White-Negro relations . . . The local white churches, the vast majority of them, have not lived up to their professed Christianity, because Christian fellowship across racial barrier is so inherent in the very nature of the church that to deny fellowship in God's House, on the basis of race or color, is a profanation of all that the church stands for.[50]

In this paragraph, Mays stressed that the associational life, which Christian fellowship fosters, is of paramount importance for the achievement of democracy in America and in Christian churches. His focus on a constructive ethic of Christian fellowship as the keynote to democracy is to inspire democratic behavior and drive among individuals and the citizens of this nation.[51] Christian fellowship is critical to the cultivation of democratic virtues of participation and communication, which Dewey in *Public and Its Problems* insisted remain the most enduring goal of a democratic society.[52] Walter Lippman in *Drift and Mastery* as-

48. Mays, "Democratizing and Christianizing America," 532.

49. Ibid.

50. Mays, *Born to Rebel*, 241.

51. Quoted in Kloppenberg, *The Virtues of Liberalism*, 81.

52. Ibid., 91.

serted that democratic vision necessitates the progressive collaboration of individuals and the development of (democratic) citizenship.[53]

In particular, Mays was concerned about the practice of segregation in white churches, which not only dehumanized black Christians, but also segregation in white churches was a defeat to Black and white unity. The fact that racial segregation existed in Christian white spaces, opportunities for white redemption and interracial dialogue and harmony were unimaginable for both whites and blacks. Hence, he could write, "Secular organizations make no commitments, nor do they prate about brotherhood among men and a gospel of redemption and salvation. When the church maintains a segregated house, and simultaneously preaches the fatherhood of God and the brotherhood of man, then surely "hypocrisy" is the mildest term one can apply. "White sepulcher" comes to mind."[54] In the era of racial segregation and public lynching, Mays pointed out white clergy were spreading the message "on living in order to be assured of God's blessings and of eternal salvation, while at the same time Negroes were being cheated, beaten, and lynched throughout South Carolina,"[55] for example.

For Mays, *the gospel in white* is a bold rejection of biblical Christianity and a serious challenge to Jesus's non-negotiable moral command to "love your neighbor." As he maintained, "Segregation in the House of God has been a great strain on my religion."[56] Mays not only believed that segregation in Christian congregations was a theological heresy, as many South African Christian leaders called the apartheid, segregation was an immoral societal structure. He argued that

> there is no basis to justify consigning a man to a segregated, inferior role in the church or anywhere else in society, and that modern racial segregation is 'tantamount to penalizing one for being what God made him and tantamount to saying to God, 'You made a mistake, God, when you made people of different races and colors . . . The only basis the church has for its segregated policy is the wickedness of church people themselves.[57]

53. Lippman, *Drift and Mastery*, 16, 66.

54. Mays, *Born to Rebel*, 241.

55. Ibid., 242.

56. Ibid., 243.

57. Ibid., 260–61.

Comparatively, Cone's theological vindication against the White American church is also pronounced in the paragraph below:

> It is a sad fact that the white church's involvement in slavery and racism in America simply cannot be overstated. It not only failed to preach the kerygmatic Word but maliciously contributed to the doctrine of white supremacy. Even today all of the Church's institutions—including its colleges and universities—reveal its white racism character. Racism has been a part of the life of the church so long that it is virtually impossible for even the "good" members to recognize the bigotry perpetuated by the church. Its morals are so immoral that even its most sensitive minds are unable to detect the inhumanity of the Church on the black people of America . . . To be racist is to fall outside of the Church . . . If there is any contemporary meaning of the Antichrist (or "the principalities and powers"), the white church seems to be a manifestation of it. It is the enemy of Christ. It was the white "Christian" church which took the lead in establishing slavery an institution and segregation as a pattern in society by sanctioning all-white congregations.[58]

Hence, interracial fellowship has always been a major issue in black and white churches. Based on Mays's careful research, many white Christians did not see it as a Christian duty to deal cordially with their black brothers and sisters nor have they even bothered to pursue interracial cooperation based on a Christian ethics of mutual exchange and reciprocity, and a theology of goodwill and mutual care.[59] On the other hand, black ministers believed that white ministers needed "a new (true) conception of the brotherhood of man . . . [and] to act like decent human beings."[60] The fundamental ideology associated with this unchristian attitude was that white Christians believed that they were superior and therefore made the primary work of interracial cooperation and relations more difficult for both races.

Finally, white ministers insisted, "Negroes should have their definite localities in cities. The churches of the whites and the government should assist them in their educational, religious and social program."[61] Here, white Christians defined cooperation in terms of racial segregation. The

58. Cone, "The White Church and Black Power," 72–73.

59. Mays and Nicholson, *The Negro's Church*, 159.

60. Ibid., 162–63.

61. Ibid., 202.

only solution to the Black problem according to these Christian clergy is "complete segregation with no possible encroaching on white territories. Give him his section, schools, churches, etc., and see that he stays there."[62] In other words, they believed that blacks should be kept in their place. In a detailed and informative paragraph, Mays summarized the power and omnipresence of the race concept in the American conscience as well as on the psychology of the white world, even beyond the American border:

> For the race problem is so universal that it has to be considered wherever people meet . . . For the race problem is ubiquitous; and I have never been able to escape it. It came up in every national and world Christian conference I ever attended. It is ever present. One often hears that Negroes never forget the race problem, that they talk about it all the time. This is equally true of white people. In church and state alike, the black man has been continually in the white man's mind. One need only read anti-Negro newspapers reaching back a hundred years, and anti-Negro books written over the decades, or study the laws the various states and the federal government have enacted against the Negro to find that the black man has dominated the white man's thinking since the first Africans landed here in 1619. The Negro, I am convinced, is the white man's obsession.[63]

Moreover, he argued that the concept of race is a modern invention and that racial discrimination and segregation in Christian circles and assemblies is anti-thesis to Christian fellowship and the Gospel of unconditional love. Modern racial categories were not part of the early Christian church, he added. There is no historical record in the church annals that the early Christians excluded other Christians from Christian fellowship based on their skin color. He contended that there is no theological basis and scientific proof to support racial segregation and discrimination in ecclesiastical communities. While the racial problem is connected to Western imperialism and conquest of the brown and black populations in Africa, Asia, and the Americas; this racial hegemony has produced dire implications in the life of the church. Mays observed keenly:

> It seems clear, then, that the color or racial bar in the church is a modern thing. It was not, in fact, until the seventeenth century that the outlines of the modern race problem began to emerge. It is the modern church that again crucifies the body

62. Ibid., 164.

63. Mays, *Born to Rebel*, 255.

of Christ on a racial cross. Race and color did not count in the early existence of the Protestant Church. It was when modern Western imperialism began to explore and exploit the colored peoples of Africa, Asia, and America, that the beginning of segregation and discrimination based on color and race initiated. It was then the color was associated with "inferiority," and whiteness with "superiority."[64]

Both racial discrimination and segregation, according to Mays, carry tremendous effects on the person or group being segregated. Mays outlined six major impacts or consequences of segregation upon the disadvantaged race or blacks:

1. it is conceded that segregation and discrimination hurt the pride of the person discriminated against, that they retard his mental, moral, and physical development;

2. they rob society of what the disadvantaged group might contribute to enrich humanity;

3. imposed separateness breeds ill-will and hatred;

4. it develops in the segregated a feeling of inferiority to the extent that he never knows what his capabilities are;

5. His mind is never freed to develop unrestricted. The ceiling and not the sky become the limit of his striving;

6. It scars not only the soul of the segregated but the soul of the segregator as well.[65]

In addition, Mays also criticized the white church for its failure for not condemning the lynching of black citizens and defending their human dignity and rights as Americans. He called lynching "the most evil of my early years."[66] Mays stated that he has never read any article by any white Christian minister or a group of white ministers or anyone in the name of the white Church and Christianity "who condemned the horrible crime of lynching."[67] Regrettably, he lamented that American white Christianity resembled the culture that it imitated and produced it. Substantially, it was influenced by the racial politics and moral decay of the day; the

64. Ibid., 352.
65. Ibid., 354–54.
66. Ibid., 243.
67. Ibid.

White church failed to take a different route to campaign for racial justice and condemning the lynching of black citizens in society. He reiterated, "I found no record of a church voice raised in protest. The church was so much a part of the system that lynching was accepted as part of the Southern way of life just as casually as was segregation."[68]

Given the concerns Mays had raised about American Christianity and American democracy, did he make any proposal to help improve both institutions in America? What was Mays's vision for American democracy and American Christianity in the future? To these two vital concerns we shall now turn to in the subsequent paragraphs.

Constructing a Truly Democratic America and Prophetic American Christianity

Democracy as Responsibility and Mutual Reciprocity

Foremost, Mays articulated his concept of democracy in various writings, but in a historic speech he delivered on January 1, 1963, one hundred years after Lincoln's Emancipation Proclamation on January 1, 1863, he advanced his clear vision of democracy as it pertained to the African American experience in the 1960s and henceforth. Mays's speech occurred in the context of an ecumenical religious conference that took place in Chicago, and the event was sponsored by the National Council of the Churches of Christ in America, the Synagogue Council of America, and the National Catholic Welfare Conference. Mays's unified goal in that conference was twofold. First, he wanted "to get to heart of this country's racism" and second, to "appeal to the conscience of the American people."[69] As we have noted in previous analysis Mays was critical about the prevalence of anti-black racism in the American culture and his thesis that America's problem was a moral crisis. Yet Mays saw that race affected every area of the human life in the American culture, especially America's experiment with democracy and human rights issues. He proceeded to describe his democratic dream in seven objectives:

1. We are called for a reign of justice in voting rights;

2. for equal protection of law;

68. Ibid.
69. Ibid., 262.

3. for equality in educational and cultural opportunities, in hiring and promotion, in medical and hospital care;

4. and for open occupancy in housing.[70]

As previously observed in Jean-Bertrand Aristide's "Ten Commandments" of democracy to democratize and humanize the Haitian society, in the same line of thought, Mays's first four democratic goals are legal and ethical. Just like Aristide's thesis on moral and political theology, they are specific demands that will maximize America's democratic ideals in the best interest of African Americans and these ethical imperatives are grounded on the principle of equality of opportunity. The next three are both moral and theological. All these seven objectives connected to his democratic philosophy cogently presented as a series of appeals in the rhetorical style of David Walker's *Appeals* (1829). They are well-grounded on Mays's theological ethics and anthropology. Generally, they appeal to Christian moral theology that intersects the topics of brotherly love, Christian eschatology, and caring for one another.

5. We are called for a reign of love in which all barriers based on race would be eliminated, in which the stranger would not only be welcomed but sought after,

6. and in which "any man will be received as brother—his rights, your rights; his pain, your pain; his prison, your prison"

7. We call upon all the American to work, to pray, and to act courageously in the cause of equality and human dignity while there is time to eliminate racism permanently and decisively, to seize the historic opportunity the Lord has given us for healing an ancient rupture in the human family, to do this for the glory of God.[71]

The common themes between Aristide and Mays, as t[their belief coincide to democratic ideas and principles, include education, employment, human rights, safety, freedom, and human flourishing. Elsewhere, Mays elaborated on the practicality of democracy to contribute to the welfare and thriving of the black population in the United States. He underscored specific areas in both the civil and political societies where American democracy should be inclusive and indiscriminate, and reign supreme.

70. Ibid.
71. Ibid.

> What the black man needs most are: a better education; technical skills to enable him to succeed in a highly competitive society; decent jobs that pay enough to enable him to live comfortably above the poverty line; adequate housing, with the consequent abolition of slums and ghettos; political strength to influence voting to his benefit and to defeat racist politicians; a sense of pride, self-respect, and self-identity; and a sense of solidarity.[72]

Mays's observation brings us to the conclusion that America's democratic problem is an issue of the collective will of the American people. Mays connected the issue of the collective will to moral principles and ethical values. Therefore, he could reason that one cannot afford to join the exploiting class because one is the exploited; one cannot afford to be prejudiced against a certain ethnic group or race because you are victims of prejudice; and one cannot afford to join the forces of fascism because fascist forces are against you.[73] To put it simply, one cannot fix an error with another error, and one cannot bring justice with an act of injustice. Mays established a close rapport between democratic ideals and moral virtues; hence, he could tell his audience at Howard University to "be men and women of integrity and honor—standing first, foremost, and always for principles and not that which is expedient."[74] Mays did not detach morality from social responsibility and collective service. It is within this context Black liberation theology is historically connected with the writings of Benjamin Mays. Black liberation not only makes moral and democratic demands upon America to benefit Black people. African theologian John Mbiti observes that advocates of Black liberation theology insist that "Black Americans should have had from the start—freedom, justice, a fair share in the riches of their country, equal opportunities, in social, economic and political life."[75]

Mays's biographer John Herbert Roper explained that Mays was not only inclined to the Social Gospel movement and Christian Democratic ideology, he also labored substantially to bring social gospel to black congregations to foster social salvation in the black community. He qualified that Mays had compelled black ministers not to divorce belief and action because "hard work had to be grounded in firm belief."[76] He also added,

72. Ibid., 308.

73. Mays, "Democratizing and Christianizing America," 532.

74. Ibid.

75. Mbiti, "An African Views American Black Theology," 380.

76. Roper, *The Magnificent Mays*, 90.

"Mays resolved things by emphasizing actions, doing good, practicing good, doing the right" to solve the dilemma of grace and "works of salvation" in biblical Christianity.[77] Another Mays biographer Randal Maurice Jelks remarked that Mays "viewed theological argumentation, preaching, and teaching as crucial in defining the pathway to black American freedoms"[78] and democracy.

Mays's decisive commitment to a prophetic vision of the American church and to a democratic order in the American society were the catalyst for his relentless campaign toward racial and economic justice for the black population and progressive interracial relations between blacks and whites. Also, he understood that for a society to be fully functioning for its citizens, it must include the various elements essential to human development and conducive to the democratic project. These things might include a stable government, equal access to economic resources, social activities, educational institutions, and civic and recreational facilities; comparatively, he proposed that just public policies, and equitable resources will contribute to the common good and a constructive democratic order.[79]

Mays believed that to democratize Christianity, it will entail that Christians and any non-religious individuals in America must exercise the power of the will, assume personal and individual responsibility, and live a life of interdependence and reciprocity. In the Commencement Address he delivered at Howard University, which we already alluded to in our previous analysis, Mays exhorted the Howard graduates to cultivate a democratic mind based on the democratic virtues already discussed in this chapter. First, Mays believed that the democratic order entails that people in a given culture should believe that human beings share the same human nature. He believed that everyone is teachable and able to learn, and as volitional agents, individuals have power to foster changes in society. In other words, effective education, willingness to change, and the recognition of our common humanity are important ingredients in the process to construct an operative democracy and thriving political state. As he declared, "If people can be changed for the worse, it is reasonable to suppose that they can be changed for the better. If men can be evil purposes, it is safe to assume that they can be educated for goo

77. Ibid., 115.

78. Jelks, *Benjamin Elijah Mays*, 168.

79. Matthews, "Mays and Racial Justice," 277.

purposes. If human nature is essentially the same the world over, it is fair to presume that the German people are by nature no better and no worse than other human beings."[80] Mays's idea of social evolution and change (i.e. political, economic) is related to John Dewey's notion of democracy and community. According to Dewey's definition:

> The very idea of democracy, the meaning of democracy, must be continually explored afresh; it has to be constantly discovered and rediscovered, remade and reorganized; while the political and economic and social institutions in which it is embodied have to be remade and reorganized to meet the changes that are going on in the development of new needs on the part of human beings and new resources for satisfying these needs.[81]

Dewey established a distinction between democracy as a social idea and democracy as a political system of government. He reasoned that these two manifestations of democracy are closely linked and both relate to human relationships and community. Dewey believed that in order for democracy to be actualized, "it must affect all modes of human association, the family, the school, industry, religion. And even as far as political arrangements are concerned, governmental institutions are but a mechanism for securing to an idea channels of effective operation."[82] The notion of community is significant in Dewey's articulation of democratic framework and principles. He stated that "government exists to serve its community, and that this purpose cannot be achieved unless the community itself shares in selecting its governors and determining their policies . . . They are not the whole of the democratic idea, but they express it in its political phase."[83]

Mays was not a utopian thinker who believed that the democratic order was without fault or needed space for improvement—given the possibility for individuals to develop evil dispositions in their hearts, harm each other, and create oppressive systems and institutions. Yet he was an optimistic Christian social democracy who held that the democratic system and just public policies could help alleviate the economic conditions of the poor and the future of individuals in this country. For Mays, American democracy was tied to American pragmatism to the degree he

---

80. Mays, "Democratizing and Christianizing America," 527.

81. Dewey, *The Later Works of John Dewey*, 182.

82. Dewey, *The Public and Its Problems*, 143.

83. Ibid., 146.

could assert that "We are not slaves to the traditions and the mores of society. Men have been smashing mores and traditions for centuries above them . . . As we fight with might and main to overcome Jim crow, segregation, and every form of discrimination, we must not forget that the human mind can rise above its environment and change its environment."[84]

To create a democratic system that functions for all people, the power of the collective will is of paramount importance and everyone in society should aim for (the) "worthy ends"[85] of the collective. Mays maintained that "If a democratic government really wanted its democracy to function more perfectly, it would find ways and means within the democratic framework to make it function more perfectly."[86] The work of democracy involves both the will and conviction of the Federal government to democratize its institutions and to democratize its political systems. This political intervention will correlate with the self-interest of the people to actualize democratic standards in society. Alluding to President Franklin Roosevelt's historic 1941 State of the Union Address about the meaning of the American democratic freedom, Mays insisted that if the United States were to maintain the integrity of its democratic principles and national soul, the American government must "deliberately bring to full fruition the four freedoms"[87]: the freedom of speech and expression, freedom of religion, freedom from what and freedom from fear. These democratic virtues are essential to the triumph of democracy in the American society.

Second, Mays stressed that to construct a more humane and democratic order that reflects the desire and the will of the people, it would require that the American people live "in a cause for which they were willing to die."[88] Democracy not only means self-sacrifice, but also self-giving for the cause of human flourishing and transformation. The idea of collective self-sacrifice is based upon the coveted human virtues of empathy, fellowship, mutual support, and relationality. As he recapitulated, "If we are willing to fight and die for democracy and the four freedom abroad, we should be willing to teach them in the schools of this country. We would realize the fact that what hurts one, hurts all and that the

84. Mays, "Democratizing and Christianizing America," 533.

85. Ibid., 527.

86. Ibid., 528.

87. Ibid.

88. Ibid., 527.

destiny of each American is tied up with the destiny of all Americans."[89] Mays also discussed the significance for Americans to forge a democratic character and conscience to actualize democratic ideals and promises in everyday human interactions. The democratic hope is contingent upon the actions of both Christianity and the Federal government "to become exponents of the democratic way,"[90] Mays sustained.

Nonetheless, the critical reader would want to know why did Benjamin E. Mays assign the work of democracy in America to the Christian religion and the Federal Government? One might reason rightly that the Federal government as a political entity is responsible to champion a democratic life and effect it in society. Why does this have to do with a religious body such as the Christianity? What are the reasons behind Mays's argument? What makes Christianity an eligible entity or a qualified body to participate in the work of democracy? Why did Mays argue that the American nation needs to be Christianized? Notice that he suggested a twofold process to redeem, safeguard, and advance the American society: democratization and Christianization, correspondingly. We must first explore Mays's idea of the church and its function in society before we can address the inseparable affinity he coordinated between American Christianity and American democracy.

The Church and the Social Order

Mays's concept of the church falls under the category of spiritual and social. From the spiritual aspect, in numerous writings, he argued that the role of the church is to provide spiritual formation to the people of God. From the social outlook, Mays believed that the church should be an agency for social reform, and that Christians should stand against all forms of human maladjustment and alienation in society.[91] In his Howard Commencement Address, Mays articulated four central reasons why the Christian Church is an important agent of democratic transformation and human progress in the American society.

These motives cover disciplines of theology and ethics and topics relating to the origin of the church, its peculiar allegiance, its view on human life, and its philosophy about humanity. Mays declared that (1)

89. Ibid., 531.
90. Ibid.
91. Mays, "The Religious Life and Needs of Negro Students," 337.

Christianity is a unique institution by the virtue of its origin and nature, and claims a supernatural origin, that is, God for its author, and it exists in two major branches: Protestant and Catholic Christianity; (2) Christianity proclaims its ultimate allegiance to God, and its loyalty is not to a political state, not a system of government, not an economic structure, or an ideological worldview; (3) the Christian Church, before the grand scientific discoveries and technological advancements in modernity, unapologetically asserted the common origin of all people and that Christians have called this originator God; (4) prior to the major scientific breakthroughs in modern times, the Church flagrantly proclaimed that God created the human race as one global family (the belief in the fatherhood of God and the brotherhood of all people), and from one common blood God made all nations, peoples, races, and ethnic groups to live together in the earth; and (5) the Christian Church boldly argues that every individual is a person and the life of each individual is sacred and that God has endowed each individual with intrinsic dignity, worth, and value.[92]

The Christian Church boldly argues that every individual is a person and the life of each individual is sacred and that God has endowed each individual with intrinsic dignity, worth, and value. Mays also added "Any institution that has the nerve to make such claims is obligated—if for no other reason than to maintain integrity of soul, to strive with might and main to make good on its pronouncements."[93] Because of these underlying theses about the role of the church in society and the cause of democracy, Mays lamented over America's white churches for being one of the most visibly racially-segregated and undemocratic institutions in the American society. In this case, the white church has failed to be a positive public witness in society and an agent of peace and democracy. As a result, Mays could pronounce:

> On the question of democracy and Christianity, the Church should go further than night clubs, hotels, theaters, and restaurants. If the Christian forces of this country really wanted to do so, and if they really believed what they preach, they would make the Church Christian within a single decade. Then it would earn the right to speak to the secular order—not only in the area of race but in the area of social and economic affairs. It would be not only a priestly church but a prophetic church.

92. Mays, "Democratizing and Christianizing America," 528.
93. Ibid.

Mays established a link between the democratic tradition and prophetic tradition, as these two visions relate to the role of religion in society and politics. For Mays, the contemporary church has not displayed any prophetic character nor has it participated in social activism. The church has turned its back from some of the most urgent concerns and existential crises in society and remained unengaged to the pressing issues in society. The church should be regarded as the conscience of the nation and the hope of the people. These shortcomings of the church justify Mays's basic claim that the American church needs to become Christian so it could be used by God. They also validate his other claim that the American church, not just the American society, is subjected to the democratic process. If the church is not democratized, how could one expect it to contribute to the democratization of the American culture? The democratization must first begin in the church, and that Christians have the sacred social duty to provide "ethical grounding and ethical direction for the people in a modern democracy."[94]

If the Christian church is unable to stand against all forms of injustice and oppression, Mays concurred, "The church has no right to exist."[95] The project of a democratized church is to carry out its social vision, which entails the abolition of war, the promotion of justice in the economic and legal sphere, the ending of racial discrimination, and the campaigning for political rights and emancipation on behalf of the disfranchised groups and oppressed populations.[96] Thus, Mays could project the idea that "It goes without saying that a religion which ignores social problems will in time be doomed."[97] Why did Mays believe that religion was important to the democratic process and in the realization of the American democratic ideals? We should now consider seven major reasons he outlined in an article he published in 1940, "The Religious Life and Needs of Negro Students."

Religion, Society, and Democracy

First, religion is essential to the democratic process because it helps to bridge in society the economic and class gaps between "high" and the

94. Roper, *The Magnificent Mays*, 81.

95. Mays, "The Religious Life and Needs of Negro Students," 337.

96. Ibid.

97. Ibid., 344.

"low."[98] For example, Christians of economic affluence are able to attend the same congregation with other Christians who live on the economic and social margins in society. Both the poor and rich Christians are united by faith but divided by class or race. Yet they share a common set of beliefs and practice a set of rituals associated with the same religious tradition they all embrace. Second, Christianity is a religion that transcends race and gender, and that no one, because of her race or gender orientation, should be denied participating in corporate worship with other Christians. The limits of democracy are tested when an individual's character is assessed exclusively base on his or her racial, gender, or religious identity. This human attitude is detrimental to the democratic progress in the church and delays the promises of democracy in society

Third, because democracy is an on-going process and entails human experiment, discovery, and renewal, religious education is fundamental to the triumph and maintenance of democracy. According to Mays, "the human spirit throughout all time has been reaching out toward something beyond itself. He will discover things beautiful, noble, and inspiring. He will understand that man is incurably religious."[99] Since democracy is a process of human discovery, similarly, religion is a process of self-discovery. The rapport between democracy and religion is paramount for the progress of society and human flourishing, Mays maintained. Fourth, Mays argued religious education must be integral to the intellectual advancement of society and human civilization, and without which, democracy cannot and will not blossom. As he put it, "if education is to deal with the whole of culture, with every aspect of the student's life, the college can no more escape its responsibility in the area of religion than it can escapes its responsibility in the area of literature and mathematics."[100] Thus, Mays connected religious education with the project of citizenship and civic responsibility and engagement. He believed that religion has the potential to produce "good men and women" in society and contribute to mutual respect among the citizens of the same nation.

In addition, the religious experience may contribute to the democratic life and religious resources that could be used to foster human understanding and could be deployed as a tutor to instill in individuals and communities the ethical values of compassion, relationality, and

98. Ibid., 338.
99. Ibid., 339.
100. Ibid., 340.

sympathy.[101] Another way the religious knowledge might contribute to a democratic nation-state through the establishment of networking and "contacts with people who demonstrate in their person the fact that religion counts."[102] If the democratic order is dependent upon people for its survival, individuals in both civil and political societies must embrace and practice the core principles of democracy such as the idea of interdependence and coming together for a common cause or to reach a shared objective, and without which democracy is not democracy the same way religion is not religion without human connection and sensibility.

Sixth, the religious knowledge is connected to the notion of authority. Mays claimed that individuals in society "need authority and this authority is to be found in religion."[103] By the concept of religious authority, Mays referred to a governing moral system that provides direction and guidance to religious people in determining moral choices, ethical behavior, leadership principles, and political principles and ideologies. He supposed that if someone "throws aside all external authority he or she must create authority from within."[104] He offered further elaboration on the function and imperative of religious authority to attend to the needs of the individual and the collective:

> An individual, if he is to be a personality that counts, must keep forever the lines of his destiny in his own hands. And that means some kind of inner authority. At certain points, if the individual is to maintain the integrity of his own selfhood, he or she must defy the mores, refuse to be used, whether by men or systems, and decide within himself or herself that there are some things which he will not brow-beaten into doings. Ethics and morals may be relative terms. But if he is to count, [he or she] must build up for himself a system which for him is final authority. And this system must be an ever-expanding system but always built up in that light of the highest and the best that he knows.[105]

There is an evident rapport between religious authority and democratic authority. Religion is useful to democracy because like democracy, religion provides leadership and "direction to life—a direction that is neither communistic nor fascistic—not even the direction of a capitalistic

101. Ibid.
102. Ibid., 341.
103. Ibid.
104. Ibid.
105. Ibid., 341–42.

individualism,"[106] Mays consented. The democratic faith, according to Mays, "give one balance and direction however desperate the times. With such a conviction one will strive for the establishment of a righteous order; but he will understand that if the righteous order is not established; both the unrighteous and the more nearly righteous will suffer."[107]

Additionally, the democratic faith is predicated upon the proposition that the democratization of the Church is an on-going process that comprises a period of trial and error and the process of deconstruction, redirection, and re-imagination. He defined the inclusive role of the democratic church in society as (1) to bring justice, peace, and fairness in society; (2) to improve human dynamics including interracial relations; (3) to protest against the possibility of future wards; (4) to cooperate and work together with local communities and organizations and institutions, both civil and political, to enrich human life, and finally, (5) to forge global and international alliances and networks to effectuate global peace and create an engaged and relational humanism.[108] Mays was also convinced that it was also the public role of the Christian church to campaign against the exploitation of the unfortunate groups and races. Caribbean Theologian Korthright Davis employs the phrase "The community of the Realm of God" not only to refer to God's guiding leadership in the Christian Church; it is a key concept that describes the work of the church to "challenge the socio-economic, cultural, ideological, and political heritages of our times toward their transformation into instruments of life that are fully human."[109]

We should point out that Mays believed in the promise of Christian democratic socialism. For example, Gary Dorrien contends that "Christian socialism paved the way for all liberation theologies that make the struggles of oppressed peoples the subject of redemption,"[110] and Mays as a forerunner of Black liberation theology did not separate the liberation of black people and the Social Gospel movement. It is not an overstatement to infer that for Mays, "democratic socialism is the ethical passion for social justice and radical democratic community."[111]

106. Ibid., 342.

107. Ibid., 343.

108. Mays, *Seeking to Be Christians*, 68.

109. Davis, *Serving with Power*, 106.

110. Dorrien, *Social Democracy in the Making*, 3.

111. Ibid., 4.

Correspondingly, Mays envisioned the role of the church as global and transnational, and that Christianity had a moral responsibility to stand against the powerful and imperial nations that attempt to violate the political rights and national sovereignty of weak societies and darker nations. Mays defined democracy as "belief in action" the same way he crusaded for the transformative role of the Church in society and in the public sphere. He held that the democratized Christianity would help to bring into fruition the highest democratic ideals in the American society.[112] We must also point out that Mays established a distinction between political rights, which we have highlighted in the previous paragraph, and human rights. Briefly, he claimed that individuals could not forego their human rights since they are inherent in every living person and that "human rights are equal because all men are required to perfect their moral nature."[113] Davis also claims that the public advocacy of the Church constitutes to insists that "human rights are more than legal conventions. They are demands of the divine right to be human. They are also the rights of demand by others on our own humanity."[114]

In the same way, he explained that political rights enable individuals "to buy where one pleases, freedom to worship in the church of his choice, and to attend public places without discrimination."[115] Mays' conception of freedom is a counter thesis to the practice of racial segregation and the violation of the political rights of black people. Freedom is essential to the democratic experiment, and Mays construed freedom in its cultural, legal, and global optic. In the same line of reasoning, his concept of human rights and natural rights is historical, particular, and universal—as he considered the Black struggle for freedom and civil rights in this country:

> There is no such thing as "Negro Rights." The essential human rights of Negroes do not appertain to them as Negroes, but simply as members of the human family. Human rights are not Negro rights, any more than they are white rights or red-haired persons' rights. They flow from the essential constituents of our nature, not from its accidental characteristics.[116]

112. Mays, "The Religious Life and Needs of Negro Students," 338.

113. Mays, "Review: A Catholic's View of Race Relations," 632.

114. Davis, *Serving with Power*, 106.

115. Mays, "Review: *A Catholic's View of Race Relations*," 632.

116. Quoted in Mays, "Review: *A Catholic's View of Race Relations*," 632–33.

By consequence, a democratized Christianity involves not just intellectual approbations or theological commitment, but "convictions, and
convictions involve action. We believe what we do, and what we are what
we do."[117] The actualization of democracy in society necessitates the belief
that the life of the individual has intrinsic value and worth regardless
of race, gender, sexuality, or religion. A democratized faith must commit itself to the defense of human life—be it black lives or the life of the
poor and the economically-underrepresented population—because life
is sacred. The democratic faith correlates with Christian public witness
to advance democratic justice and equity and equality of opportunity for
all people. According to Mays, the democratized Church stands against
discrimination at the workplace or any area of opportunity in the common life of the American society. Mays could declare that "If we believe
that every American should have equality of opportunity to develop his
mind and character and do not work toward that end, we do not believe
what we say."[118] This is what he called democracy in action. This belief,
according to Walter Lippman, "does not live by logic, but by the need it
fills."[119] This void is democratic, moral, and religious.

Moreover, Mays construed the democratized church as an entity
that acts upon its responsibility in society. Not only the democratic faith
calls for collective responsibility, it places an urgent call upon the individual in the church to be a responsible and active Christian citizen. In
his articulation of the idea of democracy that bears both individual and
collective responsibility, Mays inferred that in a country like the United
States the individual might be forced to go against his or her belief such
as going to war and killing a person for the sake of national freedom and
sovereignty. Second, he reasoned that the individual might find himself or herself in a situation where heavy penalties might be imposed
on him or her if the individual goes against the current practice, what
we may call democratic suicidal—a notion Mays challenged. In such
cases, Mays suggested two options to the individual: "One must find
ways of keeping alive his beliefs through action or he may accept his
environment and lose his beliefs."[120] Within this sacred responsibility
of the church, Caribbean theologian Edmund Davis could write about

117. Mays, *Seeking to Be Christians*, 76.
118. Ibid.
119. Lippman, *Drift and Mastery*, 114.
120. Mays, *Seeking to Be Christians*, 77.

the work of democratic church as contributing "the moral, spiritual, cultural, economic, and social consciousness and development"[121] of a nation. He reiterates that the Church in action, by its very nature, must "contribute to the spiritual and social advancement of the society through its involvement in the fields of medical care, social and religious activities, and educational programmes."[122]

This reasoning recapitulates the notion of democracy as convictional belief. As a Christian theologian remarks, "Convictions are not merely beliefs we hold; they are those beliefs that hold us in their grip. We would not know who we are but for these bedrock beliefs, and without them we would not know how to lead."[123] This is illustrative in the example Mays furnished below about the intricate interplay between segregation and integration in relation to the virtue of Christian fellowship:

> A person who does not believe in segregation of the races but lives in a community where segregation is prescribed by law must find ways to have fellowship with those of other racial groups despite the law. He must act on his belief in Christian fellowship or he will cease to believe it. And the true Christian find ways to act. There are no known laws requiring churches to segregate races in their worship and membership. Here is an opportunity for the true Christian to act on his belief in Christian fellowship.[124]

Toward Better Race Relations

In this paragraph, Mays is calling Christians to act according to Christian conviction that does not discriminate morally and theologically against someone else's racial background. This provides an opportunity for Christians to change society, challenge unjust social patterns, and engage civically for the common good; he could write:

> The Christian can also do his share to get laws of segregation repealed and decisions of the Supreme Court obeyed . . . It matters not how unyielding the social pattern, how bending the law, how terrible the possible social ostracism, the Christian who really believes in God and man will do something about his

121. Davis, *Roots and Blossoms*, 110.

122. Ibid.

123. Mohler, *The Conviction to Lead*, 21.

124. Mays, *Seeking to Be Christians*, 77.

beliefs. He will recognize what so few people seem to see—that there is an area in every man's life, however small, over which he has complete control.[125]

Not only Mays was calling Americans to act democratically, he was insisting that Christians should behave according to biblical command and conviction that God wanted his people to treat everyone with dignity, justice, and fairness. This convictional belief embraces both theological persuasion and ethical value, and it must be demonstrated in public: "If the Christian will act in those areas where he has complete control, his power to act will grow and he will be able to act his beliefs in more dangerous zones."[126] Mays maintained that the democratization of the Christian faith entails the idea of living together in community, what Martin Luther King, Jr. called "the Beloved community." He also inferred such democratic faith is not only Christian, it is founded on the concept of the goodwill.

The Christian faith should be a catalyst that persuades followers of Christ to think democratically, respond Christianly, and act responsibility. Christian engagement in public should always be the demonstration of faith in action, and the action of the Christian is predicated on his faith or theological belief. It is from this premise Mays could declare boldly "The basic issues of lie are not political nor economic. They are religious—God, man, ethics, and spiritual values."[127] Mays substantiated this thesis by making it an urgent need for Christians not only to act theologically but for their actions to be premised on democratic ideals and sound ethical principles. A democratized Christianity is a faith at risk because it is predicated on a strong theological system, a set of moral conviction, and religious obligations; the authentic faith is redemptive and demonstrative in the public sphere:

> It would be surprising to know how few people would lose their jobs, positions, prestige, or popularity by taking a courageous stand or acting on beliefs and convictions that they know are right . . . One of the deepest facts of spiritual experience lies in the ultimate success of apparent defeat. The greatest fears are

125. Ibid., 78.
126. Ibid.
127. Ibid., 79.

frequently fearing of things that never happen. The true Christian will act on his faith and trust God for the results.[128]

Elsewhere, he condemned the racial segregation and miscarriage of justice in white American churches because transgressions are anti-democratic and unchristian. For him, the American church had a severe lack of democratic clarity and had misappropriated the liberating teachings of Jesus. Yet Mays was optimistic about the future of the American church and believed that it was possible to alter its ways and embrace the ethics of Jesus by way of "Christian fellowship" and "Christian relationality":

> The first stand, therefore, that the Church should take, in its effort to Christianize America in this generation, is on the question of Christian fellowship. The Church should be the one spot in America where all men are free and equal. It should be the one spot in America where artificial barriers, whether of group, class, or race, do not count. There should never by any doubt in the mind of any man that the Church is open to him; whether it be located in the bottom of Mississippi or in the upper right hand corner of Maine; and this applies to the Negro Church as well as to the White Church. On the point of segregation, the Church should not be subservient to the State nor to society. But as it stands today the Church is subservient both to the State and to Society. Instead of setting the standard for the secular order, it stands in awe of the secular order and is led by it.[129]

Mays's strong conviction to appeal to Christianize America is a call to action, and this call to action must involve political involvement, democratic participation, and civic engagement. In the same line of thought, Christian conviction to democracy must be commitments of permanence that pursue unnegotiable freedoms and human rights as well as political alliances and arrangements; it would also bring about immediate demands upon society—duties and prohibitions, commitment and collectivity, sacrifice and participation—that individuals would not be able to ignore without a firm call to serve and transform the social order.[130] One should remember that the democratic order makes life worth living and grants meaning to life itself, but "the meaning of life is the meaning of the collective"[131]—in the words of Paul Tillich. One should also

128. Ibid., 80.

129. Mays, "Democratizing and Christianizing America," 529.

130. Mohler, *Culture Shift*, 5, 15.

131. Tillich, *The Courage to Be*, 101.

bear in mind that democratic action toward human development and democratic progress are inseparable and necessary for a Christianized America and democratized Christianity.[132] For Mays, a democratic faith is grounded on the prophetic tradition of the Bible. Without a prophetic Christianity, there won't be a democratic state.

Toward a Prophetic Christianity

As part of his democratic vision, while Benjamin E. Mays was tolerant to other religious traditions and practices in the American society, he primarily relied on the transformative teachings of Christ, and the moral virtues and ethical force of Christianity to foster practical change in the American society. He envisioned that the United States could be both "a truly democratic" nation-state and a "truly Christian" society. Mays also construed Christianity and democracy distinctively as a twin (renewal) power and as the very engine of change for societal progress and for ameliorating race relations and human dynamics in culture. As he once declared, "If Germany through brutal means can build a kingdom of evil one decade and if Russia, through brutal processes, can construct a new order in two decades, we can democratize and Christianize in one generation."[133]

Mays's courageous and unapologetic claim that the prophetic Church in America has the adequate resources to "Christianize" America and be a "prophetic church," would also render the American society a truly democratic state. Mays's conviction is very appropriate and relevant for today's American Evangelicalism, as Christianity is progressively declining in the American society, and the American people are leaning more toward the secularist worldview.

> The basic issue of life is not political nor economic. They are religious–God, man, ethics, and spiritual values . . . If we could ever get the proper attitude toward God and man, we could more easily settle our political, economic, and social questions. I am talking about a belief in God that expresses itself in action. The true Christian not only has faith that leads to action, but he has faith that ultimately the results of his action will be good.[134]

132. Ibid., 109.
133. Mays, "Democratizing and Christianizing America," 528.
134. Ibid.

Mays put forth the idea that a democratic society and a democratic Christian faith encourage cooperative participation and reciprocity in the democratic life.[135] In *Democracy in America*, French political scientist Alexis de Tocqueville emphasized the practice of deliberation and the ethic of reciprocity, which he associated with relational life, makes the work of democracy functional in the American life; for Tocqueville, "the experience of associational life inclines Americans toward benevolence, or sympathy, whether they are virtuous or not . . . interests as well as sympathy prompts a code of lending each other mutual assistance at need. The more similar conditions become, the more do people show this readiness of reciprocal obligation."[136]

Mays believed that the church must embrace the prophetic tradition, and that like the ancient Prophets of the Hebrew Scripture, American Christians must bear witness even though people in this nation do not repent[137] of cultural sins and political transgressions such as anti-black racism, xenophobia, church segregation, the practice of injustice and social oppression, etc. A prophetic church is a church that is "called upon to recognize the urgency of the present situation," [138] he noted. The biblical notion of distributive and retribution justice makes the issue of economic justice for all people an urgent demand and ethical imperative in contemporary times.[139] Mays maintained that it is the Gospel that Christians announce and embody in their lives that "demands interracial justice and an unsegregated church" and that Christians should move toward more interracial progress in ecclesiastical practices because the benefits of the atonement of Christ created the unparallel conviction, that is, a sense of Christian brotherhood and fellowship among all believers.[140]

The death of Christ created the obligation upon believers to pursue each other, walk together in a common faith, and redefined political citizenship and cultural allegiance. Mays could reiterate, "It has always been the responsibility of the church and the gospel to plow new ground, smash, traditions, break the mores, and make new creatures."[141]

135. Mays, "Review: *A Catholic's View of Race Relations*," 634.

136. Quoted in Kloppenberg, *The Virtues of Liberalism*, 77.

137. Mays, *Born to Rebel*, 259.

138. Ibid., 354.

139. Ibid.

140. Ibid.

141. Ibid.

The moral and theological responsibility of contemporary Christian churches in America is

> to show how the gospel of Christ can be presented and lived so as to make new creatures of men and women in the area of race and bring hope and abundant life to all men—not only beyond history but in history. We refuse to believe that God is limited in history and that we must wait until the end of history before his mighty works can be performed . . . The individual Christian will be responsive to the gospel and he will act on his Christian convictions. There is no dichotomy between what we believe and what we do. We do what we believe.[142]

Mays used the concept of "prophets of social righteousness"[143] to refer to zealous individuals who understood their role in the public sphere as agents of transformation grounded on the exemplary life and liberative teachings of Jesus Christ. These individuals, according to Mays, must do their work outside the Church. Prophets of social righteousness strive collectively to dismantle social proscriptions imposed on the marginalized groups in the United States, especially the economically-disadvantaged black population; they appeal to the moral imperatives of Christianity to address both "social and economic problems on a larger scale."[144] Mays also established connection between the activist work of prophets of social righteousness and advocates of the Social Gospel movement. He inferred that these individuals embodied a democratized Christianity in which the "beginning of new social sciences" emerged in the society.[145] The prophetic church produces prophets of social righteousness and prophets of moral conscience to the nation.

> These aroused the churches to a sense of their responsibility for the social wrongs inherent in society. Thus, the efforts to create a fellowship across racial lines which would be in every sense Christina is a part of this larger awakening on the part of the church and religious forces. They could not turn to these larger problems without seeing definitely that most the practices with reference to the Negro were unchristian.[146]

142. Ibid., 354–56.

143. Mays, "The American Negro and the Christian Religion," 535.

144. Ibid.

145. Ibid., 536.

146. Ibid.

According to Mays, the prophetic church is the church that will consciously and actively pursue constructive projects to "support a growing consciousness of needed social adjustment" in the American society. Mays identified three areas of social development the prophetic church must work toward, including (1) social adjustment that is universal in scope but inclusive of the needs of the brown and black population, (2) social adjustment that is confined primarily to the social and economic needs of the disfranchised and marginalized populations, and (3) A psychological adjustment in which Christian theological belief and practice are interpreted creatively to support the growing democratic conviction that black people are not an inferior people; rather they are bearers of God's image, and they are entitled to the same social, educational, economic, and political benefits as other groups and races in this country.[147] Similarly, Caribbean Theologian Idris Hamid draws the connection between eschatology, change, and development as he calls upon Black people in Caribbean Christian communities to humanize the Caribbean experience and to create a new vision of the future that will not lead to resignation but to action; "We must be relenting in 'making and keeping human life human' in our society. That must be the norm of all our activities."[148]

Conclusion

At the conclusion of his autobiography, Mays's optimism about the end of the race problem in the Untied Stated is dubious, and his cynical spirit about interracial unity and harmony in the church is quite evident. For example, he declared: "I do not know whether there is a solution to the Negro-white problem. Whether racism in the United States can be abolished, I am not omniscient enough to say."[149] Mays was profoundly discontent about the state of American Christianity in ending anti-black racism and its silence on social justice issues. He certainly was not hopeful that better education and cultural resources could drastically alter human dynamics and interracial interplays in the country.

> To date, education and religion have abolished racism, despite the fact that education is supposed to enable a man to find truth

147. Mays, *The Negro's God*, 15.

148. Hamid, *In Search of New Perspectives*, 8.

149. Mays, *Born to Rebel*, 320.

and follow it, while religion is designed to make men good . . . I
find no comfort in history for the Negro's plight.[150]

On the other hand, Mays's cynicism is not ultimate despair nor
should it be regarded as the triumph of human nihilism in the American
society and in the Church. He had hoped it was possible for both white
and black Americans to move forward toward racial progress, and for
American Christianity to be the avant-garde of progress and success.

> It seems to me, however, that we have no choice but to con-
> tinue our efforts to make this country a decent place for all
> Americans . . . I have the faith to believe that white and blacks
> can improve their relationship to extent that they can live to-
> gether in peace, each respecting other. I am convinced that any
> program designed to solve the black-white problem by provid-
> ing a geographically segregated place for twenty million blacks
> is destined to failure.[151]

Mays concurred that non-violent actions in the ways of Mahatma
Gandhi and Martin Luther King, Jr. are the most promising means to
achieve racial progress in the American society and democratize America's institutions. He rejected the idea that the redemption of black and
brown people in the United States is dependent upon the total destruction of America's contemporary social, economic, and political systems;
he did not believe this form of activist drive would foster "a new order of
justice, freedom, and equality for all Americans."[152] Hitherto Benjamin
E. Mays was convinced that both white and black Americans belong to
this country and their lives and destiny are bound together. He also held
that democratic evolution in the church was necessary if this country
is going to live up to its ideals, as embedded in its Constitution and Bill
of Rights. Not only he conceived the future of democracy as a matter of
individual responsibility, he stressed that it was the collective effort of
American Christians to actualize the benefits of American democracy
for all people. In the same line of reasoning, there is a particular vision of
the American society and compatibly a sense that the American people,
regardless of their race, gender, and religion:

> have a shared destiny, a common commitment to opportu-
> nity, and fairness, where the words "liberty and justice for all"

150. Ibid., 528.
151. Ibid., 320.
152. Ibid.

actually mean what they seem to mean, where we take seriously the Universal Declaration of Human Rights, which emphasizes the importance not just of civil rights but of economic
rights, and not just the rights of property but the economic
rights of ordinary citizens.[153]

This is the society Mays envisioned within his democratic framework. For him, democracy demands that the American government, the
American Church, and the American people should plan together the
future of the nation and set up a timeliness to ameliorate the country's
socio-economic conditions and the political ills that hinder human blossoming and paralyze a large segment of its population. His democratic
vision lies in the general will of the American people and the collective
conviction of Christians that the United States could be a better country for all. For him, American democracy should promote the virtue of
equality, equity, and justice as fairness; correspondingly, he underscored
the value of community and racial difference to fortify the American
democratic experiment. Equality as justice is a democratic promise
which "stems from the political equality of all citizens . . . It is the key
to the response from the bottom, and to the prevention of disruptions
in a democracy."[154] In the last pages of his autobiography, he made this
insightful observation that is relevant to our contemporary discourse on
democracy and human rights:

> If the governments, private businesses, schools, churches,
> individuals, and the American people have the will, they can
> contribute to the solution of this problem. We can, within a
> ten-year span, provide decent housing for every family, make
> adequate jobs available for every able-bodied person, provide
> the kind of education that each child is able to absorb, make ac-
> cessible medical care for all, abolish poverty and malnutrition,
> and permit each man to advance on his merit without his being
> penalized because he is black.[155]

While May advocated for a more democratic American society and
a more progressive and democratized Christian church, he rejected the
idea that America's progress and success in the areas of economy, politics, and military can save the American people nor could these assets

153. Stiglitz, *The Price of Inequality*, 289.

154. Brigham, *Civil Liberties*, 262.

155. Mays, *Born to Rebel*, 321.

be deployed to foster spiritual transformation. In an important book on *Seeking to be Christian in Race Relations*, published in 1957, Mays reasoned that America's central problems are both spiritual and moral, not technological or scientific. He asserted, "Nothing can save us now except repentance, good will, justice, love, and forgiveness."[156] He projected the Christian church in America should lead the country to acquire and practice these virtues. Elsewhere, he affirmed that "It is indeed strange that when man does evil, he has the will, but when he faces a moral crisis and needs to do what is right, he calls on God to give him the strength to do it."[157] He also maintained, "Cultural attainment, scientific achievement and economic power are not solutions to race problems."[158]

We must continue fighting for the work of (Christian) democracy to be fully effective in Christian (public) spaces in America. Without passion and conviction, democracy will die and vanish before our eyes. In other words, democratic commitment demands both personal and collective responsibility and a strong collective impulse toward the common good. As Glaude suggested, "We have to become better people by fundamentally transforming the conditions of our living together. This will require setting aside our comforting illusions . . . What we put in and leave out of our stories tells us something about who we are."[159] Mays believed that God invaded human history in order to liberate human beings and this divine scheme also included the transformation of the social order so that human flourishing might be an existential and practical experience in this present life and the abundant life might accrue to all.[160]

156. Mays, *Seeking to be Christian*, 67.

157. Mays, *Born to Rebel*, 245.

158. Mays, "The Color Line Around the World," 142.

159. Glaude, *Democracy in Black*, 46–47.

160. Mays, *The Negro's God*, 248.

Bibliography

Achebe, Chinua. *Things Fall Apart*. New York: Anchor, 1994.

Adegbola, E. A. Adeolu. "The Theological Basis of Ethics." In *Biblical Revelation and African Beliefs*, edited by Kwesi A. Dickson and Paul Ellingworth, 116–36. London: Lutterworth, 1969.

Ahlstrom, Sydney E. *A Religious History of the American People*. New Haven: Yale University Press, 2004.

Anderson, Victor. *Beyond Ontological Blackness: An Essay on African American Religious and Cultural Criticism*. New York: Continuum, 1999.

Antoine, Jacques Cameleau. *Jean Price-Mars and Haiti*. Boulder, CO: Lynne Rienner, 1997.

Appiah, Kwame Anthony. *The Honor Code: How Moral Revolution Happens*. New York: Norton, 2011.

Aristide, Jean-Bertrand. *Aristide: An Autobiography*. Jean-Bertrand Aristide with Christopher Wargny. Maryknoll, NY: Orbis, 1993.

———. *Eyes of the Heart: Seeking a Path for the Poor in the Age of Globalization*. Monroe, ME: Common Courage, 2000.

———. *Théologie et politique*. Montréal: CIDIHCA, 1992.

———. *Tout homme est un homme*. Paris: Editions du Seuil, 1992.

———. "Umoya Wamagama (The Spirit of the Word)." PhD diss., University of South Africa, 2006.

Assmann, Hugo. *Theology for a Nomad Church*. Translated by Frederick Herzog. New York: Orbis, 1976.

Awolalu, J. O. "What is African Traditional Religion?" *Studies in Comparative Religion* 9/1 (1975) 1–28.

Azevedo, Mario Joaquim, ed. *Africana Studies: A Survey of Africa and the African Diaspora*. Durham, NC: Carolina Academic Press, 2005.

Baldwin, James. "Dialogue in Black and White (1964–1965) by James Baldwin and Budd Schulberg." In *James Baldwin: The Legacy*, edited by Quincy Troupe, 135–60. New York: Simon and Schuster/Touchstone, 1989.

———. "The Fire This Time: Letter to the Bishop." In *James Baldwin: The Cross of Redemption*, edited by Randall Kenan, 215–18. New York: Pantheon, 2010.

———. "The Last Interview (1987)." In *James Baldwin: The Legacy*, edited by Quincy Troupe, 186–212. New York: Simon and Schuster/Touchstone, 1989.

Baptist, Edward E. *The Half Has Never Been Told: Slavery and the Making of American Capitalism*. New York: Basic Books, 2014.

Barth, Karl. *Church Dogmatics*. Edited by Helmut Gollwitzer. Louisville: Westminster John Knox, 1994.

Bellah, Robert, et al. *The Good Society*. New York: Vintage, 2013.

Benitez-Rojo, Antonio. *The Repeating Islands: The Caribbean and the Postmodern Perspective*. Durham, NC: Duke University Press, 2006.

Bennett, Lerone. *Before the Mayflower: A History of the Negro in America, 1619–1962*. New York: Martino Fine Books, 2018.

Berlin, Ira. *Many Thousands Gone: The First Two Centuries of Slavery in North America*. Cambridge, MA: Belknap, 1998.

Bigo, Pierre. *The Church and Third World Revolution*. New York: Orbis, 1977.

Blackburn, Robin. *The American Crucible: Slavery, Emancipation and Human Rights*. New York: Verso, 2013.

———. *The Making of New World Slavery: From the Baroque to the Modern 1492–1800*. New York: Verso, 1997.

———. *The Overthrow of Colonial Slavery: 1776–1848*. New York: Verso, 2011.

Blount, Brian K. *Then the Whisper Put on Flesh: New Testament Ethics in an African American Context*. Nashville: Abingdon, 2001.

Boesak, Allan A. *Black and Reformed: Apartheid, Liberation, and the Calvinist Tradition*. Eugene: Wipf & Stock, 1984.

Boff, Clodovis. *Theology and Praxis: Epistemological Foundations*. Eugene: Wipf & Stock, 2009.

Boff, Leonardo. *Church: Charism and Power: Liberation Theology and the Institutional Church*. New York: Crossroad, 1984.

Bonino, José Míguez. *Toward a Christian Political Ethics*. Minneapolis: Fortress, 2007.

Brigham, John. *Civil Liberties and American Democracy*. Washington, DC: CQ, 1984.

Burrow, Rufus. *Extremist for Love: Martin Luther King Jr., Man of Ideas and Nonviolent Social Action*. Minneapolis: Fortress, 2014.

Burton, Orville Vernon. "Born to Rebel." In *Walking Integrity: Benjamin Elijah Mays, Mentor to Martin Luther King Jr.*, edited by Lawrence Edward Carter, 33–80. Macon, GA: Mercer University Press, 1998.

Bujo, Bénézet. *Foundations of An African Ethic: Beyond the Universal Claims of Western Morality*. New York: Crossroad, 2001.

Carter, J. Kameron. *Race: A Theological Account of Race*. Oxford: Oxford University Press, 2008.

Casseus, Jules. *Eléments de Théologie Haïtienne*. Port-au-Prince: La Presse Evangélique, 2007.

———. *Toward a Contextual Haitian Theology*. Port-au-Prince: Imprimerie Media-Text, 2013.

Chancy, Myriam J. A. *Frame Silence: Revolutionary Novels by Haitian Women*. New Brunswick, NJ: Rutgers University Press, 1997.

Clormeus, Lewis Ampidu. "L'Église catholique face à la diversité religieuse à Port-au-Prince (1942–2012)." *Archives de sciences sociales des religions* 166 (April–June 2014) 155–80.

Cone, James H. *Black Theology and Black Power*. San Francisco: Harper & Row, 1989.

———. "Black Theology and the Black Church: Where Do We Go from Here?" In *Black Theology: A Documentary History, Volume One: 1966–1979*, edited by James Cone and Gayraud S. Wilmore, 266–75. Maryknoll, NY: Orbis, 1993.

———. *A Black Theology of Liberation*. Maryknoll, NY, Orbis, 2010.

———. *The Cross and the Lynching Tree*. Maryknoll, NY: Orbis, 2011.

———. "Epilogue: An Interpretation of the Debate Among Black Theologians." In *Black Theology: A Documentary History, Volume One: 1966–1979*, edited by James Cone and Gayraud S. Wilmore, 425–39. Maryknoll, NY: Orbis, 1993.

———. *For My People: Black Theology and the Black Church*. Maryknoll, NY: Orbis, 1991.

———. *God of the Oppressed*. New York: Seabury, 1975.

———. "Looking Back, Going Forward." In *Black Faith and Public Talk: Critical Essays on James H. Cone's Black Theology and Black Power*, edited by Dwight N. Hopkins, 246–59. Waco: Baylor University Press, 2007.

———. *Martin and Malcolm and America: A Dream or A Nightmare?* New York: Orbis, 2012.

———. *My Soul Looks Back*. Maryknoll, NY: Orbis, 1999.

———. *Risks of Faith: The Emergence of a Black Theology of Liberation, 1968–1998*. Boston: Beacon 2005.

———. *Said I Wasn't Gonna Tell Nobody: The Making of a Black Theologian*. Maryknoll, NY: Orbis, 2018.

———. *The Spirituals and the Blues*. Maryknoll, NY: Orbis, 2003.

———. "The White Church and Black Power." In *Black Theology: A Documentary History, Volume One, 1966–1979*, edited by James Cone and Gayraud S. Wilmore, 66–85. New York: Orbis 2004.

Costas, Orlando E. *The Church and Its Mission: A Shattering Critique from The Third World*. Wheaton, IL: Tyndale, 1977.

Danfulani, Umar Habila Dadem. "West African Religions in European Scholarship." In *European Traditions in the Study of Religions in Africa*, edited by Frieder Ludwig and Afe Adogame, 341–64. Gottingen: Hubert, 2004.

Danticat, Edwidge. *Create Dangerously: The Immigrant Artist at Work*. Princeton: Princeton University Press, 2010.

Davis, David Brion. *Inhuman Bondage: The Rise and Fall of Slavery in the New World*. New York: Oxford University Press, 2006.

———. *The Problem of Slavery in the Age of Revolution, 1770–1823*. New York: Oxford University Press, 1999.

———. *The Problem of Slavery in Western Culture*. New York: Oxford University Press, 1988.

———. *Slavery and Human Progress*. New York: Oxford University Press, 1986.

Davis, Edmund. *Roots and Blossoms*. Bridgetown, Barbados: Cedar, 1977.

Davis, Korthright. *Emancipation Still Comin': Explorations in Caribbean Emancipatory Theology*. Maryknoll, NY: Orbis, 1990.

———. *Serving with Power: Reviving the Spirit of Christian Ministry*. New York: Paulist, 1999.

Davis, Zachary, and Anthony Steinbock. "Max Scheler." *The Stanford Encyclopedia of Philosophy*. 2014. http://plato.stanford.edu/archives/sum2014/entries/scheler/.

Dewey, John. *The Later Works of John Dewey*. Vol. 11, *1925–1953: Essays, Reviews, Trotsky Inquiry, Miscellany, and* Liberalism and Social Action. Edited by Jo Ann Boydston, et al. Jackson: Southern Illinois University Press, 2008.

————. *The Public and Its Problems*. Athens, OH: Swallow, 1954.

Dorrien, Gary. *Breaking White Supremacy: Martin Luther King Jr. and the Black Social Gospel*. New Haven: Yale University Press, 2018.

————. *The Making of American Liberal Theology: Crisis, Irony, and Postmodernity, 1950–2005*. Louisville: Westminster John Knox, 2006.

————. *The Making of American Liberal Theology: Idealism, Realism, and Modernity, 1900–1950*. Louisville: Westminster John Knox, 2003.

————. *The Making of American Liberal Theology: Imagining Progressive Religion, 1805–1900*. Louisville: Westminster John Knox, 2001.

————. *The New Abolition: W. E. B. Du Bois and the Black Social Gospel*. New Haven: Yale University Press, 2015.

————. *Social Democracy in the Making: Political and Religious Roots of European Socialism*. New Haven: Yale University Press, 2019.

Douglas, Kelly Brown. *Stand Your Ground: Black Bodies and the Justice of God*. Maryknoll, NY: Orbis, 2005.

————. "Womanist Theology: What Is Its Relationship to Black Theology?" In *Black Theology: A Documentary History Volume Two: 1980–1992*, edited by James Cone and Gayraud S. Wilmore, 290–300. Maryknoll, NY: Orbis, 2005.

Dube, Musa W. *Postcolonial Feminist Interpretation of the Bible*. St. Louis: Chalice, 2000.

Du Bois, W. E. B. *Black Reconstruction in America 1860–1880*. New York: Free Press, 1998.

————. *The Negro Church: With an Introduction by Alton B. Pollard III*. Eugene, OR: Cascade, 2011.

————. *The Philadelphia Negro: A Social Study*. Philadelphia: The University of Pennsylvania Press, 1996.

Dupuy, Alex. *Haiti in the New World Order: The Limits of Democratic Revolution*. Boulder, CO: Westview, 1997.

Dussel, Enrique. *Beyond Philosophy: Ethics, History, Marxism, and Liberation Theology*. Lanham, MD: Rowman & Littlefield, 2003.

————. *Ethics of Liberation in the Age of Globalization and Exclusion*. Durham, NC: Duke University Press, 2013.

————. *Twenty Theses on Politics*. Durham, NC: Duke University Press, 2008.

Dye, Thomas R. *The Politics of Equality*. Indianapolis: The Bobbs-Merrill, 1971.

Ellis, Marc H., and Otto Maduro, eds. *Expanding the View: Gustavo Gutiérrez and the Future of Liberation Theology*. New York: Orbis, 1990.

Erskine, Noel Leo. *Decolonizing Theology: A Caribbean Perspective*. Maryknoll, NY: Orbis, 1981.

Evans, James H. *We Have Been Believers: An African-American Systematic Theology*. Minneapolis: Fortress, 1992.

Evans-Pritchard, E. E. *Theories of Primitive Religion*. Oxford: Clarendon, 2004.

Fils-Aimé, Jean. *Vodou, je me souviens: essai*. Québec: Les Editions Dabar, 2007.

Foner, Eric. *The Fiery Trial: Abraham Lincoln and American Slavery*. New York: Norton, 2010.

Fontus, Fritz. *Effective Communication of the Gospel in Haiti: Its Inculturation*. Pembroke Pines, FL: N.p., 2001.

Francis, Leah Gunning. *Faith: Sparking Leadership and Awakening Community*. St Louis: Chalice, 2015.

———. *Faith Following Ferguson: Five Years of Resilience and Wisdom*. St Louis: Chalice, 2019.

Franklin, John. *From Slavery to Freedom: A History of African Americans*. New York: Knopf, 2000.

Frazier, E. Franklin. *The Negro Church in America*. New York: Schocken, 1974.

Glaude, Eddie S. *Democracy in Black: How Race Still Enslaves the American Soul*. New York: Crown, 2016.

Glissant, Edouard. *Caribbean Discourse: Selected Essays*. Charlottesville: University Press of Virginia, 1999.

———. *Poetics of Relation*. Ann Arbor: The University of Michigan Press, 1997.

Gordon, Lewis Ricardo. *Existentia Africana: Understanding Africana Existential Thought*. New York: Routledge, 2000.

Grant, Jacquelyn. "Black Theology and the Black Woman." In *Black Theology: A Documentary History, Volume One: 1966-1979*, edited by James Cone and Gayraud S. Wilmore, 323–38. Maryknoll, NY: Orbis, 1993.

———. "Womanist Theology: Black Women's Experience as a Source for Doing Theology, with Special Reference to Christology." In *Black Theology: A Documentary History, Volume Two: 1980-1992*, edited by James Cone and Gayraud S. Wilmore, 273–89. Maryknoll, NY: Orbis, 2005.

Gregory, Howard, ed. *Caribbean Theology: Preparing for the Challenges Ahead*. Kingston, Jamaica: University of West Indies Press, 1995.

Grenz, Stanley. *Theology for the Community of God*. Nashville: Broadman & Holman, 1994.

Gutjahr, Paul C. *Charles Hodge: Guardian of American Orthodoxy*. New York: Oxford University Press, 2012.

Gyekye, Kwame. *Tradition and Modernity: Philosophical Reflections on the African Experience*. New York: Oxford University Press, 1997.

Hackett, Rosalind I. J. *Art and Religion in Africa*. London, Cassell, 1999.

Hamid, Idris. *In Search of New Perspectives*. Bridgetown, Barbados: Caribbean Ecumenical Consultation for Development, 1971.

———. *Troubling of the Waters: A Collection of Papers and Responses*. San Fernando, Trinidad: Rahaman, 1973.

———. "Theology and Caribbean Development." In *With Eyes Wide Open*, edited by David I. Mitchell, 120-33. Kingston, Jamaica: Cadec, 1973.

Hick, John. *An Interpretation of Religion: Human Responses to the Transcendent*. New York: Palgrave Macmillan, 2004.

———. *God and the Universe of Faiths*. Rockport, MA: Oneworld, 1994.

Holifield, E Brooks. *Theology in America Christian Thought from the Age of the Puritans to the Civil War*. New Haven: Yale University Press, 2008.

Hopkins, Dwight N. *Being Human: Race, Culture, and Religion*. Minneapolis: Fortress, 2005.

———. *Shoes That Fit Our Feet: Sources for A Constructive Black Theology*. Maryknoll, NY: Orbis, 1993.

Hurbon, Laënnec. *Dieu dans le Vaudou haïtien*. Paris : Payot, 1972.

Idowu, E. Bolaji. *African Traditional Religion: A Definition*. New York: Orbis, 1975.

———. *Olodumare: God in Yoruba Belief*. New York: African Tree, 1999.

James, C. L. R. *The Black Jacobins: Toussaint L'Ouverture and the Santo Domingo Revolution.* New York: Vintage, 1989.

Jelks, Randal Maurice. *Benjamin Elijah Mays, Schoolmaster of the Movement: A Biography.* Chapel Hill: The University of North Carolina Press, 2012.

———. "Mays's Academic Formation, 1917–1936." In *Walking Integrity: Benjamin Elijah Mays, Mentor to Martin Luther King Jr.*, edited by Lawrence Edward Carter, 111–29. Macon, GA: Mercer University Press, 1998.

Johnson, James Weldon, and J. Rosamond Johnson. *The Books of American Negro Spirituals.* New York: Viking, 1926.

Johnson, Luke Timothy. *Sharing Possessions: Mandate and Symbol of Faith.* London: SCM, 1986.

Jones, William R. *Is God a White Racist? A Preamble to Black Theology.* New York: Anchor, 1973.

———. "Theodicy and Methodology in Black Theology: A Critique of Washington, Cone, and Cleage." In *Black Theology: A Documentary History Volume One: 1966–1979*, edited by James Cone and Gayraud S. Wilmore, 141–52. Maryknoll, NY: Orbis, 1993.

Joseph, Celucien L. "Prophetic Religion, Violence, and Black Freedom: Reading Makandal's Project of Black Liberation through a Fanonian Postcolonial Lens of Decolonization and Theory of Revolutionary Humanism." *Journal of Race, Ethnicity, and Religion* 3/4 (August 2012) 1–30.

———. "The Religious Imagination and Ideas of Jean Price-Mars (Part 1)." *Journal of Race, Ethnicity, and Religion* 2/14 (December 2011) 1–31.

———. "The Religious Philosophy of Jean Price-Mars." *Journal of Black Studies* 43/6 (2012) 620–45.

———. "The Rhetoric of Prayer: Dutty Boukman, The Discourse of 'Freedom from Below,' and the Politics of God." *Journal of Race, Ethnicity, and Religion* 2/9 (June 2011) 1–33.

Keller, Catherine, et al., eds. *Postcolonial Theologies: Divinity and Empire.* St. Louis: Chalice, 2004.

Kendi, Ibram X. *Stamped from the Beginning: The Definitive History of Racist Ideas in America.* New York: Nation, 2016.

Kimball, Charles. *When Religion Becomes Evil: Five Warning Signs.* New York: HarperCollins, 2009.

Kloppenberg, James T. *The Virtues of Liberalism.* New York: Oxford University Press, 1998.

Lebron, Christopher J. *The Making of Black Lives Matter: A Brief History of an Idea.* New York: Oxford University Press, 2017.

Lewinson, Barbara Sue. "Mays's Educational Philosophy." In *Walking Integrity: Benjamin Elijah Mays, Mentor to Martin Luther King Jr.*, edited by Lawrence Edward Carter, 215–31 Macon, GA: Mercer University Press, 1998.

Lincoln, C. Eric. *The Black Church Since Frazier.* New York: Schocken, 1974.

Lincoln, C. Eric, and Lawrence H. Mamiya. *The Black Church in the African American Experience.* Durham, NC: Duke University Press, 1990.

Lippman, Walter. *Drift and Mastery: An Attempt to Diagnose the Current Unrest.* Madison: The University of Wisconsin Press, 1985.

Long, Charles H. *Significations: Signs, Symbols, and Images in the Interpretation of Religion.* Aurora, CO: Davies Group, 1999.

Lowe-Ching, Theresa. "Method in Caribbean Theology." In *Caribbean Theology: Preparing for the Challenges Ahead*, edited by Howard Gregory, 23-34. Kingston, Jamaica: University of West Indies, 1995.

Ludwig, Frieder, and Afe Adogame. "Historiography and European Perceptions of African Religious History." In *European Traditions in the Study of Religions in Africa*, edited by Frieder Ludwig and Afe Adogame, 1-22. Gottingen: Hubert, 2004.

Magadla, Sphokazi, and Ezra Chitando. "The Self Become God: Ubuntu and the 'Scandal of Manhood.'" In *Ubuntu: Curating the Archive*, edited by Leonhard Praeg and Sphokazi Magadla, 2-28. Pietermaritzburg: University of KwaZulu-Natal Press, 2014.

Magesa, Laurenti. *African Religion: The Moral Traditions of Abundant Life*. Maryknoll, NY: Orbis, 1997.

———. *Anatomy of Inculturation: Transforming the Church in Africa*. Maryknoll, NY: Orbis, 2004.

Magloire, Gerarde, and Kevin A. Yelvington. "Haiti and the Anthropological Imagination." *Gradhiva* (2015) 127–52.

Masolo, D. A. *Self and Community in a Changing World*. Bloomington: Indiana University Press, 2010.

Mather, Cotton. *The Negro Christianized: An Essay to Excite and Assist that Good Work, the Instruction of Negro-Servants in Christianity (1706)*. Edited by Paul Royster. 2007. https://digitalcommons.unl.edu/cgi/viewcontent.cgi?article=1028&context=etas.

Matthews, Verner Randolph. "Mays and Racial Justice." In Lawrence Edward Carter, *Walking Integrity: Benjamin Elijah Mays, Mentor to Martin Luther King Jr.* Macon: Mercer University Press, 1998. pp.263-288.

Mays, Benjamin E. "The American Negro and the Christian Religion." *The Journal of Negro Education* 8/3 (1939) 530–38.

———. *Born to Rebel: An Autobiography*. Athens: The University of Georgia Press, 1987.

———. "The Color Line Around the World." *The Journal of Negro Education* 6/2 (1937) 134–43.

———. "Democratizing and Christianizing America in This Generation." *The Journal of Negro Education* 14/4 (1945) 527–34.

———. "Higher Education and the American Negro." In *African American Political Thought: A Historical Reader*, edited by Marcus D. Pohlmann, 38–69. New York: Routledge, 2000.

———. *The Negro's God as Reflected in His Literature*. Eugene: Wipf & Stock, 2010.

———. "The Religious Life and Needs of Negro Students." *The Journal of Negro Education* 9/3 (1940) 332–43.

———. "Review: A Catholic's View of Race Relations: Interracial Justice by John La Farge." *The Journal of Negro Education* 6/4 (1937) 631–34.

———. *Seeking to Be Christians in Race Relations*. New York: Friendship, 1957.

Mays, Benjamin E., and Joseph William Nicholson. *The Negro's Church*. New York: Arno, 1969.

Mbiti, John S. *African Religions and Philosophy*. Portsmouth, NH: Heinemann Educational, 1969.

————. "An African Views American Black Theology." In *Black Theology: A Documentary History, Volume One: 1966–1979*, edited by James Cone and Gayraud S. Wilmore, 379–84. Maryknoll, NY: Orbis, 1993.

————. *Introduction to African Religion*. Portsmouth, NH: Heinemann Educational, 1991.

McKinney, Karyn D. *Being White: Stories of Race and Racism*. New York: Routledge, 2004.

McKivijan, John R., and Mitchell Snay. *Religion and the Antebellum Debate Over Slavery*. Athens: University of Georgia Press, 1998.

Menkiti, Ifeanyi A. "Person and Community in African Traditional Thought." In *African Philosophy: An Introduction*, edited by Richard A. Wright, 171–82. Lanham, MD: University Press of America, 1979.

Mignolo, Walter D. *The Darker Side of Western Modernity: Global Futures, Decolonial Options*. Durham, NC: Duke University Press, 2011.

Mohler, R. Albert. *The Conviction to Lead: 25 Principles for Leadership That Matters*. Minneapolis: Bethany, 2012.

————. *Culture Shift: The Battle for the Moral Heart of America*. Colorado Springs: Multnomah, 2011.

Mosala, Itumeleng J. *Biblical Hermeneutics and Black Theology in South Africa*. Grand Rapids: Eerdmans, 1989.

Mudimbe, V. Y. *The Idea of Africa*. Bloomington: Indiana University Press, 1994.

Nicholls, David. "A Work of Combat: Mulatto Historians and the Haitian Past, 1847–1867." *Journal of Interamerican Studies and World Affairs* 16/1 (1974) 15.

Niebuhr, Reinhold. *The Children of Light and the Children of Darkness: A Vindication of Democracy and a Critique of Its Traditional Defense*. New York: Scribner's, 1944.

————. *An Interpretation of Christian Ethics*. Louisville: Westminster John Knox, 2013.

————. *Moral Man and Immoral Society: A Study in Ethics and Politics*. Louisville: Westminster John Knox, 2013.

Noll, Mark A. *The Civil War as A Theological Crisis*. Chapel Hill: University of North Carolina Press, 2009.

Page, Hugh R., Jr. "The Africana Bible: A Rationale." In *The Africana Bible: Readings Israel's Scriptures from Africa and The African Diaspora*, edited by Hugh R. Page Jr., 3-10. Minneapolis: Fortress, 2010.

Pannenberg, Wolfhart. *Anthropology in Theological Perspective*. Edinburgh: T. & T. Clark, 1999.

————. *What Is Man? Contemporary Anthropology in Theological Perspective*. Philadelphia: Fortress, 1970.

Paris, Peter J. *The Social Teaching of the Black Churches*. Philadelphia: Fortress, 1985.

————. *The Spirituality of African Peoples: The Search for A Common Moral Discourse*. Minneapolis: Fortress, 1995.

Parrinder, Geoffrey. *African Traditional Religion*. London: SPCK, 1978.

————. *West African Religion: A Study of the Beliefs and Practices of Akan, Ewe, Yoruba, Ibo, and Kindred Peoples*. Eugene, OR: Wipf & Stock 2014.

————. *World Religions: From Ancient History to the Present*. New York: Facts on File, 1984.

Patterson, Orlando. *Freedom in the Making of Western Culture*. New York: Basic, 1991.

————. *Slavery and Social Death: A Comparative Study*. Cambridge, MA: Harvard University Press, 1982.

p'Bitek, Okot. *Decolonizing African Religions: A Short History of African Religions in Western Scholarship.* New York: Diasporic Africa Press, 2011.

Pfaff, Fancoise. *Conversations with Maryse Conde.* Lincoln: University of Nebraska Press, 1996.

Pinn, Anthony B. *The Black Church in the Post-Civil Rights Era.* Maryknoll, NY: Orbis, 2002.

———. *Why Lord? Suffering and Evil in Black Theology.* New York: Continuum, 1995.

Price-Mars, Jean. *Ainsi parla l'oncle suivi de Revisiter l'oncle.* Montréal: Mémoire d'encrier, 2009.

———. *Formation ethnique, folklore et culture du peuple haïtien.* Edited by Celucien L. Joseph. Port Saint Lucie: Hope Outreach Productions, 2016.

———. "From So Uncle Said." In *I Am Because We Are: Readings in Black Philosophy,* edited by Fred Lee Hord and Jonathan Scott Lee, 145–51. Translated by Raymond F. Betts. Amherst: University of Massachusetts Press, 2016.

———. *La République d'Haïti et la République dominicaine. TOME II. Essais D'Ethnographie.* Edited by Celucien L. Joseph. Port Saint Lucie: Hope Outreach Productions, 2016.

———. *So Spoke the Uncle.* Translated by Magdalene Shannon. Washington, DC: Three Continents, 1983.

———. *Une Etape de l'Evolution haïtienne. Essais D'Ethnographie.* Edited by Celucien L. Joseph. Port Saint Lucie: Hope Outreach Productions, 2016.

———. "The Vocation of the Elite." In *Caribbean Cultural Thought: From Plantation to Diaspora,* edited by Yanique Hume and Aaron Kamugisha, 13–27. Translated by Bernadette Farquhar. Kingston, Jamaica: Ian Randle, 2013.

Rabaka, Reiland. *Against Epistemic Apartheid: W. E. B. Du Bois and the Disciplinary Decadence of Sociology.* Lanham, MD: Lexington, 2010.

———. *Concepts of Cabralism: Amical Cabral and Africana Critical Theory.* Lanham, MD: Lexington, 2010.

———. *Forms of Fanonism: Frantz Fanon's Critical Theory and the Dialectics of Decolonization.* Lanham, MD: Lexington, 2010.

Rawls, John. *A Theory of Justice.* Cambridge, MA: The President and Fellows of Harvard College, 1971.

Rediker, Marcus. *The Many-Headed Hydra: Sailors, Slaves, Commoners, the Hidden History of the Revolutionary Atlantic.* New York: Beacon, 2013.

———. *The Slave Ship: A Human History.* New York: Penguin, 2008.

Rey, Terry. *Crossing the Water and Keeping the Faith: Haitian Religion in Miami.* New York: New York University Press, 2016.

Roberts, J. Deotis. *A Black Political Theology.* Louisville: Westminster John Knox, 2005.

———. *Black Religion, Black Theology: The Collected Essays of J. Deotis Roberts.* Edited by David Emmanuel Goatley. Harrisburg, PA: Trinity, 2003.

Rodriguez, Ruben Rosario. *Dogmatics After Babel: Beyond The Theologies of Word and Culture.* Louisville: Westminster John Knox, 2018.

Roper, John Herbert. *The Magnificent Mays: A Biography of Benjamin Elijah Mays.* Columbia: The University of South Carolina Press, 2012.

Rowland, Christopher, ed. *The Cambridge Companion to Liberation Theology.* New York: Cambridge University Press, 2007.

Segovia, Fernando F. *Decolonizing Biblical Studies: A View from the Margins.* Maryknoll, NY: Orbis, 2000.

Shannon, Magdaline W. *Jean Price-Mars, the Haitian Elite, and the American Occupation, 1915–1934*. Basingstoke, UK: Macmillan, 1996.

Sider, Ronald J. *Just Generosity: A New Vision for Overcoming Poverty in America*. Grand Rapids: Baker, 2007.

Sidhom, Swailem. "The Theological Estimate of Man." In *Biblical Revelation and African Beliefs*, edited by Kwesi Dickson and Paul Ellingworth, 99–104. Maryknoll, NY: Orbis, 1969.

Smith, E. W. *African Ideas of God: A Symposium*. London: Edinburgh, 1966.

Staffin, John. "A Brief and Candid Answer." In *The English Literatures of America: 1500–1800*, edited by Myriam Jehlen and Michael Warner, 821–24. Hoboken: Taylor and Francis, 2013.

Stiglitz, Joseph E. *The Price of Inequality: How Today's Divided Society Endangers Our Future*. New York: Norton, 2012.

Surgirtharajah, R. S. *Asian Biblical Hermeneutics and Postcolonialism: Contesting the Interpretations*. Maryknoll, NY: Orbis, 1998.

Tasie, George I. K. "The Heritage of the Mouth: Oral Sources and the Study of African Traditional Religion." *International Journal of Humanities and Social Science Invention* 2/3 (2013) 26–34.

Taylor, Keeanga-Yamahtta. *From #BlackLivesMatter to Black Liberation*. Chicago: Haymarket, 2016.

Tillich, Paul. *The Courage to Be*. New Haven: Yale University Press, 1980.

———. *A History of Christian Thought*. New York: Harper & Row, 1968.

———. *Systematic Theology*. Vol. 1. Chicago: University of Chicago Press, 1973.

Todorov, Tzvetan. *On Human Diversity: Nationalism, Racism, and Exoticism in French Thought*. Cambridge, MA: Harvard University Press, 1993.

Torbett, David. *Theology and Slavery: Charles Hodge and Horace Bushnell*. Macon, GA: Mercer University Press, 2006.

Torgovnick, Marianna. *Gone Primitive: Savage Intellects, Modern Lives*. Chicago: University of Chicago Press, 1997.

Torres-Saillant, Silvio. *An Intellectual History of the Caribbean*. New York: Palgrave Macmillan, 2006.

Townes, Emilie Maureen. *Womanist Ethics and the Cultural Production of Evil*. New York: Palgrave Macmillan, 2006.

Tracy, David. *The Analogical Imagination: Christian Theology and the Culture of Pluralism*. New York: Crossroad, 1998.

———. *Plurality and Ambiguity*. New York: HarperCollins, 1989.

Tutu, Desmond. *God Is Not A Christian: and Other Provocations*. New York: HarperOne, 2011.

Universal Declarations of Human Rights (1948). http://www.un.org/en/udhrbook/pdf/udhr_booklet_en_web.pdf.

Vellem, Vuyani. "Black Theology of Liberation: A Theology of Life in the Context of Empire." *Verbum et Ecclesia* 36/3 (2015) Art. #1470, 6 pages. http://dx.doi.org/10.4102/ve.v36i3.1470.

———. "Interlocution and Black Theology of Liberation in the 21st Century: A Reflection." *Studia Hist. Ecc.* 38, suppl.1 (2012) 1–9. http://www.scielo.org.za/pdf/she/v38s1/02.pdf.

Young, Josiah Ulysses. *A Pan-African Theology: Providence and the Legacies of the Ancestors*. Trenton: Africa World, 1992.

Washington, Joseph. *Black Religion: The Negro and Christianity in the United States.* Boston: Beacon, 1964.

West, Cornel. *Prophesy Deliverance! An Afro-American Revolutionary Christianity.* Philadelphia: Westminster, 1982.

Wilmore, Gayraud S. "A Revolution Unfulfilled, but not Invalidated." In *A Black Theology of Liberation*, by James H. Cone, 145–63. 40th anniversary ed. Maryknoll, NY: Orbis, 2010.

Woodson, Carter G. *The History of the Negro Church.* Baltimore: Black Classic, 2016.

Index